The LORD,
Bless you
and keep you;

The LORD,
Make his face
to shine upon you,
and be gracious to you;

The LORD,
Lift up his countenance
upon you,
and give you peace.

ELIOENAI SAHARA

OF AN
UNRIGHTEOUSNES
DONE TO A PEOPLE
OF G-D

ELIOENAI SAHARA

AN
AWAKENED
1492
NATIVE <u>*AMERICAN*</u> INDIAN

A MEMOIR

ELIOENAI

Hebrew name is **אליועיני**
meaning, **"Mine Eyes are Toward
The Creator"**

SAHARA

Hebrew name is **סהרה**,
meaning **"Moon."** It is also of Arabic
origin, where its meaning is
"Wilderness."

OF AN UNRIGHTEOUSNESS
DONE TO A PEOPLE OF G-D

ELIOENAI SAHARA

AN AWAKENED

NATIVE AMERICAN INDIAN

1492

A MEMOIR

אליועיני

ELIOENAI

BOOKSTORE.COM

BOOKSTORE.COM
A Division of Elioenai Sahara

704 Milano Drive
North Las Vegas, NV 89081

For information about special discounts for bulk purchases,
please contact Elioenai Sahara Special Sales at 702-251-4080 or
business@ElioenaiBookstore.com.

The Elioenai Sahara Speakers Bureau can bring The Author to
your live event. For more information or to book an event contact
the ElioenaiSahara Speakers Bureau by contacting
ElioenaiSaharaSpeaks@elioenaibookstore.com or visit our
website at www.elioenaibookstore.com or call 702-251-4080

Designed by Elioenai Sahara

Manufactured in The United States of America
ISBN 978-1-63972-115-3
ISBN 978-1-63944-518-9 (pbk)
ISBN 978-1-63972-114-6 (ebook)

From The Author

I Decree and Declare. The Supreme Superiority of G-D, The Father. G-D, The Son. And G-D, The Holy Spirit over my life. Thank you for purchasing this book. It makes my whole journey worthwhile. Each purchase has a special place in my heart, it reminds me of when I first started asking G-D to write a book, not knowing that G-D would fill the empty pages with himself. All thanks and praises to The Most High G-D.

This book is not intended to offend or give any false information. Just my opinion and experience. I hope that after reading this book you will have a better understanding of how one person's day to day life can be changed.

The Author wishes to express. The words in this book are from my personal relationship and experience with The Almighty G-D of Heaven. The Creator. The Great Spirit G-D of יִשְׂרָאֵל Yisra'EL יְהֹוָה Yahweh. (Yo'way, Yaya, Yah, Jah) The TETRAGRAMMATON, Yodh, Heh, Waw, Heh. There are over 100 biblical scriptures that says. "No man shall add to or diminish from G-D's words." For this reason, The Creator's conversations with The Author, and his G-D's conversations with the Author. G-D, HaShem, EL, EL, EL Elyon. G-D, HaShem, EL Adonai. G-D, HaShem, EL Jehovah. G-D, HaShem, EL Gibhor. Including other words spoken by The Holy (Kachina/Archangels) of The Creatir has not been changed or altered. Therefore, page count is not strictly regarded.

This book is written in a colloquial expression format, to reach a broad demographic of people scattered around The World.

1

ELIOENAI SAHARA
BOOK DISCLAIMER NOTICE

Within the moment I had stopped writing. The Creator, The Great Spirit G-D of יִשְׂרָאֵל Yisra'EL יְהֹוָה Yahweh, The TETRAGRAMMATON, Yodh, Heh, Waw, Heh came at my side saying.

"OK Daughter. Have you finished the book?" I said. "Yes Holy Fathar, I have." Then The Creator G-D say's. "OK. Now! Don't forget. OK?"

I said. "Don't forget? What is it Holy Fathar?" (I readied my pen to receive from The Creator the other things, he wanted to say beyond all that he said from 2012 to 2019.)

Then The Creator, The Great Spirit G-D says to me again. "Now don't forget. OK Daughter?

I AM THE AUTHOR. And you? YOU ARE THE ARTHUR of this here book. I laugh. And The Creator laugh with me. We laugh together even the more. When I discovered The Creator. My Holy Fathar was serious.

Therefore, He who is Greater than I. The Creator. The Great Spirit G-D of יִשְׂרָאֵל Yisra'EL יְהֹוָה Yahweh is The Author. And I am The Arthur of this here book. Just like G-D said. Blessed Be He.

DEDICATION

This book is dedicated to _all_ my relations with
reverent love.

To
My beloved
Late Matriarch & Patriarch
Mamie "Mrs. B"
& Daddy "Mr. B"

To
The Native American Indian Nations
scattered around The World.

The Assimilated
Native American Indian Descendants
Including
The Native American Indian Descendants of
The Commonwealth of The Bahamas, and
The Greater & Lesser Antilles islands in
The Caribbean Sea.

To
The 12 Tribes of יִשְׂרָ אל Yisra'EL,
The Chosen, The Righteous,
And The Adopted
Kingdom Citizens.

3

Table of Contents

I AM
HERE

CHAPTER I

Boom! The reverberation echoed throughout our six-bedroom house followed by darkness stealing all regular sense of normalcy. Many firm rigorous steps made its way to the destruction. Yelling. Panic. And hopelessness filled the room. As the dust begin to settle. And debris removed. A howling expression of grief filled the room. It was my mother. Overcome by the sight of the destruction. And just as it happened? Silence. Calm. Not a pin drop.

I was three months old lying in my crib when the attic boards laying across was removed. My Aunt Melvoin and her hidden stash came through the attic. Tangled up in the live wires, like a strangled whale, tossed violently onto dry land. My Uncle Derek raced to shot off the electric. And get Mr. B. The Ten commandments lawgiver.

Aunty Melvoin had the gumption, to hide her stolen stash. Unfortunately, that was not the right thing to do. My Daddy (Granddaddy) Mr. B. The monarchy monitored our obedience to G-D's ten commandment laws. Statues. And ordinances. He retired a 50-year veteran Police Sergeant. Mr. B. walked in last. Chest inflated. Carefully parting the wooden plank boards like Moses parting the red sea. While holding a makeshift Chaney brier tree baton. With the rest of the family trailing behind him for the verdict.

Mr. B. looked up at the giant hole in his ceiling. He looked down on Beverly. Then the sentence came for failure to _obey The LORD's Ten Commandment_ number eight. Mr. B pointed his makeshift at Auntie spell Melbourne's face and said in his constable voice of authority. "Fry dry? You have made your bed up hard. Now! You will have to sleep in it hard." Which meant Auntie should have never touch the bitter fruit called sin by way of stealing.

And because she did? She would have to clean up the mess. Get the attic repaired. And pick herself up from the floor. Those who wanted to remain eating Mr. B's food and living in Mr. B's home. Avoided her like the plague. We would know her sins were forgiven by G-D. Only when Mr. B. acknowledge her again openly. Mr. B walked away. He usually handed down harsher punishment for disobeying G-

D's laws. But it was her grandaunt's evergreen 100-year-old exotic manikara zapota, sapodilla fruit tree. So technically. She didn't steal the fruits. Even though she took it without asking. Melvoin stopped over groaning and said. "Yes sir. Daddy sir. Thank you, sir." Accepting the verdict.

When the dust settled. For the first time. I saw my family. Leaning over me. With illuminated bodies. And seven glaring suns. Shining from their faces. Looking down on me smiling. I remember watching a jolt of light leave them and entered me. Hitting me deep within. That brought me to life. Instantly, I became awake. And aware. Around the room my eyes went in a circle. I remember laughing in hysteria of my great fortune from The LORD Most High. Then a voice from The Holy Spirit spoke. Guided, and instructed me saying. "This is your Aunty. This is your Aunty. This is your cousin. This is your cousin. This is your mother. This is your grandmother. And this. This is your Granddaddy. He oversees you. And he is in charge of *all* the others. Obey his words and all will go well with you. And the voice that you heard in the distance? that's your Uncle Derek. They seemed supernatural in every way. A people whose appearance was as The Sun. Seeming to wear their souls (a brilliant light) outwardly. A magical people. Watching the miracle unfold? I remember thinking. "Wow." "Am just now alive. And things are already as good as this? Then I should not hesitate to follow The LORD. I became anxious to see just what The Holy Spirit of G-D had in-store for the rest of my life. With overwhelming contentment from deep within. I laugh in hysteria while in that crib. I was in awe of the blessings of The LORD Most High. That he would plant me with such a people. As The People that I saw in the room. So, I turned mine eyes toward G-D. And I asked The Holy Spirit forces that consumed the room. To take full control of my life. That my latter end would be much like my first. Filled with The Holy Spirit. Somehow, I knew. While lying in that crib. Watching The Holy Spirit move before my eyes. If I wanted

to be OK from that moment forward. I needed to follow this Holy Spirit. That dominated the room. And I did.

"Are you ready?" He says at my bedside. Each night for thirteen years. I opened my hands and extended them up. Placing my hands in Jesus outstretched right hand. He took me away from the world. To be with him. Around The World we would fly. Sitting upon the clouds of Heaven. Looking down below. He said to me. "Do you see the people?" I would look down to earth. And the people would look up at us and point to us in The Heavens. And I would answer him. "Yes. I do." "They are yours. And you are mine Jesus would say to me." I say. "Yes LORD.

When we flew? I tried letting Jesus right hand go. I felt experienced. Years of flying hand in hand. When he held me. I didn't fall. When I let go? I fell slowly. I became afraid. Jesus caught me. Because of my efforts to branch off and to learn. Jesus was pleased. But he said, "you are not ready to fly." And he smiled. I smiled back at Jesus. We were in love. I never let Jesus right hand go again. And he never let mine. One morning as Jesus returned me to my bedroom, he says to me while holding both my hands "tell your mother her Aunty Rose will die tonight. I went at my mother's bedroom door between two or three am. I knocked. My heart stated beating fast. Needless to say, I was nervous. My mother was not the one to be disturbed while sleeping. But I decided that she would want to know what Jesus told me. I knocked on the door and said. "Mommy, Mommy, Jesus said Aunty Rose will die tonight. My mother answered me immediately saying. "Get to your bed child. If you know what's good for you little girl. You hear me?

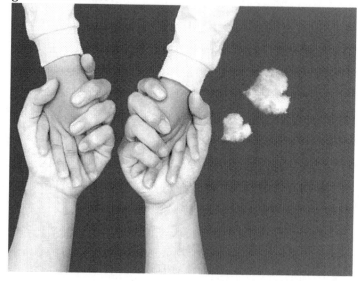

In her mind "what would I know, I was only a six-year-old child having a bad dream. Until the morning came, and my grandmother Mamie came to our home with the same bad news. This time. That Aunty Rose was dead. Not that she was *going* to die. Then I became overnight a mysterious Golden Chick-charney bird that Mamie and Mommy stared at in astonishment. Mommy was the worst. She placed me in the living room chair for days on end. She feed me from there. And pretended not to be staring at me from a distance. Then she would pass by me now and again. And ask me over and over. "Now how did you know my Aunty Rose was going to die?" My response never changed. It was always. "Jesus told me.

I said Jesus told me so much, until I became upset with Jesus for telling me. It bring me grief. A feeling I had never had before. I didn't like not being able to go outdoors. My seeking G-D through the butterflies, the lizards, the ants, and the wind that blew the trees. My love for outdoor meditations and imagining had come to an end. All things that meant everything to me had vanished. So I said to G-D in disapointment. "This good thing that Jesus has done. Has become bad for me LORD. So now, I will avoid Jesus voice and shot him out of my head. And never repeat anything that he says. Because it will just get me into trouble."

I muted him. I shut Jesus out. I just didn't know what other punishment I would have to endure, if I said, "Jesus said, to anyone. Or that I heard his voice and he comes to me" The more I avoided Jesus. The more he spoke. Even more, I hid myself in silence. When Jesus spoke I would cover my ears and hide myself under the sheet or in the closet. I became very sad that Jesus had cause me to suffer with his message. After awhile, I did not speak anymore to anyone.

A few weeks passed. And a travelling evangalist came to visit our Baptist Church. She said to the congregation. "There is a child here that Jesus speaks to every night. He comes by her bedside and takes her flying. I want you to come up here with me child." I got up and walked up to the podium. I watched as my mother and facial expressioned dropped. This was the first time I felt what pride and vindication felt like as a child. As I sashayed down the Church isles to the pulpit smiling with my head held high. I knew it was G-D that send down from Heaven to rescue me Because he didn't want me to shut him out. When I walked pass my mother, I heard her say while looking at me. "My G-D." As I walked toward the lady evangalist. She smiled at me. Took my hand. And started speaking to the congregation. Through the wisdom of G-D's Holy Spirit. I knew G-D was restoring me from chastisement to my regular happy, walk with G-D, talk with G-D childlike self. Which was the greatest part of me.

The evangelist then said to The Church. "You see this little girl? The LORD has need of her." Then she looked at me and said. "Little girl, The LORD had need of you." I became happy again. And stop muting out Jesus' voice. Because he vindicated me from my mother's persecution.

At times. Demonic little children the same size and height as me. Would visit trying to strangle me. I would wake up having difficulties breathing. And find scrapes and bruises on my neck from them. They hated that Jesus loved and visited me. Cleopatra the natives of the remote islands called me. Coolie at times. And mango skin gal the next.

My Dad wanted to name me after The Queen of Egypt. My Mommy met him halfway and called me Cleo. Growing up? I was a beautiful ugly duckling. Beautiful? Because I was told. Ugly? Because I was oddly different in many ways. I didn't have the look or mannerisms of a black child. And that confused everyone around me. I dealt strictly in the holy sp-

Holy Spirit Island Native American
Indian woman called "Coolie"

irit and with the holy spirit. That made me a very odd person, Living in a world where Spirituality (The Holy Spirit). Nature. And G-D had little to no friends. And I saw it as a child. And I would often ask G-D to take me away because the world seemed like a very hard place. And there was many that were not observing spirit, nature and G-D.

I filtered everything through The Holy Spirit. And in my gut. I always felt there was a missing piece to who I really was. My identity. Me on the soul level. Many wanted me to believe that my brown skin came from across the waters from Africa. I explored that, while trying to find myself, but it never added up. People tried forcing me to accept that reality. When common logic said something else. My brown skin was not brown or black. It was copper. Differences were not readily accepted. People were told their ethnicity. Not by blood. And not by ancestry. But by the color of their skin. You were either black from Africa or white from Europe. I knew I didn't have any African's American or European white's blood in my veins. Though I didn't know who I was? I knew who I was certainly not. With little to no knowledge of my Native American Indian Heritage. And nothing to work with. *I kept turning my eyes to The G-D* of Heaven to help me know myself.

TWO
SCOOPS

CHAPTER II

Saying "Sir and Ma'am" excessively. Were signs of a polite and respectful child. Or signs of a child with some-tin wong. Or a child that was fine with a couple of extra screws loose. Growing up this is what the other children would say is wrong. Either child? The elders would let us go unscathed. If "Sir and Ma'am" did not work as penance? It was because the level of our misdeed desired extra. Remission. In asking for forgiveness, we would pretend to be a wounded. Half dead calf. Hinging on for dear life.

If your mother was whipping, you and you said. "Mommy, Mommy? Am hinging on in there for dear life." Made an angry face. Bulge your eyes out. Tighten your lips. And open your nose? She would think you were seriously hinging on. To direct your anger toward her. 95% of the time our parents bite the dust on the half dead calf trick.

We had various ways to trick our elders. Laughable stories were told in Church. When I looked at all involved in deception? I determined the straight and narrow way seem more painless. And the joys of the straight and narrow road were not fleeting. And end of journey rewarding.

Trickery and deception also have joys. But fading joy. A form of fool's gold. Or a trick of the hand. Know you feel it. Know you don't. Pain and Suffering follows closely behind Trickery and Deception. Those Spirit are joined to each other. The Straight and narrow road (The Spiritual Road) was peaceful for me. And I wouldn't have to over blink. Stick out my tongue. Drool excessively. Or perform the pretend half dead calf trick. The mold was broken with me. I do believe. I looked differently from others. I acted differently also. I had copper hair and copper skin. And there was none like me for miles around that remote island. Within The Commonwealth of The Bahamas.

"Your hair looks at though, you've been diving conchs in the Atlantic Ocean child?." while violently gripping my hair. "And your skin is so dingy looking." All through my mother did not mean anything bad by those words. I saw I was different. And had no place in the world. I needed no extra help with that.

I required constant care growing up. Mosquitos' bites allergic reactions would swell my legs. Placing me on bed rest. While sores stick to my bedding and uniform socks. While sleeping, My sister Rochelle would stand over my bed. Stretch her hands over me and cry out with a loud voice. "Lazarus. Come forth." Lazarus is of the bible. John 11:43 he was covered with sores, and dogs would lick them.

I knew the bible stories very well as a child. The bible stories helped me to navigate my life and made decisions. And to understand how G-D work. And how G-D seeks things. Other kids would bully me because I was born different. Not black and not white. And my ways were not like their ways. They would always tell me that I was not good enough. I was doing something wrong. It didn't matter the task. And it didn't matter that I excel in everything that I did. It didn't matter how hard I tried to do it their way. I just did not complete a task like any other kid. Though I did it correctly, The constant feeling of not being good enough or like the others? Drove me closer and closer to The Holy

Spirit for comfort and understanding of the world I lived in. I couldn't understand why I could not be who I was

The way I saw things were different from others. I didn't measure others by physical assets. But by spiritual assets. When everyone else looked down on The Bucket family's fifteen bad kids. I hoped in their spiritual recovery. I saw the aura illuminating from their bodies to be of low estate. Very poor quality of spirit is what I saw. So, I always tried to stay away from the poor-spirited kids. And even the poor-spirited adults for that matter.

I didn't think poor was of cloths. And of food. And of shoes. Or of pocket. Spiritual morality determined a person's wealth. The morally bankrupted was real poor to me. And the greatness of spirit determined wealth. Generally? I saw the good in others. And The Holy Spirit was always there with me. Like my natural nature. Easy. There. Talking with me. And accessible always.

I didn't trespass against anyone willingly. I would often turn the other cheek. Because I knew. The powers of G-D that existed within me from a very early age. So, I would pray about it. Talk it over with G-D, like I would a friend. Then I would throw it in the sea of forgetfulness and leave it there. Which is required of you. If you love G-D. For vengeance and recompense belong unto G-D.

Therefore, I never beat the meat of my personal bully, Teressa Penniman's backside. I was stronger of Mind. Body. Soul. And Spirit. And I had G-D. Her blows weren't affecting me any. Though they were annoying. Through the laws of G-D's governing The Universe. I had the upper hand. So, I needed to apply mercy because of it. Or I would end up on the wrong side of G-D's Laws. This was the way of my thinking as a child, spirit minded. I didn't want to be on the wrong side of G-D's Laws. I wanted to always stay in The LORD's grace. Ms. B (Mamie) always taught me. One day. It will be a day to late to live right. And The LORD will *repay the* work of *all flesh hands. Good unto the good. And evil unto evil.* Which forced me to consider my actions carefully. Day by day. So, I took her blows because she needed me too. So, it wouldn't be accounted to her for a sin.

I didn't let her beat me to blood. Absolutely not. She was the frailest little thing. The level of my annoyance brought me pain. But her blows? Did nothing. I looked down on her head while she hit me. I said to The Holy Spirit. "How can a little bitty mosquito. Even consider possibly winning a fight against a big ass bomber fly." I let it happen time and time again. I didn't take the blows from her to me. As some form of her anger toward me. No. I took her soft and tender blows from her. For her. Absorbing it through The Spirit. Less her punishment would be greater from G-D for trespassing against me wrongfully. Not permitting her to drink from the same cup in return. And not attaching her evil deed to me and extending its reign of terror. I offered her the lesser of the two evils. I blessed her with her blows for both of us. My blows in her cloths would have ended her day light for sure. I was a stronger child, physically, Spiritually, and Mentally. I had control of myself. She had none.

I followed spiritual guiding principles growing up. When it seemed like everyone else around me was just winging it. With no path to travel. No road to walk. No consideration for the next man. Not even a line drawn in the sand not to cross in life. Nothing. I needed The Holy Spirit's to guide me. The Spirit was the place to know a person's attributes. I was convinced. The kids that bullied me. Were fools' pies. Used as the devil's device by the evil spirits. So, I didn't blame them. I pitted their estate always. They couldn't see themselves.

24

They didn't give their free will over to The Holy Spirit to be fill. So, I saw their deeds to be void of The Good Spirit. I only saw things as they pertained to. And in The Spirit Realm. Everything else was a distracting noise that I would flee from. I lived in a world that only saw things as it pertains to. And for. And with. The Flesh. I would always turn away and flee from flesh driven conversations.

Until one day I couldn't walk away from the bully Buckets. (The Bucket Family) children. The only child gang on the remote island. Stealing everything that could move. "Nuisance" the elders called them. Breaking into people's houses. Leading the police right to them by leaving misspelled handwritten notes in other homeowners' bathrooms that read. "Fluch da twolet. Stoop bean sew nastyie. Sing Rollin. Native American Indian children were taught to speak words of The English language. But not adequately how to spell the English word we spoke.

One day I got of the school bus. And saw Roland Bucket. And his barefooted amigos. They always moved in a group. With suspicious looking critters crawling around their heads. And a tornado of flies and dirt encompassing them like a dust cloud. They couldn't see their own infirmities. Which was forever closer to their eyes than my infirmities of sores brought on my mosquito bites allergic reaction. Even as I child I knew Luke 6:42. Sacred Scriptures helped me to discover the foolish and the wise of the people at a very early age. I related everything to scripture Luke 6:42 says. *"Why do you look at the speck in your brother's eye, but fail to notice the beam in your own eye?"* They had eyes. But they did not see.

I had eyes. And was the same age as them. But I saw. Because I was a spirit minded child. While they were carnal minded children. They started singing when I passed. "Two scoops of raisins in a package of Kellogg's raisin brand. Two scoops." This day. I woke up on the wrong side of my bed. I wanted to beat the dog mess out of the Bucket's children. Ending the suffering of the elders in my community. Brought on by their existence. Enough was enough. They were not going to continue to take my kindness for weakness. I had reached the height of my discontent. What they didn't understand was. I was not engaging them. Not became I couldn't. Or because of fear. But because I didn't care too. I understood that I should not trespass against another person's landmark. Spiritual or physical. And never fight against my neighbor.

But this day. I had enough of their trespasses against me. And I needed not for them to think that I was weak by any means. For I was filled with The Holy Spirit. Fill with the strength of G-D. Concealed in my body. I dropped my school bag. Opened my arms to the sky. Turning slowly toward them. I said. "What I need from you bully Buckets is to fight me." So, I can cause the earth to open and swallow all y'all like Moses did." I beckoned with my fingers and said out loud. "Come. Fight Buckets. This way I can do away with you all forever" I ignited The Holy Spirit force field (Shield of Protection) in. And around me. That started with my right hand ignited with the Holy Spirit fire (Powers of G-D). That slowly took over my entire body. I never wanted that power that took me over to be used. I knew I had it. It was always only for last resort in times of trouble. As The Holy Spirit taught me it was.

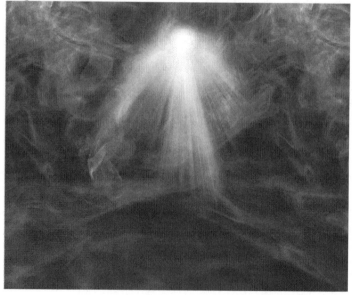

And because I understood the powers of The Holy Spirit were not able to be retracted once it came. If it didn't want to be retracted. In other words, I couldn't change my mind. I had to be sure that I needed help. Before calling upon G-D in that way. When the power of G-D came. It was like a double-edged sword. That also taught me responsibility. The two options in calling The Holy Spirit to my rescue was. The powers/The Holy Spirit would do exact to my desire. Or the powers/The Holy Spirit will do worse than anything I could have imagined. Because it had the power to justify itself. And it's actions. In the bringing about of immediate justice. It was of G-D. So, I hid G-D's power of his Holy Spirit within me from others. Because The Holy Spirit when called, could have done worst than my own thoughts or desire.

But I always knew The Holy Spirit was there for me to call on. And The Holy Spirit was greater than any human strength. And anything that existed in the world. So, I troubled no one. While understanding clearly, 1 John 4:4 "You are from G-D, Little children, and have overcome them; because greater is he who is in you than he who is in the world.

In 1984. The Holy Spirit taught me the Holy Spirit Fire. The Force Field (Shield of Protection). I learned now to activate it within me. During this time. Stephen King's American science fiction Fire-starter came into my life by divine design. I was the same age as the girl in the movie. The Holy Spirit directed me to take the good and use it. And I did. With the Buckets. I remember thinking. "Am going to use all the G-D I have in me to destroy these buckets of mischief. And I'll be finally done with these babies who have eyes but cannot see. Slowing my journey to Spiritual perfection down. Truth is. I always desired more meat than the children my age that were around me were able to

29

furnish. Which made my circle trump tight. Me. G-D The Father. G-D The Son. And G-D The Holy Spirit. Enlightening my consciousness. While renewing my strength daily in G-D. Which cause me to increase in Wisdom, Knowledge and Understanding. With the flame of the right hand of G-D's Holy Spirit fire. I worked on antagonizing the buckets to fight. So that me and the universal forces could finally get this bullying me thing over and done with. For righteousness was with me. And I knew it. I said. "Listen h-

ere. You Buckets. How far do you think I can kick y'all Buckets?" Then I started singing them a song. "One Bucket. Two Bucketth. Three Bucketth. Four. Five Bucketths. Six bucketths. Seven bucketths. More. "And who should you be? I said to Roland. "Roll-in Bucket? And you? I said to his brothers. Ice Bucket?" And you over there? "Who are you mop bucket? Get a life. Or kick the bucket. Bucketths. Am done with you babies." I lingered in the spot of The Holy Spirit Force Field. (Shield of Protection). I walked away.

When I saw it no longer needed it. Their courage was broken that day. They never troubled me again. That day I learned to use courage to overcome challenges.

PRODIGAL SON

CHAPTER III

My Grandmother Ms. B. "Mamie" took me under her guardianship. She had the time and the heart to care for me. "You are a special child. G-D has plans for you. And you are loved by me." Mamie says to me. Even though I was covered in sores and different.

One day I was feeling down because of my affliction. Mamie says. "Child don't you know you've got sugar in your blood? Your blood is pure. Therefore, the mosquitoes mostly come to you. And don't bother anyone else."

Mamie would take the time to mix blends of medicine. Using different tree leaves, saps and twigs and other green plants for my healing. And she would say to me. "G-D loves you. And I love you. You are going to be just fine. You just wait and see." She would anoint my body with her holy olive oil. Her bible was always with her. While I laid there incapacitated. She would read certain scriptures. Pray. Sing and cry over my incapacitated body. Pealing back my uniform socks from my sores.

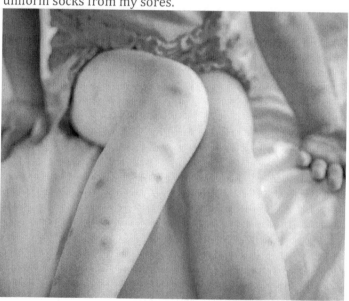

My fairy G-dmother. I saw as my Grandmother Mamie. Who turned out to be no fairy. But a faithful. Fearless woman of G-D. I had a great life growing up. My parents did their best. They were very hard-working successful people of noble blood. I was blessed to have nobility on both sides of my family.

Blessed to have families on both sides with Church Ministries. Baptist and Anglican. I was blessed to be submerged in the wealth of the knowledge of G-D at a very early age. I was blessed to be the secretary reading The LORD's minutes (the church notes). I was blessed to sing in the church choir for the LORD. All of it I loved. And I desired it more than fine gold. More than anything else in my life. The light and love I received from my elder's face? Nothing worldly was able to afford me.

Two families owned private planes on the remote islands. My family was one of them. My dad also owned a six-engine cigarette boat. A new red convertible Corvette. Three Kawasaki ninja bikes. And other luxury vehicles. He loved exotic cars. Like he loved exotic women. He married a European and had two children.

My two European little sisters came to the remote island to visit for the first time. And I knew The Biblical prodigal son story was true. As the life of The Prodigal Son. Became the life I was living instantly. I also learned that day. There was something fundamentally wrong with the way the adults build their actions; after they conclude something. That they have not given any spiritual thought to. Which is to consider the spiritual laws concerning a certain action or a certain outcome. I stood there observing the activities along with The Holy Spirit of G-D. And we did laugh. It was the most foolish thing. I had ever seen at the time. And at my age. And even as a child. I knew it was head shaking foolishness. The grown-ups had an over-the-top pomp and pageantry on the entire island. When the other kids (native children) were carrying water uphill for the sake of their families and the village elders. From the day they were born and never got a reward of such magnitude. Which would have been a just reward. Good natured, Hardworking, G-D fearing children. In service of their families. For the love and respect of them.

Mama Rita took out all the fine China. And made the island natives to celebrate like the even was of biblical proportion. And I did laugh with G-D. Today? It reminds me of Coming to America. The wedding scene. Whenever I saw that movie? I would burst out laughing, while remembering the galore my family had over our European relatives visit.

While listening to the beat of the goat skin drums and the cow bells. I recognize then. The different behaviors toward the European children. And The Native children. I remember getting put aside by the adults also. It was as though the holy grail was at the house. People of the islands were racing to ensure that a European child happened for them. Mothers were taking their daughters into it. And fathers were telling their sons. Having a European child elevated your family's social statues. You were somebody or something. At the time. That was the way of the world.

The adults went away with my sister's luggage. Mama Rita called out to me. I ran from the bushes to her and said. "Yes Grammy?" She says. "Look after the kids." I was a kid myself. But they knew. I was no fools pie with hollow insides. I was strong of heart. And wise of mind. And I walked with G-D. And his presence was always with me. So, I was always treated with respect by my elders. I took them to the playroom. Shortly after entering. My European little sister walks in for the first time. I guess she didn't know what to expect and felt awkward. It felt a little awkward for me also. I decided to observe her, so that I would learn how to treat her. She spun around wildly in the center of the room. Completing a circle on one leg. Landed on both. And said first to me. While pointing. "You? "F*** you. You? F*** you too. You? F*** you. And you? You? F*** you?" Which covered the four of us in the room.

I stood up on my feet with both fists bold. My pressure rose. And my blood boiled. I said. "Little whipper snapper? Those words are fighting words." I had never heard the 100-pound words before. Which was the limit. How could she at 6 years old. Arrive at the limit? Not even the elders reached the limit. But the younger did? In my haste I said. "One more word out of you little whipper snapper. And I promise you. I will knock all your teeth clean out your mouth." Which was the standard threat for cursing. The adult would tell you that they would knock all your teeth clean out your mouth. And if you did not want to be gum lee, you would not try it.

Cursing was a sin to us. We understood that it defiled us. Especially the females. Boys took a chance at cursing. But girls? It was always expected never to happen. We understood our senses to be gates to The Soul. To be used for The LORD's purpose. The mantra of our home was. "If you don't have kind words to say? Then you ought to be quiet." We were good gentle spirited people. Naturally. And we were spirit. Before we were anything else. What she said was called 100-pound words. Before you caught a bible concussion. In hopes that the sacred scriptures upside your head would give you knew encouraging words to use.

The little whipper snapper was only six years old. When the grace of G-D rest on me and enlightened my understanding. And removed my anger. The voice of The LORD came to me saying. "Look. And see. She is overwhelmed." Just then I was taken above in The Spirit. I looked down on earth from up above. Into an open field. I saw natives of the island dressed in all black. Moving around

in a circle. Overwhelming two white dots in the center that appeared trapped. And I understood the vision instantly. I relied on The LORD to teach me as he did always. I didn't understand the world and the people around me without him. Which saved the little whipper snapper from having to potentially learn the pretend half dead calf, Indian trick her first day with the family. I pitied her. I didn't tell the elders. My father's last name was powerful. And his family was respected. And I was also. Because of them. I knew I was not a poor child, by any means. From a very early age. We didn't leave our estate to get anything. My dad's parent owned more than half of the remote island. The grocery store next door. The restaurant. The liquor store. The pool hall and lounge. The hotel. The Beach Villas, The Apartment rentals, The airport shop, the dive shop, and the cargo ships. The farmlands and the fields.

"Which one would you like to go to school in today princess?" My dad burst into the room elated to take me to school. His face lite up in my direction like a Christmas tree. When he drove the red corvette. Of his exotic vehicles and Kawasaki ninja bikes? I would select the red corvette because I knew it make him happy. And free. His laughter could be heard from miles around.

My mother's parents were Deacon and Mother of The Baptist Church they founded. My Mothers dad. I call Daddy (Mr. B). And My Grandmother. I call Mamie, (Ms. B). She was a cook of over 50 years. For a prominent Hotel on the island. She cooked also for celebrities and dignitaries. Even international superstars and film producers that would travel to The Bahamas. The former Prime Minister of The Commonwealth of The Bahamas. Sir Lynden O. Pindling. Sir Lynden made private trips on his plane to dine at Mamie's restaurant E & G's. And I would be right beside her setting the tables, serving the water and aiding her in the kitchen prepping. As her restaurant was always crowded. At times because of the customer's fame. I would be afraid to go at the table with Mamie because I was just a little girl. But she would always force me by her side to greet the customers and see after their needs. Some Bahamian artists make records singing Mamie (Ms. B) praises because of her great cooking.

Mamie and Daddy and the other elders. Always sent to collect me to dance around their late-night campfires. It was exciting. But I never understood, why they had to hide to have their ceremonies and rituals only at night. But it was a real privilege that I was always selected above the other children in the village. While I dance. I observed that it always made them happy. They were always smiling at me and clapping. They rewarded me with as many roasted corns as I was able to carry. But what I didn't know at the time was. The attendees were not only those that were seen, but also one who was unseen. G-D. The Creator. I saw dancing for my elders made them happy. And I was the only child permitted at their late-night ceremonies. So, I slowly started dancing for G-D in the spirit during the day, my thinking was. It would make G-D happy as well. I would imagine myself above. In the open universe. While still dancing below. I would always bow as though; I was bowing before G-D each time. At the start of my spiritual dancing. Growing up, I always felt like there was a higher power observing me in silence. I always felt there was someone there listening and writing my and our deeds. But in silence. I just never knew who exactly was there. I knew that a higher power had made me and everything I saw. So, I would say after bowing, and through faith. In believing that a higher power existed. I would say to G-D "I have come that you should find delight in me." And at other times after bowing before dancing for a G-D that I could not see. I would say. "I am here to ensure your happiness. And to check-up on you LORD, to see how you are doing today." Even when I didn't know who the heavenly father was. I believed he existed as a great and holy one that created the world. I had nothing I was able to offer G-D as a child. but I checked in with G-D every day to ensure he was always happy and delighted with me, as I was delighted in him.

MARQUICEE'S
YO'WAY

CHAPTER IV

One day. After mandatory eastern sunrise prayer. And gratitude to the other cardinal directions. West, North, and South. Grammy Mama Rita said. "Let me show you something." She returned with some items in her hand.

Her smile was regal. Instantly I loved her. She looked like me. And she wore a long deerskin wrap around skirt with fringe sleeves. And her skin was copper looking. I admired her radiant skin. It wasn't brown and it wasn't black. With a feather in the back and a band around her head. With two long braids hinging down. I stared in admiration. As my heart beat slower. I felt a connection to myself for the first time. As I looked down on the picture. Mama Rita says to me. "Child? This is your Marquicee. Your Great grandma. Your granddaddy's mother. She's a Native American Indian. You ain't see. You look just like her?

She is them set over there in the US. The Cherokee Indian in them. She's from The Wolf Clan. That's who your Great-grandma people is. From the Hopewell in Tennessee. your Great Grandma was a priestess. She was a beloved healer, known for her beauty. I took care of her throughout her old age child. A lot of your Great Grandma people died. Including your Great Granddaddy. He got killed by the soldiers.

I said. Mama Rita? "Why did the soldiers kill Great grandpa? Mama Rita said. "For their land. Thousands of them made it here safe. Marquicee was so afraid the soldiers would kill the rest of her family. So, they came on them canoes. You know child? Them canoes like what you and your Dad got out there on the beach? That's like what your Great grandma and them came here on."

As I look at Marquicee's beautiful face. My heart sunk. Just to think of the journey across the ocean Marquicee had to endure. On such a small craft. When I couldn't swim. Not even the shoreline shallow water could I swim. I said. Mama Rita? "When did this happen?" She said. "Back in 1838. They came here The Native American Indians from Georgia, Tennessee, Florida, and Mississippi. And all around those

46

places. They started new villages. Some in red bay. And others right here. And some down the road there in Key Short Bay."

"Marquicee say life wasn't good. Marquicee tell me one day The G-D she offered prayers. Named Yo'way would come and save the Indian people. Marquicee say Yo'way is The Creator. The Great Spirit. I worship him in secret. She said some Indians call him by other names.

I say. "Where did she come from Mama Rita? I've never seen anyone like her before." Mama Rita said. "From Egypt. On seven ships. That landed in these islands. And in the US. Marquicee say. They spoke the Hebrew language.

My Great-grandma Marquicee's Yo'way G-D, The Creator. I didn't know. And other children didn't worship. Like all the other native Indian children. I only knew Jesus Christ. And Church seven days a week. Teaching mostly, of Jesus Christ.

I didn't know it was not the adults and elders that was fueling us with Church, day and night to get rid of us kids from being around the house. but I was a steady and habitual Church goer not knowing that I was going there within the assimilation of my ancestors long before me. Brought on by others. I knew Church as the only place on earth to find G-D. It seemed the name The Creator or The Creator G-D was for the elders and senior men and women to use. And the name G-D was used by the catholic missionaries and priest when they were teaching us. My Marquicee's G-D, The Creator? Was kept from the children. As a form of a secret. But Jesus was given to the native children to reverence and observe in kind. We didn't have a name for Jesus G-D. We just called him G-D. And was taught that Jesus was the son of G-D, and G-D is made in our image, and likeness. Yet we were brown skin, and our G-D was white. His picture was all over our homes and Churches in the village. We were taught to strive to be like Jesus. And to have an everlasting relationship with him. So that one day we would meet his father. Through him. For no one comes to The Father except through Jesus John 14:6. We native kids knew this by heart. And we strive for the ultimate relationship. To arrive at the presence of his Father. Well at-least I did.

In Mama Rita's hands. Was a plaque from The Queen of England. Acknowledging Mama Rita's Red Cross Society contributions. On every board. Mama Rita was the Chairwoman. Founder or Co-founder. A most distinguished person. And wherever we went unannounced? We were given the royal treatment. Everyone knew my grandmother was the representative of G-D on the island. People song her praises. And sorted her counsel. And she healed the sick. Even families with infertility issues. By mixing a blend of medicinal plants with prayer, rituals and ceremonies.

Families would show up in my presents and say. "Mama Rita. You remember us? And I would look up at their faces shining in admiration of her. And they would bless her with gifts and money for something she did in the name of The LORD Most High. Ten years earlier.

So, wealth does follow you. Which always reminded me of _Ecclesiastes 11:1. "Cast your bread on the surface of the waters._ For you will find it after many days." Prophesies Mama Rita gave to the community holding up the bible in her right hand. And they would all come to pass in the eyes of the people. When she traveled and prophesied. Many would laugh at her. Especially the men. They laugh the loudest. Mama Rita was a female doing something predominantly done my males. I learned. It was the way The LORD had it. So that he may cast down all high looks. Ensuring his dominion. Over the selection process of his servants.

Though they would treat her poorly. She would never lose sight of why we were visiting their Church, and what message G-D had given her for The People. She was a strong woman of G-D. I often said to The LORD. "LORD? If I could only grow up to be just like my Grandmother Mama Rita, A strong woman of G-D? I would have done the best thing I could possibly do with my life." She was the grandma of my soul. We loved each other in an extra special way. I was her favorite. And she was mine. Everyone knew that. We were two of a kind. I was taught of G-D. And the bible every waking minute by her and Ms. B. There was no conversation without G-D's guiding principles. Every day, they told me. "There will be a day that is called to late child. So always sow good and righteous seeds with G-D. That you may reap the reward." What I didn't know was. I was under the tutelage of two experience women of G-D by G-D's instructions. As an apprentice.

In the country. People offered Mama Rita G-D's tithing. Gifts and offering. When she went into any city. I was there. On the remote island. She owned fur coats and an extensive wardrobe and jewelry collection. From around the world including England, and Paris. I understood later she needed those to travel along with dignitaries as their spiritual adviser.

Whenever we traveled? I would return to the remote islands with a caravan filled with clothing, toys and precious keepsakes from other countries. It happened so much. It was as though Santa Claus visited me every other day on the remote islands. I observed that. And I was humbled.

BLENDING
IN

CHAPTER V

Mama Rita and I would dress up in our boots. After my lessons with her. And dance the night away to our happy lyric. "Boots" by Nancy

Sinatra. The people cared for her. And bless her with abundance.

Mama Rita was never without. She had generational wealth to boot. If she showed up? The people wouldn't close the event without acknowledging our presence. Which was a drag for me at times. It prolonged me ditching the itchy leggings. And puffy princess dresses. Flow shine shoes. The gold bangles. And the diamond earrings.

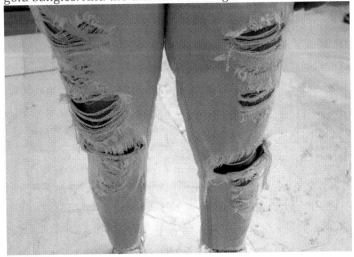

For a fly rod. Crab legs. A barked jelly coconut. A freshly picked mango. Fins, snorkels. And a pair of wildly ripped blue jean pants. I was ripping wholes in blue jeans. Long before it became a fashionable thing to do.

One day Mr. B. saw my riches to rages look. He walked up to me. Snatch both my arms violently. Shook me up. Stared me in the eyes and said. "Child, what happen to you? Did the neighbor's dogs attack you child?" I said. "No Daddy." Mr. B said. "Then you have lost your head. Do you see how you look?" Then he let my arms go. And slowly walked away whistling. I stood there and watched him walk. My Daddy

(Granddaddy) Mr. B. was always provoking my thoughts with playful drama. He always made you smile and think. I swear he knew the end of something long before it's beginning. I laugh. Checked myself and said. "it's my new look Daddy. It would take you sometime to get use to me like this. But I like it. Am blending in." Mr. B stopped looked back and said. "No child. It is not for me to get use to you like that. It is for you to get use to yourself. As you are. Now what you look like? You look like you just step out of a blender. But blending in? He pointed from my feet to my face. He says. "I don't see it." Throwing his hand up in the air. As being done with me. He turned and walked away. I didn't enjoy the attention I received in luxurious apparel. When others where near naked. It troubled me inwardly. It made me feel guilty of something. I would often ditch them. Deep in the bushes. On any given day I had a change of attire hidden in the bushes. So, I could blend in.

Off with the gold bangles and chains. I would throw them in the sea and watch the tide take them away. Dad and Mama Rita would replace the gold, within the week. I tried to tell them I never liked it. But they never listened. Each time. I felt defeated that I had to wear such things when others had none. I stopped ditching the gold. Because it kept coming back from the ocean like a boomerang.

My toys were to new looking. I hated them. I needed them to blend with the other kids' toys. So, I'd drag them on the beach road behind my bicycle. Or I'll dash barbie & ken's head on the coconut tree for a good bruising. They were only good if they looked like ragamuffin dolls. Handed down a few generations. Blending in meant everything to me. My ways were always called different. I remember doing the fancy table setting Mama Rita taught me. The other kids laugh me to scorn. Viciously knock me to the ground and said. "Stop acting white." I never stopped setting the table. I just ignored the world that chastise me for who I was. And I continued setting the table for two. Me. And an extra placement for G-D. For many years while dinning out I would have the waiter or waitress place an

extra placement before me for G-D. When they ask me if I was expecting someone? I would answer, "yes". I never stopped making room for G-D. Because I needed G-D to known that he was always on my mind. Because indeed, and in action?. G-D was.

In 2017 as I was dinning at a restaurant in Ohio with a friend. I had the usual placement set for G-D. It was something the friend had seen me do before. While enjoying my dinner and speaking to G-D ever so softly. Giving thanks for his abundance of blessing to have afforded me the fine dining restaurant meal.

At the same time of my gratitude, the shadow of large wings came through the restaurant. Causing the lights to flicker. And the earth rocked ever so gently. In the same time The LORD said to me, "You will be with me forever. It happened so quickly. The spirit of The LORD dipped in, said those words to me, and was gone, just as quickly. I had heard G-D's voice before, but never to the point where anyone else heard G-D's voice at the same time as I did. A female and a male patron sitting at different tables said to me. Wow, did you hear that? Did you see that? I said, "Yes, I did" Then both said to me. "Should we call someone? In dismay, of hearing the voice of G-D and the supernatural event. The male said. "Who should we call?" I smiled at him and said. "Who would believe you?" The friend that I was with hear The LORD's voice and repeated what The LORD said to me, back to me.

Shortly after laughing at the fact that no one would believe us. And anyone we call to share with the public what we had experience? Would properly take us away in strait jackets because of their own unbelieving hearts. So the perfect strangers and I made the best out of our respective

56

meals, it seemed neither one of us was hungry anymore. G-D stole the show. I set a placement for G-D at the restaurant's dinner table. And G-D made himself the main course.

I saw differences between me and other kids. But I was not acting white. I was simply trying to be myself. I feared there was something wrong with me. I started to think I might have arrived at the world broken. I couldn't do anything the way other kids would do it. Though I would arrive at the same conclusion as they did. And at times, even faster and more proficient than they did. My way of getting there was always different, but good. I tried hard to fit in. I started saying to myself. "You are broken." "You have come to the world, broken." "Why is there no one else around you like you?" If I saw a dead animal. I could not pass it by. I would stop and thank G-D for the animal's life. Because I was sure no one else acknowledge the life that was given to the animal that was lost. I would ask G-D to accept the dead animal soul back unto himself. I never saw or knew anyone that did that. For me, it always seemed like the good, reasonable, and natural thing to do. That also made me appear differently.

And I did not kill for fun like other children. Their killing helpless birds, lizards and frogs made me angry. I would often say to the other children. "How would you like to come home one day, and your parents are no longer there? Because someone bigger and stronger than them kill them for absolutely no reason? Not for food and not for survival. Do you not understand that these birds, lizards, and frogs have families also? Like you have a mother, a sister, and a brother?

Instantly I would get beat up, because I was a kill joy of a child. Telling them things that they could not comprehend. It was just a stupid animal to them. To me? I had no part in the animal's life. Therefore, I could not take part in its death. How could I destroy that which I had no part in creating? I met the animal on earth when I arrived. Therefore, I was to go my way (about my business) without being a disturbance to the animal. And he me.

I practice at home to not act the white that I was not acting in the first place. This happened for years. When I should have been spending the time getting to know myself better.

I would often ask. While looking up to the sky. "Who am I?" Until one day at age 36 years old. My life changed. When I walked into a room unannounced. I heard my sister say. "So, Mommy? Your daddy. The white man. Tell me more about him. Mommy said. "And what are you asking me about this again for? "Well, I know you have sisters and brothers in the US. And I just want to know more about your daddy. My Granddaddy. He was a full-blooded white man, right? Mommy said. "Yes." No one wanted me to learn that my real granddaddy was a white man. I say. "What Granddaddy Mommy? "What white man? "Hoping that she would clarify. I say. "What is this I am hearing about your daddy being a white man? When were you going to tell me this? Mommy says. "Well honey. Our women were frown upon. If she went outside of our race. So, it was important for everyone to keep it a secret." I say. "What about this is a secret? Everyone knows your daddy is a white man. And not the black man I call Daddy. Everyone but me. So apparently there is no secret. You knew I've been struggling for years to understand myself and my identity. And this is how you let me find this out. Is this why all my

life am being told to stop acting white. You held the missing piece of my puzzle away from me all these years. For what? That I must walk in here to learn. My Granddaddy is not really my granddaddy. And my real Granddaddy I don't even know? And the only person in this family that doesn't know this information is me? Come on family. Come on. Y'all can do better than this." I turned and walked away.

I was not at peace within myself. I withdrew even further to seek G-D. So, I started having longer extended meditations. Where I would leave my current existence. And levitate above myself. While seeing myself sitting still below. I would gently lift and toss aside all distractions and obstructions to my view. Buildings. Cars. Streetlights. And all things made of men's hands. I soon perfected mentally removing all things that seemed artificial within nature. I felt that was the only way, I was able to see beyond clearer for a better understanding of just how things came into being. And who I was also. For some reason beyond my own understanding. I started searching for answers even more. After meeting Marquicee. I stretched the limits of my own imagination. So that I was able to see for myself how creation came into being, before the distractions that exist within nature. This I would do daily. Sometimes, three or four times a day for hours. And I believed the results of my own process of elimination.

Each time I would get to the end of my meditative elimination of the worlds distracting objects and noises. To see within G-D's Creation. I would be sitting along, with the open universe, and I was always left to think. There must be an architect of all that I saw. A Grand Designer, An Infinite, Intelligent One. All that was left that was real. The things that were beyond man's ability in all of their infancy wisdom. Both individually and collectively to make The Universe. "Someone must have made this." Was my thinking as a child. I say to myself. It seems impossible to have been created on its own.

Using this same method of elimination. I would go back to Adam's time period. And other times. Noah. And even Jonah in the belly of the whale. Where I learned certain breathing techniques. As a child, I was busy looking and searching out the stores of the bible and the architect of The Universe. The Ultimate Intelligent One.

SEEKING BEGGAR

CHAPTER VI

One day. As I was seeking. Not knowing how to find the one responsible for The Universe. That he should tell me who I was. My Mama Rita said to one of her lodge sisters who presented her with a problem and not a solution. She said loudly. "My Father G-D. Is KING OF THE WORLD!" Expressing that she had no limitations, but that which she gives herself. My Mama Rita was bold like that spiritually. She considered herself belonging to G-D, That statement vibrated through me. And changed my life. I knew without a shadow of a doubt. The ground I walked on. That was firm under my feet and the universe I saw within me when I would get to the end of my eliminating imagination. Did not make itself. And all this I knew because of my own daily mental elimination meditations.

I had heard many childhood stories growing up about certain beggars sitting on the doorsteps of The King and finding favor. So, I went to find "THE KING OF THE UNIVERSE." That he should make me one of his hired servants. To learn from him. And know me. I decided I would much rather be a door keeper in the house of The LORD. Than to dwell in the tents of wickedness for all eternity.

I wrapped some clothing in a cloth, like a beggar would have done in Jesus' time. I place it at the tip of a stick. And tossed it over my right shoulder. I walked to my extra special place on the beach. Sat down. And started imagining and meditating.

And I imagine myself speaking with strangers while on my way happily to The King of The World's castle so that I make speak with him. I knew that the universe would recognize my actions because they witness beggars with a pure and a clean heart received the attention of Kings in times pass. With their aid? I knew that if I was faithful to the task. The Universe would help me.

I was very cleaver in my seeking of The King of The Universe. Because I knew? He would be fill with wisdom. As a King should be. I arrived at his palace I imagined for him. There were many guards. And people moving around outside in my imagination. I imagined many steps to the upper-level entry door. Though others were rushing to get in the door of the castle just like I had imagined? I was in no hurry. I intended through imagination to take my time. So, I would spend an entire day imagining. Basically, camping out in a peacefully manner at The King of The World's doorstep to gain entry. I wanted to be noticed from up above. Not down below. So, I made the crowd of people bum-rush The King's door. And I took a seat on the first step. Alone. Just so I can be noticed in a peace-loving way. I alone sat down with my back to The Kings door as though I didn't care to go in each day. I would move up one step at a time daily. Playing my flute. And waiting patiently.

It took my imagination many days to complete what I had in-visioned. When I arrived at the top of the step something happened. I was there alone. All the people I had rushed the Kings door daily to create a disturbance. Were tired. And laid out on the floor. But I did not imagine them tired. As I walked over the sleeping bodies on the steps of The King's castle. The double doors of the castle opened to

me. As I walked to the open door. I looked back at the bodies, and I realized by saying to myself. "I didn't imagine any of this?" Neither did I imagined any part of what happened

next. Two extremely large guards invited me inside. I walked in the middle. They were frightening to look upon. And they needed no weapons, their size was weapon enough they were so huge. But they still had 10 to 15 feet swords in their right hand. They walked me over to a high table. And showed me three items made of gold. A golden helmet. A golden breastplate, a golden sword.

While at the table one guard turned to me and said. "My G-D. THE KING OF THE UNIVERSE has sent you three gifts. That he would like you to have. You may select only one. That you would like to have." The massive guards stepped back and says. "Make your selection." I selected the gold helmet. And place it on my head. Instantly I was returned into my body. I was never so happy as in that moment. I begin to recognize this KING OF THE UNIVERSE to be the greatest force that existed in all Things.

This was the day. In my heart, the KING OF ALL THE UNIVERSE, became my friend. Because he met me inside of my own orchestrated imagination. I knew. This KING OF

THE UNIVERSE was strong. Because he came to me through my unreal and made it real. I found The architect I was seeking. And he gave me a gift. I was over the moon happy.

The following day my dad came up to me and say. "What would you like to eat today?" I love his questions about dinner. He was such an exceptional fisherman and diver. I was able to have anything that was under the sea. In the Atlantic Ocean. It was an adventure for me as a kid. To decide a challenge for my dad. I say. "Today I would like to go out in the boat Dad. And spend the day fishing. My Dad replied. "You've got it princess!"

We enjoyed ourselves. And stayed on the boat overnight. The following morning. We ran out of bates, hooks and sinkers. And needed ice to refresh ourselves. The nearest town was in the direction of home. We were catching too many fish to leave. My Dad says. "Are you ready?" I say. "No. We will get the things we need. It's too good to leave now. We should stay. And THE KING OF THE UNIVERSE will provide our needs. Here. And now."

My Dad smiled at me. And said. "OK daughter. If you say we stay? We stay." He knew that G-D worked miracles around me. He had seen enough to his own good fortune over the years. He just didn't know what would happen. I also didn't know. But I had unwavering faith. After THE KING OF THE WORLD met me in my own imagination. A day earlier. I went in the galley to meditate privately. After stilling myself. I levitate above the boat. To show the LORD myself. On the boat. In the middle of the ocean. And to speak and be heard. After I levitated and showed The LORD where I was. I called on the LORD. I said. "KING OF THE WORLD? If it be your will. May it please you to supply my need for hooks, sinkers and ice? I will wait upon **THEE** all day. As I have done before indeed and in action. For **THOU** art my sure delight. And my ever-present help in times of trouble."

I returned to my body in the galley's chair. Then I make myself comfortably like I did at the Kings doorsteps." I was not going to move until my request was fulfilled. Intentionally affirming to the LORD. I will not be move. For I know. Without a shadow of a doubt. The LORD did watch and keep. After I said that to the LORD. I said. No more! A short time after I was sitting there with my eyes closed. I heard a male's voice speaking with my dad, and I hear multiple footsteps on our boat. But I stayed in silent meditation. I had my eyes fixed on the LORD. Supplicating before him for the fulfillment of my request. That he should meet me in my situation like he met me in my imagination prior. Seconds later my dad came in the galley. He was holding a large bag of ice. And a large clear bag of hooks and sinkers. Then he said to me. "A gentlemen brought these things and says to me. "Give these to the female on the boat." I smile at my dad. He smiled back at me, and we continued another day out at sea. Only by G-D (THE KIG OF THE UNIVERSE) grace. At the end of the day. At sunset. We sat watching the horizon. A gently voice spoke in my right ear and says to me.

"What would make this time memorable for you?" I say. "Well LORD? if I can see..." Before I was done speaking. A dolphin emerges out of the water just for me. Before I told The LORD that I desired to see a dolphin. And I Blessed the LORD for his powers. And for making my dream come through. From that day forward. I never stop believing in miracles. And the powers of The LORD.

After heading home from a long adventure. I joined my Auntie Vicky and my cousin Zelrona walking on the beach. It was Sunday. The Natives beach day. Our blended family was now bringing our estate European tourist traffic. While walking. I turned away for a second. Looked back again and Zelrona and my Auntie was down the beach like lightening. So, I dash behind them to see what made them run so fast. They dove in the sand and started digging it up frantically. Suddenly. The fun stopped on the beach. All eyes were on the sand.

Then I saw other beach goers running toward Zelrona and Aunt Vicky. As I got nearer to the commotion. I hear. "White gal?, white gal ya deaf? Cover your pork. Cover your pork white gal." I looked and saw a white woman lying on her back wrestling to stay alive from sand strangulation. As the natives thought she had washed up on the beach a mermaid. As they did in the movies. Or her lack of clothing was the direct result of being attacked by someone or shipwrecked and floated onto their beach in the dead of night. When they learned she was nude by choice, and not by force? Her nudity offended the Natives, they were all obedient to G-D's laws given to Moses as ways for females to live by. They were angry that she had committed the sin openly, No pun intended. She did not follow the guiding principles of The Bible set forth by G-D, that a woman should only be exposed to her husband. This incident was the first time the natives on the remote island had seen a law of G-D broken publicly. That day, I learned the word, "nudist beach." That's when it was planted in out that nudity was ok, everyone in Europe was doing it.

The Natives of the island did laugh at themselves when they discovered their error. But walked away from the lady felling contented that she was now fully clothed with the finest pink sand beach on the remote island.

ZERO
SIR

CHAPTER VII

My friend Prudence and I decided to walk to my Mamie's restaurant at lunch time. We had prearranged plans. We were excited for the bell to ring. As we got closer to my family's restaurant. I heard Mr. B say in his normal loudest voice. "Am the best. From The EAST. The WEST. The NORTH. And The SOUTH. No man has beat me yet!" Immediately I knew Daddy, Mr. B was playing backgammon.

When others ran away from him. I ran to him. The only way to beat the best. Was to play the best. I needed to have what he had. And what he knew? I needed to know. I walked in and observed The Manager of The Water Company getting up from the table defeated. Straight away my Daddy challenged me to a game of backgammon. No one else would play him. He was that good.

The more I lost. The more I wanted to play again. I knew I was only able to lose just so many games. Before the wheel started turning in my favor to win. I knew if I was able to win just one. I would strive to win them all. Because with

winning one, I understood there was also the possibility of winning more, and more, and more. Until I was winning all. Eventually I did. I never stopped winning. "Come on Cleo." Mr. B said to me. He loved rushing me along to make a move. Only when I put the squeeze on him. Making moves harder and harder for him to make would he give up.

Mr. B. would leave the game open for hours. He would wait until I fell asleep in the chair. Then sneak out the room. Or pretend to need Mamie. To avoid having to concede to his grandchild. I enjoyed the games with Mr. B.

But it was time to head back to school. Prudence and I strolled back singing and eating ice cream sundaes. As we turned the corner, we didn't see anyone on the school grounds. We panicked. Dropped our ice creams. And washed our hands on our skirts. With ice cream covering our mouths. We scrambled up the hill to our respective classes. In the distance the Principal Mr. Newly called out to us. He

says. "Cleo? Prudence? Come here." Mr. Newly was among the teachers that came to the remote islands from Britain. I tried whispering a quick-thinking plan. To concur the situation ahead of us. As Prudence rushed. Looking straight ahead. I looked at her face and said. "Prudence? This is what we must do to get out of this. Before I was do-ne strategizing I saw fear enter Prudence changing her facial expression at the same time. I shuck my head in dismay. I couldn't believe how quickly prudence gave up the ghost before the battle. We were already defeated. This I knew for sure. Because I was following G-D's guiding principles. **Matthew 18:20.** For where two or three are gathered in my name. There I am in

the midst of them to bless. So I often applied his principles. And as I saw the outcome successful as G-D says in scripture. I kept on applying more and more each time. We were two in the midst of G-D until Prudence jump ship and fear of Mr. Newly overtook her. We couldn't win. The minute prudence let fear in amount us. We were finish. Well not all of us.

Prudence said. "Yes sir Mr. Newly." Mr. Newly said. "Where were you?" "We were at the restaurant for lunch sir." We say. "Do you know what time it is?" Mr. Newly did not want to know the time of day. But he wanted to make sure we knew it because we were late back from lunch. "No sir" we said sweetly hoping to get off with a warning.

Mr. Newly said. "Prudence? How many whips would you like from zero to three? How Prudence? Remember. From zero to three." Which spelled out to me that zero was available from Trebek for 100. Only thing was. Prudence didn't seem to think so. I looked up to the sky in advance dismay.

"Two sir." She said in haste. Then she started rubbing her hands together and looking at me in anticipation of her good fortune. Of two out of three lashes. With zero as an option. Mr. Newly liked tricking the native children with words. He had a serpent's tongue with two edges. One that twist and turned easily. He never succeeded in tricking me with words. "Words" belong to my heavenly father to be used at my disposal. I didn't allow Mr. Newly to complete the question. Mr. Newly says. "Cleo?" I say. "Zero sir. Zero. I require zero sir. Zero from zero to three sir. Mr. Newly sir. Yes sir."

If he hated that I was right and still wanted to whip me? I was going to kill him with kindness and double up on the sirs." Either way. I was going to win the pass without punishment. Mr. Newly whipped his bamboo stick in the air. Pointed the way and says. "Get to your class. You smart butt."

I felt he had it in for me. I was not easily tricked. The spirit of G-D was there inclining my ear that I should hear and understand properly. If he was going to ask another question, I was not going to leave time for him to formulate or pontificate for that matter. I was out-tar-there.

The following day there was a sporting events that make the neighboring schools all come together. And everyone on the school grounds would instantaneously become friends just to beat the other teams. So, I felt honored. I was chosen to be the track and field substitute. My physical education teacher knew that I hated to perspire and to appear disheveled. Which resulted from PE. If I was forced to run in a race? I would forfeit mid-race. The minute I felt the first drop of sweat hit my forehead.

This time. I felt obligated to beat the other schools. I ran home. I couldn't wait to show of my team spirit to my mother and sister Rochelle. I say. "Mommy? Mommy? Mommy? They want me to be the team's prostitute!" Incidentally. I didn't know the scope of a team prostitute. But I intended to be the best.

After getting laughed at to scorn. By my mother and sister. I decided I was not going to be a team prostitute after all. Not even a substitute for that matter. I even question going to a College Institution after that humiliation that lasted years.

At that time Mama Rita's Husband. My granddaddy had a stroke. So, I was called overnight by my sister Rochelle. "A stroked prostitute." And my mother would laugh. I looked at them and thought? "They cannot think I don't understand those words. I was an advance child." So, from that moment onward. I consider the words they were offering me. "Stroked prostitute." So, I called them a word of my own that described their actions. "Dysfunctional."

I hated that my tongue was tied. Or at least this is what the foreign British teachers told us was wrong with us. When you had a mispronunciation of a word. Or a misinterpretation between two words. That sounded similar. While these things happened to me and so many others. We were not told the English language was not the language of our ancestors.

For example. My Aunt Emma told a European white woman when she was prompted to tell the white lady what the name of her mother was. My Aunt Emma said. "My Mamie's name is *Midget*" instead of. "My Mamie's name is *Mildred*." Or Mr. B for example. He went to the city to look for a particular food truck that was called "*Esther* meals on wheels." He went around the city until night fall. Looking around and asking for "*Easter* meals on wheels."

All we were told was The Native American Indians. Our Ancestors? Had all died out. But I would often question being told that by our teachers. I filtered everything through my meditative imagination, process of elimination while searching for the truth.

One race dying out. And another similar near exact race living in the same lands? but with no connection to the people prior? And they did not come from any other lands? Seemed like it was propagated information to me. All I didn't know was. W*hy did it happen!* So, my thoughts were always very deep. But my tongue as they made us to believe. Was often very tied.

There was very little to no information about my ancestors The Native American Indians. In fact, we were taught more about The Pirates of The Caribbean, and the movie. Namely Black Beard. And Huckleberry Fin and Tom Sawyer.

I never forgot. My ancestors The Native American Indians, The Indigenous People of The Earth. Because some of my elders. Didn't permit me to forget.

Her name was Ms. Leila Stuart. Every time she saw me. She calls out to me saying. "Marquicee? Which was her name for me. My name didn't matter to this lady. Don't know if she even cared to know my name. I was always my great grandmother's name. Marquicee the Indian to her. She would say to me. "How are you doing Marquicee?" Hugging me tightly to her chest saying "Child? You look just like your great grandma. You know she was an Indian?" She told me enough. That I should never, ever forget.

REPENT
REPENT

CHAPTER VIII

The day started unlike any other. A continuation of seven days of fasting and praying by my uncle and Pastor's instructions for his congregation. Though it would have been the first time for me. It was easy. I ate very little anyway. And was often required too as skinny. Living in the City at our vacation home. I had no need to cook for anyone else. Which was great for my fasting and seclusion with G-D.

I continue to fast. Pray and anoint my head unto G-D The Father. G-D The Son. And G-D The Holy Spirit daily. From the third day onward into the fast. I develop from weakness to strength. Which was a weird feeling for me because I was not eating. My very first manifestation of the Holy Spirit visitation during my fast started at my computer as I was searching the internet passing the time. The Holy Spirit came upon me the heaviest I had ever felt. And says to me. "Write these things!"

I went over to the word document page. Readied my fingers on the keyboard awaiting the master's instructions. And he spoke through his Holy Spirit and says to me. And I wrote. **"Children in the world are suffering. Suffering by**

the hands of their own parents. Their own teachers. Their own preachers. Their own peers. And the circle goes on and on from there. I beach you brethren. End the suffering Now. Or else the LORD your G-D will come in a mighty way to save the innocent ones.

You have been loved of me for a lifetime. Death. Hatred for your brothers. Jealousy. Greed. Malist. Adulterous. Thieves. Murderous. The land is dying.

Cast away all this! I am your Savior. I am your G-D. Hear me! Do my will! I love you. Heed my words! Repent! Repent! Repent! Be saved. I love you. I am G-D! Repent! Repent! Repent! Repent! Repent! Repent! Repent! Repent! My fingers had never moved so swiftly as it did while typing the Holy Spirit's message for The World. Because the Holy Spirit had spoken the message. I kept it original. I did not edit it. I looked at the message. And thought. "Wow." Then I said to myself. "Who will believe that I have a message from G-D? So, I started typing next to the Holy Spirits these words of my own.

"My brothers and sisters in The LORD Most High. I wish only to prove to you that this message is from G-D. And as I sit in my home typing this the greatest type of my life." I stopped there. Then the Holy Spirit sent from G-D returned to me again. Took over the message. And says to me. Say this unto them. **"If you love. And trust me my faith? So should you show faith to my messenger."** So, I typed. In tears and with the spirits permission. I beg the people. I said. "Please, please. Repent. People of The World. Repent. The spirit of G-D when further and said to me. Say unto them. **"Lay down your burdens and come to me. For I, I am your G-D. I toil with what to do with you. The sickness. The diseases. The way you have turned your backs against me. You have forgotten. Out of the lion's den you have been** taken. I have saved you from all evil. You have forgotten the LORD your G-D.

Less I bring you home! You have caused me pain. Toil. Heartache. Do you not know the measure of my love for you? Do you not know what you mean to me? I am your father. You have been drugged through the lowest of valleys. And I saved you from it. I love you. Change from your wicked ways. I am The LORD your G-D. I will spear the righteous and destroy the wicked for my own namesake. No wicked will prosper in the Land. The Righteous should exalt the Earth. For I am G-D. Ruler of everything.

Be not afraid. For I will come as a thief in the night. To rescue my people from darkness. The righteous will inherit the earth. The wicked will be scattered about left to roam the earth. For I am G-D and above me there is none other. I have come to save and set the captives free. I am your G-D. You are my child. The righteous should be with me forever. And I in him. I live forever.

I concluded The Holy Spirit message for humanity by typing. "I am only a humble servant G-D choose to do his bidding at 7:25pm Monday August 2009. And it is at this end. That I pray for humanity that G-D would have mercy upon us all." As the Holy Spirit spoke in more details. The Spirit's hold on me became firmer. I became frighten. I felt the love for humanity. I also felt the disappointment. What overwhelming sorrow it was for me to feel the heart of G-D. It was real.

I tried everything to comfort G-D. Dancing as I did for him from my youth. Singing. Reverence. Sacrifices. Nothing worked as before. So, I offered my life while kneeling at the foot of my bed. In exchange for G-D's hurt. And as atonement for the sins of the World. Of which I did not know that the World had sinned exactly. It just seemed like the right thing to say. And I continued by saying. "And for the salvation of all your children. That they will be reconciled back to you." Suddenly a ball of light entered my room. I turn to look. And there he was. A man. I felt was THE KING OF THE UNIVERSE. G-D. That gave me the gold helmet. Sitting in my boudoir. Though he sat? His cloak did not rest. His frame was made of a turquoise and greenish color light. And he held his hands together forming a triangle. As though he was contemplating. I felt the weight of the heart of The LORD in the room. And it was heavy. Sorrow was upon him. I ran to his feet to comfort him. Fell down on my knees and said. "My LORD? "How can I take this pain away from **THEE**? And as The LORD cried while sitting in my bedroom chair.

I said. "My LORD? I am so sorry for whatever it is. Speak to me LORD, and THY servant heareth. Tell me how I can fix whatever it is that has happened, that has brough you to this grief? And what can I do? I offer you myself. As a living sacrifice for your pain. My life I give unto you LORD in atonement for your pain. That it shall go away. That you should feel pain like this no more LORD." Then The LORD spoke while crying and said to me.

"My children are scattered throughout the world. By others. And I love them. I made a covenant with

them. And they are my very own. But <u>others put my children to death without a cause</u>." This is when it hit me. That The World was in trouble with G-D. Because of his children that were scattered. I remember thinking. "Who are these children that died without a cause The LORD is speaking off?. As the LORD permitted me to comfort him, because of his sorrow. The LORD spoke again and said to me. "<u>Though I had chastened my own children? I did not put them to death. But many others throughout The World have put my children to death.</u>

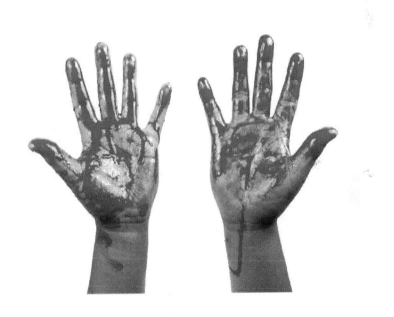

Then The LORD, THE KING OF THE UNIVERSE took me up with him into a place. And I looked and saw rivers of blood. Thick red flowing blood. And The LORD dipped both his hands in the blood. And brought his bloodied hands to his face. Then he reached out his bloodied hands to me. That I may witness the blood of his innocent children. I weep. Because of _Romans 12:15 "Be happy with those who are happy, and weep with those who weep."_ And The LORD did weep. And I also cried with The LORD. The LORD then showed me many buried. With unmarked graves. Of those whom the rivers of blood belonged unto. And I watch as the KING OF THE UNIVERSE, G-D sobbed. Like any Father. Over the death of his decease children. Whom he said to me. "Their deaths were not of natural cause."

I had unquenchable sorrow on all sides. For my love. The LORD, & KING OF THE UNIVERSE. And for Humanity. Of-which I am a part. I just knew without a shadow of a doubt humanity was in trouble with G-D. And many people would die because of it. *Because of Matthew 5:38-39 – Ye have heard that it hath been said, An eye for an eye, and a tooth for a tooth.* But it was him (The LORD) that had spoken those words in Matthew, experiencing the offence brought on my others. Therefore, I understood fully through The Holy Spirit, that *the rebuke for the offense must come into The World from him that gave the warning*.

While at the river of blood with the LORD. He placed in my spirit Genesis 1:1. *In the beginning was the word and the word was with (G-D).* In this case the words were, "An eye for an eye, and a tooth for a tooth and The LORD was warning me of the outcome."

While at the rivers of blood with The LORD. His Holy Spirit came to me saying. "**As many that have died of these rivers of blood?. So should many other bloodied rivers flow. But this time! By G-D. And not by men. He has spoken. Should he not uphold that which he spoke?** I became instantly nauseated. I understood coming calamities would befall mankind sent by The LORD while standing at the river with The LORD and his bloodied hands.

It seemed to me. The murdering of those The LORD said was his children was an act of waging war on G-D. And those he says he loved. And I knew. It would end in monumental catastrophe. And death would be humanities portion for crossing The LORD's landmark. Which is his people. The lot of G-D's inheritance, *Deuteronomy 32:9 says, Do ye requite the LORD, O foolish people and unwise? Remember the days of old, consider the years of many generations; ask THY father, and he will shew THEE, THY father, and he will show THEE; THY elders, and they will tell THEE. When The Most High divided to the nations their inheritance, when he separated the sons of Adam, he set the bounds of the people according to the number of the children of*

91

Israel. For the LORD's portion is his people (his children); Jacob is the lot of his inheritance."

I didn't know exactly who the children were that G-D had this enormous anguish over their deaths. I tried hard to think who the children where that died. Then G-D said to me **"My children are scattered throughout the world. By others. And I love them. I made a covenant with them. And they are my very own."** When I heard this, I suspected changes in The World. Because of G-D's sorrow

over the death of his children. I had never seen The LORD as sorrowful. And as brokenhearted over anything. As he was over these children he spoke off when he came to my boudoir. And I had never seen The LORD as angry and as dreadful looking. As when he turned away from my side to go out into all The World. When The LORD took his eyes of me. He turned from me and he became a consuming fire. Fire surrounded The LORD. Because of his anger. I saw upon The

LORD, that he was displeased. And filled with angry rage. And The LORD went through the Earth with his fire. I somehow knew. Days of trouble was ahead. I began to expect trouble sent by G-D to The Earth. And I would pray and cry daily to The LORD for mercy on us.

A few days later. After The LORD's visit me. I turned on the TV and heard on the news a report. That found 200 unmark graves of slaves buried after 1859 in Winston Salem, NC in 2018. On the very seem day in 2021 breaking news reported by Cadmus Delorme, Chief of The Cowessess First Nation said in a news conference that 751 unmarked graves were found at the side of The Marieval Indian Residential School. A month earlier 215 Native American Children, some as young as 3, were found buried on the side of indigenous residential schools that operated from 1899 to 1996 by The Catholic Church. The nearby cemeteries at the unmarked graves have been run by the Roman Catholic Church,

My prayer still yet today. Is that no one will. And I mean not one single solitary person will come face to face with the wrathfully dreadful anger. I saw. On the face of The LORD G-D and KING OF THE UNIVERSE. That day. Over the death of his children. As one unfortunate soul that troubled and kidnap me came to find out of G-D's wrath over those he love.

One day I was being driven home in my car. Being chauffeured by my fiancé's butler. We lived on Paradise Island. One of the most exclusive residence in The Commonwealth of The Bahamas. As The Butler was taking me home to my fiancé. He said. "Can I stop at the foot of the bridge? There is a restaurant I would like to grab some take out?" I say. "Yes." While I continue looking down at my computer. The Butler was visible. So, I was not concerned.

I saw a person walk over to the butler and shared an embrace. Others were ordering food from the restaurant also. When our Butler returned to the vehicle to drive us home. Over the bridge. He said to me. "My high school friend. That I have not seen in many years has invited me to his house tonight. It's his birthday. Would you mind if we pass by his house? He is having a party tonight. I will not be long there. It is just that if we go at the house. Owen (my fiancé) expects that I will not leave." I said. How far away is it? He said. "It's just around the corner." I said. "Yes. You many, But for a short time only."

We had an exceptional butler. He worked hard. He knew everybody. He always looked out for me. He never gave me any trouble. So why not. I was in good hands. Or at least I thought so. We arrived at our butler's friend house. It was a huge white house. Several levels. When we got inside. Our butler left my side. I took a few steps inside the house that opened to the back of the yard. It was a nice house. But

I had seen better. To me? It was just a regular house. I saw many people moving around. But nothing out of the ordinary. They seemed happy and having fun. Like a regular party. Everyone was wearing white. I stood in one spot for a minute. Then I left and went back to my vehicle. And waited for my butler to drive me home. He came. And we left.

And the end that should have been history? Was not. The following day. While at my other apartment. Our butler had just driven me too. An apartment that I went to as a leveling place of peace. When I wanted to break free from the "High Life." As blending in. Being grounded. And remaining humble. Still meant everything to me.

I started walking from my bedroom to the front door of my apartment. Just as I open it? In from of my door were four men. One to the left of the door. One to the right, One a few steps behind the two nearest the door. And. One in the driver's seat. Looking anxious. While looking up and down the street. Left and right. The one nearest me on the right says. "We need you to come with us." I say. "For what?" The other one to my left said. "Never mind what for. We just need you to come with us. Now. You can do that on your own. Walking. Or you can do that by force. And that will mean others will get hurt." The other man said. "Everyone around here."

The neighboring kids used my front porch as a congregating stop. When they knew I was visiting my second home? They would come to see what treasures I brought them. They sat between me and the four men. I only needed a second to consider what they were saying to me. I knew. There was no way I would have allowed the kids to be hurt by trying to escape or scream for help. So, I unwillingly walked silently with the men to an awaiting vehicle.

I saw they had guns without seeing the guns. I could tell by the one on the right's jacket. I walked to the waiting kidnapper's car, and they showed me to a seat. The one that was closest to me at my front door? Sat beside me in the front seat. I was still holding my cellphone in my hand. They didn't seem to care. The driver? He was doing a lot of driving and turning. He went what felt like everywhere with the vehicle. Trying to confuse me. The front seat passenger was busy talking on his phone. Using the word. "Boss." And playing with the radio. When I looked up at the men sitting beside me? They would look down at me. They were huge. My phone stated to ring. It was Owen on my caller id. One look from the man on my right? And I knew I couldn't answer it. I watch as Owen called and called. Which had never happened. That I didn't answer his calls. So the more, he called.

We finally arrived at a house. I didn't recognize. I had a
general Idea. It was the western direction. They walked me

into a house. One said to me." Where is it?" I shrug my shoulder and say. "Where is what?" The other man that sat on my left in the car took over. Advance toward my face and said to me. "You know what." I waited for a second. And very calmly said. "No. I do not."

We waited in that house for what felt like eight hours. As the sun begin to set. My optimism began to fail. I felt I would not be rescued. Then they took me on another drive that felt like a day had pass. It was obvious they were trying to confuse my mind again on the locations, we were driving in.

We arrived at a location. I had remember seeing before. It was the home I had visited the night before. I was placed in a chair. In a part of the house, I had never seen before. This is when my heart failed me. And I left as though I was going to die. As they left me there to sit. I said to G-D. "LORD?. Look upon me. My soul is drawn out. I am cast down to the ground. Many are they that are my adversaries. Many are they which desire to remove my footsteps from the land of the living. And I am only one. Whatever is laid to my charge G-D? I am innocent." I closed my eyes and said Look LORD? I place my two hands in the air toward Heaven (In the Spirit). That the G-D would examine them for my innocence. Then I said to G-D. "But yet my soul is cast down to the grown and they (the voices of my kidnappers in the other room I directed The LORD to hear) wait for my soul to devour it. I say. "Save **THOU** me Oh LORD. For I am innocent."

When I opened my eyes. A man was sitting in the chair directly in front of me. He was wearing a tiger print shirt. He says to me. "Where is it?" I say. "I don't know what any of you are talking about. Where is what?" He said to me. "You are the only one that was at my house that I don't know. And I know everybody. Now where is it? "A man w-

alked in, And the one in the tiger print said to him. "Where were you? I've been waiting for you."

He looked at me and says. "Boss? Why is she here? The boss in the tiger print said. "She stole from me." Which was the first time I had heard that. The one that walked in and was talking to the boss I had seen before once or twice. I didn't know his name. I was a VIP at his girlfriend's nail parlor. And we saw each other in passing at other VIP social events around town. But we never spoke. He said right away to his Boss. "Boss? I don't think his girl stole anything. There must be a mistake. She has it like that. And where she doesn't have it? Her people have it. I don't think she does roll like that Boss." Then he thought for a minute and says. "No. She wouldn't do something like that, am sure of it." The boss says to him. "You know her?" He says. "No. Well not like that. But I have seen her around. Everywhere she goes. She's straight. And she moves all the time with people who have it boss. So, I don't think she did it."

The Boss say. "Just do your F**king job. What? What? Is the henchman getting soft? The Henchman said. "No Boss. But she can get anything she wants. Why steal? The Henchman hesitated. And the boss kept pressuring him. To do something he did not want to do. Which was to harm me. The henchman took a deep breath and pulled out a knife. I observed the boss became excited that I was about to be tortured. Instantly I developed a hateful passion toward the boss's lack of respect for life. As he was not the life given to require my life from me. His actions regarding my life make me to instantly disrespect his life in the spiritual realm. I observed the Henchman was like a prisoner to his boss. What I saw and heard? Let me to feel as though. I was not

100

the only person not free to leave. In the room. But the henchman was also. Not free. Just as he was about to threaten me by force. The Boss was called to the other room. And I was able to catch my breath.

Then the henchman that held the blade? The Boss called into the next room. Before the henchman left. He said to me. "Look. Am sorry this is happening to you. Something in my heart says to me. You didn't do this. Am going to get you out of this." The henchman looks down to

the floor and said to me. "Am trying to leave all this behind me. Am working on it every day." With a heavy heart. The Henchman left the room. While alone? My phone rings. I open the line quickly that no one should hear it ring. It was my best friend, Sheila. She says. "Are you all, right? Owen is calling me looking for you." I whisper. "Sheila? Am in trouble. I've been kidnapped. I am in The Western part of town. I am in a huge white house with multiple steps at the front door. There are henchmen, bosses, and other bad guys. I need you to send the police. To the biggest white house in the west. Come quick. There is not much time. I believe they are going to kill me." Sheila said. "Don't you worry. I know just who to call. I used to date the second in command of the army. I will get him on the phone." Sheila and I disconnected the line.

The boss came back and said to the four that brought me there. "Get rid of her." I remember looking at the boss's face on my way out the door. And He smiled proudly at me and adjusted his robe. He had this look on his face. I can do away with your life this is what I do. Like killing and taking a life was just a regular day in the life of him look. What he didn't know was I had a personal relationship with HIM (G-

D) who gives life and was able to take it away. So instantly. Because of his arrogance. I hated that guy spiritually, because he portrayed himself as The Master. G-D. One thing I knew for sure. My life did not belong to me. It belonged to G-D.

They walked me at the front door to exit the house. I knew what was coming next. As the door of the house open. I heard bullets going into hundreds of chambers. Then a voice came over a bullhorn saying. "All of you there? Step out of the house with your hands up." I stepped out also with my hands up. I saw a sea of armed men. All had machine guns. Wearing army uniform. Three helicopters rested in the sky before our eyes. Directly in front of the house. Fully loaded and ready to go. I passed out on the floor.

The one that spoke on the bullhorn stepped forward. And crossed the street. He walked up the stairs to the top and came directly to my face. He said to me. "I believe you are why we are here. If you are in danger. I need you to give me a sign now." I became frozen in place. He said to me as he looked deep into my eyes. "Madam? Can you hear me? Are you all, right?" Just give me a sign that you are in danger, and this will all be over. Are you who we are looking for?" With my hand in the air. And tears flowing from my eyes. I couldn't speak. I was so relieved. I couldn't bring my hands down from the sky. I suffered shock. bullhorn brough me back to life. He said with his Bullhorn. "Get them out of here. And the army men moved into the house and arrested all the occupants. And took them away"

At the time. My ex of 10 years was a very prominent attorney. 10 Minutes into custody. He had already heard what had happened to me. He called my phone while in protective custody. He came to me. He says. "Do you know who did this to you?" I said. "No. I don' t know his name." My ex said to me. "He is James." He is only the biggest dealer on the island. Then the officer in the room said. "You don't know who he is? I said. "No" The officer said. "Well only all the females on the island knows him." I said. "But I don't. I have never seen or heard of him before." The office said. "Well, this is their last strike. And they would get the book throw at them for this. They all will be going to jail now for a long time this time around. We must keep moving them to different jail locations every hour on the hour."

My ex said to me. "Listen. I know James. Am his lawyer. He has me on retainer right now on a case. I will speak to him and let him know. Whatever it is. It is a mistake. He doesn't know you've been like a wife to me for over 10 years. I don't think he knows that. I will speak with him.

I said to all in the room. While I was still in shock. I said. "Listen. Here it is. I really don't care about any of this. I just want to go home. The thing I have been saying all day. Is the thing I am going to say right now. "I don't know anything about what is going on. I don't even know why I am here. I don't even know what am being accuse off by them."

Then I began to think. If I would press charges. Everyone and their mother would know. I brought them down. My friend at the nail parlor would be without her daughter's father. The Henchman. Who in the end? Tried to defend me. In my heart I forgive the Henchman. He asked me for forgiveness. By saying he was sorry.

I said to my ex. The bosses Attorney. "Say this to the boss. Let him know. It is because of the Henchman. That they would all go free. I have nothing for the rest of them. And this deal? I place before G-D with all my heart. For the sake of peace. Not because of fear. But I don't care to see or hear from anyone of them again. And if I do? The deal is off. Even before G-D. Tell him. It is not because I am afraid of them that I will drop the charges. For it is them that has done me wrong. And now that his life and the lives of his men is in my hand? I offer him a trade. I never. Ever. Want to see. Or hear from them again." I went home to Owen. The following day. My ex. The Attorney for the boss called me. He said. "James wants to thank you. He said that he would like to give you $10,000.00 Dollars. I answered quickly. It made me angry. I said. "I don't want his blood money. He was going to harm me. Now he wants to pay me for that? You tell him that. He made me feel like death was coming to me. And no amount of money can make that feeling subside. He was going to kill me. For what? I still don't know to this day. He can't pay me for trying to kill me. Where in the world can you pay someone for trying to kill them? No one should have to go through feeling like that. He is used to treating people like that. Well, tell him he bucked up on the wrong one. Tell him keep his money. He cannot buy me. I am not for sale." My ex said.

"I know you. But he doesn't. I had to tell you that

because you know how it goes, I have too. You know now it goes with these things. I said." So, which part of do not contact me doesn't your client understand? I don't want to hear from him or anyone of them again. That is and was the deal. Now. If you want to take the money as a retainer for coming at the station? Do what you want. I don't want his money. Do what you want with the money. I do not care. To think that he wants to pay me. Makes me angry. I on the other hand? I don't want to hear from anyone of them again. Ever. In life." My ex said. I understand. I will tell him. Well just know that he recognizes he made a mistake. I said. "Sure, he does. The world is telling him he made a mistake with me. But he's a day late." I said. "What is it he had lost anyway?" My ex, The Boss's attorney said. "His diamond bezel Rolex. After hearing that. I went to my jewelry box for my favorite Rolex. A Yacht-Master oyster-steel, 37mm, in Everrose gold. That Owens had placed on my hand, and gave to me because it was special to him. And I was also. He went and purchased another Rolex for himself.

I love that Rolex watch. Though it was a man's watch. It looked good on my small wrist. I laid on the sofa and Owen cared for me while I rested from the ordeal. The doorbell ringed. As I sat up to get the door. Owen said. "No babe. Lay down. I've got it." My head was turned away from the door so I could not see who was out there. As I laid on my back on the sofa? Two faces came over head in view of my eyes. One was Owen and I smiled. And the other was The Boss? I stood up to my feet quickly in a panic. My heart started beating out of control again. Anxiety came back again. Owen said. "What happen? You know this guy?" I said. "Yes. This is the guy that had me kidnapped." I looked at the guy's hand. He was wearing a Rose Gold and Diamond Bezel Rolex, I was wearing a Rolex. And Owen was wearing a Rolex. Then I looked up at the guy's face. To see if he agreed it was him that had me kidnapped or did he disagreed. "His face said to me. "Miss? Did you have to tell Owen that?" I don't know why it seem as though he wanted me not to say that to Owen. Owen was harmless

After I said those words. Owen told the boss. "OK. Come with me." Our Penthouse was all glass. They started walking to the pool area. I could look out at them, but they couldn't see me. That was the way the glass was designed. I didn't make out what Owen was saying. But he was being very loud and ruff with the boss. He showed the boss out

around the terrace. I buried my head in the sofa. And cried. I relived the terror for the second time. And saw me dying on the floor passing out. The ordeal came back to me now renewed. Because as it seemed I couldn't shake this boss. And the ordeal was troubling my nerves again. When Owen came inside, I said. "Owen? What is he doing here?" Owen said. "I was going to set him up with my international connection. Three of us were going to put a nightclub together. I don't know him. We share a mutual friend.

Tonight, we met for the first time. I thought we could have our meeting on the terrace. This way I can be home with you.

Days later as I begin to heal from the anxiety brought on by the kidnapping. And my smile returned, My phone rings. It is the voice of the boss. And my heart started racing again. My nerves became shattered again. I didn't know if he though it was a good idea to contact me and see if he could get in Owen's good grace or not. But three times now. I am feeling the symptoms of a victim of kidnapping. And each time he contacted me whether directly or indirectly I was being kidnapped renewed.

So now. Am asking The LORD for this boss to fade away from me. Because as it seems? He does not want to leave me alone willingly for me to heal. While am feeling the worst anxiety I have ever felt in my life. The boss says to me. "You know who this is?' My heart started racing.

Here comes anxiety tremors and shattered nerves again. I said. "WHAT do you want?" The boss said. "I wanted you to know that I found my watch." I said. "So, what you found it?

When you had it. It had nothing to do with me. When didn't you have it? It had nothing to do with me. And now that you've got it? Guess what? It still has nothing to do with me. What part of that don't you understand?

The Boss said. "I remember where I had placed it. Between the sofa cushions. I said. "LORD? This man is hard of hearing. His neck is stiff. He has no understanding. Each contact me makes with me LORD. My life feels threatened all over again. This is when I began to secretly require from The LORD the boss's footsteps removed from The Earth that I should have peace. And not continually suffer by his hands anymore. As I struggled to control by trembling body. The Boss said to me. "I heard you didn't take the money. Why?" I said. "During your visit? Did it look like I needed anything from you? The Boss says. "If it wasn't enough. You just name your price. And it's yours. Whatever you want. Car? House? Many amounts of money. Anything? I appreciate what you've done." I say. "I cannot say the same for you."

I became offended again. All my life I ditched vanity. The gold and the diamonds, the princess dress and all the new stuff. Now this guy wants to take me within inches of my life. And offer me vanity to comfort me? I was pissed. And insulted. And because he gave me relapse in my healing process? And did not want to go away willingly? I beseech The King of The Universe to lose me from him. By requiring him to go away spiritually.

My heart started racing again. And I felt I needed to speak like the hearer. To be fully understood by him. So, I said. "Listen? If you call my M*****f***ing phone again? I will make sure all y'all go up under the jailhouse. You hear me? You wouldn't have to worry about that. You will get so much jail time. It will be like living underneath the M*****f***ing jailhouse. I disconnected the call.

And cried out to The LORD. "LORD? This man is a tyrant. All his life he has made people to feel fear. And he has dominated the weak. Look upon my affliction. And go between us. I am innocent. Did you place me in front of him to see what he would do with me? Others told him I was innocent LORD. He wouldn't listen. Were you trying to see what he would do with me? Whom you love? (Because The LORD works in mysterious ways. I said this to The LORD next), "Anyway LORD. The last innocent that stood before him. Is me. I believe, with my whole heart you have sent me out like a lamb unto the slaughter. I believe that you have set the righteous before him as a test. That he should chose good, or evil. I became strong again in that believe. That G-D had placed me before him.

I wiped my tears, and made a decision to not live in fear. One year later. I visited the Nail parlor that the henchman's girlfriend owned. I sat in a chair with my back to the entry door. So, I couldn't see anyone that entered. As the manicurist held my hand. Someone dropped a pamphlet on the desk suddenly over my left shoulder.

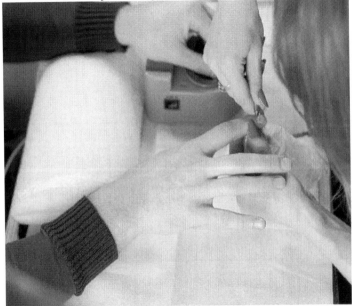

It came out of know where. Which almost spelled out to me. "You need to look at this!" Low and behold. I yanked my hand from the manicurist. Grabbed the pamphlet. Read the cover, flip through it quickly. And took in with The Holy Spirit I screamed. "Thank you, LORD. Thank You. Thank You." I knew then. I was the lamb. The LORD did place before the lion.

It was the boss's obituary I was holding. I said how did he die? A lady in the nail parlor said. "He went on a trip to Martinique. His head was chopped off and sent back on a private jet. Another lady said. "Miss? You can't thank The LORD he's dead." A voice in the parlor says. "Leave her alone." I turned around. And it was the good-hearted henchman. He walked up to me. Looked me in the eyes.

Smiled and said. "Are you OK? I say. "Yes." The Henchman said. I own you." "I said. "Whatever you think you owe me? Give it to G-D." And I walked away leaving the parlor with an incomplete manicure. While holding the obituary that The LORD delivered before my eyes. And I never returned there again. The Henchmen was free. And all the bosses' prisoners of fear were also freed. Myself included.

CHRISTOPHER COLUMBUS

CHAPTER IX

Our elders taught us. That if we ever had to tell a story? We should always tell it from the beginning. My family's history started long before Christopher Columbus. Long before Spain was formed. And even before Jesus Christ was born. We are the Descendants of Native American Indians. The natives of the land. We call Mother Earth.

In an archipelago within The Commonwealth of The Bahamas. Called "Espiritu Santo" by the Spaniards. Individually. "Espiritu" means "Spirit." And Santo. means "Saint." The English Translation for "Espiritu Santo" is "Holy Spirit. Or it's noun. Holy Ghost. So, I was born on the island of "The Holy Spirit." Also known as Andros Island. Located in The Great Antilles. Antilles were the name given to *mysterious lands.* Sometimes defined as "Islands in the ocean."

The Holy Spirit lands is the largest in The Bahamas. It has two nicknames. "The Sleeping Giant" and "The Big Yard." Located 50 km (30 Mi) west across the tongue of the Ocean. From The Bahamas national capital of Nassau on New Providence Island. Its northern tip lies 233km (145 mi) from Fort Lauderdale Florida.

The Lucayan Native American Indians a subgroup of the Tiano tribe. Were indigenous to The Holy Spirit lands. At the time of European encounters. Spain claimed The Holy Spirit lands. After Columbus' discovery of the Bahamas. The Holy Spirit lands pass back and forth between *Spanish and British* rule for 150 years.

The United States acquired Florida from Spain in 1821. Some Native American Indians. Cherokee. Seminoles and other Native American Indian Blacks escaped and sailed to the coast of The Holy Spirit lands and established settlements. In 1961 Alan Shepard. The First American in space reported he can see The Holy Spirit lands from space. Though he said "Andros and not Holy Spirit?" We the in-dwellers of those lands knew he saw. "The Holy Spirit Island" from space.

We celebrated. And talked about it for years. How faithful is the LORD? To showcase our dwelling place above all other locations in the world. We were proud. The Holy Spirit lands were seen. Which was fitting that The Holy Spirit lands be seen. Above The Holy Spirit Heavens.

The Tiano Native American Indians were the pre-Columbus inhabitants of The Greater and Lesser Antilles islands. Known as The Caribbean Islands. My ancestors were among some of the first people Columbus met upon arriving in the Americas on October 12, 1492. After their first interaction, Columbus described my ancestors as a physically tall. Well- proportioned people. With a *noble* and kind personality. Of The 12 Tribes of Native American Indian Kingdoms. Columbus mentions meeting five Native American Indian Kingdoms when he arrived at The Holy Spirit Islands (Andros Island. The Bahamas).

1. The Tianos, The Tribe of Binyamim, The people of The Bahamas. 2. The Tribe of Ephariam, The Puerto Rican

Native American Indians. 3. The Tribe of Manesseh, The Cuban Native American Indian. 4. The Tribe of Simeon, The Dominican Republic Native American Indians. 5. The Tribe of Naphtali the Samoan's Natives American Indians.

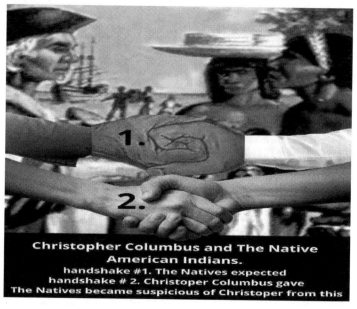

Christopher Columbus and The Native American Indians.
handshake #1. The Natives expected
handshake # 2. Christoper Columbus gave
The Natives became suspicious of Christoper from this

The Spanish priest Bartolome' de las Casas who had lived in Santo Domingo, wrote in his 1561 multi-volume. The History of the Indies: "There were 60,000 Native American Indian people living on this island (The Holy Spirit Island) when I arrived in 1508. So that from 1494 to 1508, over three million people had perished from war. Slavery. Diseases. And the mines. Who in future generations will believe this?" Columbus first attempt was on the Spanish Island. From Bahama to Cuba. Boriquen to Jamaica. The same language was spoken in various slight dialects. But understood by all."

My ancestor's language is a member of the Arawakan Native American Indian language family. Which ranges from South America across the Caribbean. It is widely said that my people were wiped out. I would often ask myself. "Then who am I? How did I get here if am from a whipped-out race? Not connected to the land or it's people?" I knew something was wrong with what society was telling me to believe about myself.

Most grown-ups didn't seem to care. I felt I couldn't grow up to act like them. Just going along with something. Just became someone said it. Or because someone else was doing it before them. Getting lead under an apple tree with other apples. When they themselves were oranges. I was different. I need to know who Heaven said that I am.

I decided. The only way to get out of the maze of lies and deception. Was to remain on The LORD's side. The LORD became my ticket. That he should help me to know what is true. And what is a lie. I made up my mind. I knew without a shadow of a doubt. If I would only trust in The

LORD will all my heart. And lean not on my own understanding. In all my ways acknowledge him. And he will make my paths straight. As he did.

My ancestor's society was divided into two classes: naborias (commoners) and nitainos (nobles). These were governed by Indian chieftain. To whom tribute was paid. They were known as caciques. Who were either male or female. And regarded as "king or prince" "queen or princess." Caciques inherited their position through their mother's noble line. This matrilineal kinship system descent. And inheritance. With social status pass through the female lines. They were advised by priests or priestess healers known as bohiques. The bohiques Priest and Priestess were extolled for their ability to speak with deities (G-DS). As a bridge. From the G-Ds to men. And men to the G-D's. They were off a royal priesthood of the G-D's. The Priest and Priestess were consulted and granted permission to engage in important tasks for my ancestors. The Native American Indians.

The civility of my people surprised Christopher Columbus. Of them Columbus said. "They will give all that they do possess for anything that is given to them. (Sounds like they had gratitude to me, which is a gentle fruit of the spirit). Exchanging things even for bits of broken crockery. They are very well built. With very handsome bodies and very good faces. They do not carry arms or know them. They should be good servants. They traded with us and gave us everything they had with good will. They took great delight in pleasing us." My people did not have enemies. And had never experience cunning, cruel behavior as displayed by Christopher Columbus.

"My ancestor's level of love. And loving-kindness was so profound. Columbus reported. About The Native American Indians *"Your Majesty. There are no better people in **ALL** The World."* As it should have been. My ancestors were living in The Land of "The Holy Spirit." Within the Holy Spirits confinement. As heirs and heiress. Seed of "The Holy Spirit." Should not their ways reflect?

Were those that entered my ancestral borders not loved? That they knew not love. And it's forms? Columbus committed to the task approved by The Queen of Spain. In so many words she said. "Go and take The Creator G-D's children. The seed of The Holy Spirit. Within The Holy Spirit borders. Take those whom The Holy Spirit love. And has formed peculiar to itself. And dash them down. And place your children. Who are prince, over their children who are savages. And subdue them.

Tear their children from the arms of their mothers. Make your children. The princes and princesses? princes and princesses over their children. Teach them of our Fathers ways. And our savior The Lord Jesus Christ and the Catholic faith. So that Christianity may flourish within those remote islands. Remove far from them the ways of their Fathers. And their fathers, fathers. That they might be a Nation unto The Creator no more." Thought the doctrine of discovery does not use the word princess, but prince. Where there is a prince, is there not a princess? So the doctrine meant to put other children. The Prince and Princess above The Creator's children. The Priest and Priestess of The 12 Tribes of Yisra'EL. The Kingdoms Columbus found in the remote islands.

One job. I have learned from G-D on my journey to self-discovery that brought on enlightenment. G-D has given to The Native American Indians and their descendants. The task of caring for The Earth. By Prays. Medication. Ceremonies. Fasting. Rituals. Sacrifices. Offerings. And Thanksgiving.

Which as it turns out. The Queen orders. That Christopher Columbus and everyone else carried out? By entering the sacred Holy Spirit lands of my ancestors. The Native American Indians? Is coming around today, to be the biggest monumental misfortune of a mistake. Anyone would have ever made. Could have ever made. And will ever make again. From The World was created. Ever. Never. Oh no!. Not Ever Again.

Well at least. That's what a voice upon a throne said in so many words. When I ascended into Heaven at The Blue Blood Moon of January 31st, 2019. And saw the works of Christopher Columbus hands on display before The Supreme Court of Heaven. And an exceedingly great assembly, and the armies of G-D looked on in silence.

G-D, The Creator intended for my ancestors The Native American Indians and their descendants. To serve only him. A reserved people. Set-apart people. Peculiar people unto himself. For the portion of the LORD? Is His people. Deuteronomy 32:9

Scriptures declare. "The LORD, the LORD G-D, merciful and gracious, long-suffering, and abounding in goodness and truth, keeping mercy for thousands, forgiving iniquity and transgression and sin, by no means clearing the guilty, **visiting the iniquity of the fathers upon the children and the children's children to the third and the fourth generation."**

COME
COME

CHAPTER X

"They are very gentle. And without knowledge of what is evil; nor do they murder or steal. Your highness may believe that in all the world. There can be no better people. They love their neighbors as themselves. They have the sweetest talk in the world. They are gentle and always laughing." Columbus said of The Holy Spirit's seed. My ancestors. The Native American Indians.

The loving **THY** neighbors as thyself mentioned by Columbus. Reminded me of the second command of The Messiah, The Son of G-D. In-which The Messiah's words says to mankind, *"Love **THY** Neighbor as Thyself."* Or where it says in 1 Corinthians 10:24, *"No one shall seek their own good. But the good of others."* These words I recited. And meditated daily as a child. As a man? Columbus and his Queen. Did not know. "For as a man thinketh? So, is he. Proverbs 23:7."

To me. It said their civilization. Was not a civilized society at all. Spiritually & morally was missing. In my opinion? This made their attempts to civilize my people. Null and void before it's conception. Under Spiritual Law? Civility was needed at home. With the Europeans that enter? Before it was needed aboard. With The Native American Indians. My ancestors. Matthew 7:5 says. *"You hypocrite! First take the beam out of your own eye. And then you will see clearly to remove the speck from your brother's eye."*

I learned very early. The World rewarded evil for good. And good for evil. *Isaiah 5:20 declares. "Woe unto them that call evil good. And good evil; that put darkness for light. And light for darkness; that put bitter for sweet. And sweet for bitter."* If the European invaders recognized love. In their daily lives? They would have recognized the spiritual signs of love my ancestral family dropped like rain drops falling from the sky. At the feet of an undeserving, ungrateful people. My people found out. It is hard to give the uncultured, culture. Finally, they did what *Matthew 7:6 declares. "Do not give dogs what is sacred; do not throw your pearls to pigs. If you do? They may trample them under their feet. And turn and tear you to pieces."* As it was with Christopher Columbus.

The Europeans did not understand the sacredness of my ancestors giving. They had never experienced that level of kindness before. Of-which the spiritual levels of their deeds through loving-kindness toward the Spaniard. Were exceedingly great. As given to LORDS, KINGS or G-DS. But they were mortal men receiving that treatment. Yet the world speaks of my people. As though they were nothing. And their blood. Has carried The World from that unfortunate day of 1492 to today's date. Come. Come. Now. Let us reason together as brothers and sisters. For refusing to see G-D's truth. Which is of G-D? Is to perish with those of the reprobate mind. Which is not of G-D. The Europeans that enter? We're not of The Holy Spirit nature. Despite them saying that they came to my people in the name of The All Might G-D and Jesus Christ. Their deeds and their actions suggested to me even as a child. They had eyes. But they saw not. Ears had they. But they heard not. *Jeremiah 15:2-22 declares. "Hear this. O foolish and senseless people. Who have eyes but do not see? Who have ears but do not hear? Do you not fear G-D?*

My people became stretched thin. To the limits of their spiritual peace offering. They wanted the pearl trampling swines to leave their land. And they cared no more to give dogs that which was sacred. My people saw Christopher Columbus ships drifting in the ocean. My ancestors didn't shot bows and throw spears first. And asked questions later. They saw people in despair. That didn't look like them. Yet my people saved their lives and brought them to our shores. Where they were hoodwinked and bamboozled for saving lives. They soon realize. The European whites were not their long-lost brothers returning as they had expected. Through tribal prophecy.

"Who were the European's G-D? Did Columbus and his men. And my Native Indian ancestors have the same G-D? I often wondered as a child and would question G-D. Saying. "If they did? Why would G-D. The G-D of love. Impose such a harsh punishment as implied by Isabella, Queen of Spain as per her words. Be it done unto us by "The All-Mighty G-D's Authority. And the Authority of The LORD Jesus Christ that these heinous deeds be carried out on The Creator's servants. Living in "The Holy Spirit lands" in The Bahamas. As to dispose of The Native American Indians of the face of The Earth. As found in the **1493 Doctrine of Discovery**.

The Europeans behaviors during 1492 and subsequent years. Did not say they followed whom they said they served. When trying the spirit as written in biblical scriptures. I saw. Men carried the bible in their hands. But not in their heads and hearts. The precepts written therein was far from them. *1 John 4:1 says. "Beloved. Believe not every*

spirit. But try the spirit whether they are of G-D. Because many false prophets are gone out into The World."

"The name "The All-Mighty G-D." A very powerful title. Given only to One. Columbus Queen did dash around the word loosely in her letters to him. "The All-Mighty G-D." Though G-Ds are many. As there are stars in the sky? There is only "ONE, ALL MIGHT G-D". Who's *Ten Commandments number ten says. "***THOU*** shall not covet ***THY*** neighbor's house. ***THOU*** should not covet ***THY*** neighbor's wife. nor his manservant, nor his maidservant, nor his ox, nor his ass, nor any thing that is ***THY*** neighbor's*. And *the Native American Indian Ten Commandments also given my G-D which says. "Enjoy Lives Journey. But leave no tracks."* So, who was The Queen of The Kingdom of Spain's. And Christopher Columbus's and his sponsors, during the Doctrine of Discovery's ALL MIGHT G-D? That they should not obey his Laws? They trample creations laws of The Universe. Given for mankind to live by, under foot for years. You see I always needed meat to live as a child. My thoughts were often very deep in trying to discover the truth about myself. Because bones were for dogs.

Which G-D's handbook were the bone collectors reading from? I learned. It was their G-D of gold handbook. And their G-D of silver's handbook. Of gold?. My ancestors The Native American Indians lived in a paradise of gold. THE ALL-MIGHTY G-D is not mocked. Nor does he take bribes. Nor did my G-D of the Ten Commandments sent them. Their G-D sent them to consume and imprison us with their ways. It's as simple as that. Wisdom is kind to us. She is here and available for the taking. Of anyone who seeks her diligently.

My ancestors did not know the ways of the European whites. And had no barbaric tendencies before contact. And they did not know any evil. As said by Christopher Columbus. Evil was not taught to them by their G-D. My ancestors the Tiano, Native American Indians called G-D. The Creator "Yaya." And my Cherokee Indian ancestors called G-D. The Creator "Yo'way." Which happens to be Hebrew for Yahweh.

He taught them love and good fruits of The Holy Spirit which was their portion. In fact, a direct translation of the word "Tiano" signified *"Men of The Good."* Yet when Christopher Columbus returned on the second voyage to "the men of the good" inhabiting The Holy Spirit lands. He began to require tribute from them.

Adults over 14 years of age. Was expected to deliver a hawk's bell full of their G-D. Gold. Every three months. When this was lacking. Twenty-five pounds of spun cotton was required. If this tribute was not brought? The European's cut off the hands of the inhabitants of The Holy Spirit lands. And left them to bleed to death. I remember learning Columbus discovered the land of my ancestors. "America." But how could he discover a land that others inhabiting it.

It's like owning your house. Placing all the things you desire within it. Your great-grandmother gave you the house. You've got your kids there with you. And one fine day your doorbell rings. It's a guy from the continent of Africa. Along with his luggage. His country's flag. And a cross of Nazareth he digs into your property's soil. Telling you.

"I have discovered your house." And he makes you his slave within your own home. That you and your kids should cook him a meal each day. And every pay day? Your check is handed over to him who said he discovered you and your house. Not only that. The authorities knows that this has happen to you. But does nothing.

We were taught more good things about The Pirates of The Caribbean. Cinderella and The Three Bears. Then we were about ourselves. None had anything to do with our heritage. I never knew why we was learning The European's heritage. Teachings that should have been prevalent to Christopher Columbus children. And his homestead. Not The Native American Indian Descendants. I saw this was being done to us at a very early age. I saw the changes that took place around me. I just never knew why it was happening. And who was making it happen.

But of our ancestors? We were taught. They were barbaric cannibalistic savages that were overpopulating the earth. And because of this? They needed to be conquered, converted and destroyed. To the point that they are all extinct. This is what the world was teaching me, the Native American Indian descendant. And or teaching that lead to this understanding. That The Native American Indians. The Indigenous people of our past and present. Is nothing. Was nothing. And will never be anything. The strangers in our lands saw prayer, courage, reverence, meditation, thanksgiving, and dancing. As unacceptable barbaric behavior.

Savages! The Native American Indian people were called. Even dogs. Pharoah of Egypt has used the word "dogs" to refer to The Creator's children as well. Pharoah no longer exists. Many still today. Close mouth. Bless with their mouths. And they curse inwardly at the copper, the brown, the red and the black skin natives of the earth. The indigenous peoples. The Native American Indians.

In 1492 Europeans entered the land of my ancestors. For their lives to be save. And became the Judge. The Jury. And the Executioners. Of a seed The Holy Spirit had planted for itself. A peculiar. Set apart people. With established forefathers of Creation Story. And G-D's Covenant Promise.

Laying on the beach with seaweed crashing between my toes one day I became perplex. And started yelling at the sky like Tom Hanks on Cast Away Beach. I needed to leave. Not only the remote island. But a feeling deep down in my soul, that kept telling me something was wrong with us. The assimilated Native American Indians living in the remote islands of The Caribbean. And others in the world knew. But us. And I felt also there were things we were not being told about ourselves, and our state as a people. Though I had no clue as to what it was. A feeling kept telling me something was wrong.

I couldn't live. Without knowing myself. And what is a life not experiencing one's own identity I often though. Experiencing my real self. The self-aligned with who G-D says that I am. Not my assimilated self. But you labor every day within a false existence. With the felling as though you are off in the boondocks of your own life. Not having a front row seat in your own life events as you watch them unfold daily. Without you. While you are there

I laid there on the beach ready to die. Loudly I said. While tears fell down my face. "The LORD should satisfy me. Or I shall lay upon this cast away looking beach until all eternity. Or my bones decay. Whichever one comes sooner LORD. And I shall never move."

I said cast away. Because somehow I knew my life was a part of an island adventure that was not being filmed. When at times. I waited for the camera crew to come out of the coconut groves. Because where I lived on the beach looked just like a great place to shoot a movie about being stranded on an island. And I did not catch a break between scenes. It was my life. And it was real. I would often ask The LORD saying, "LORD, how did we become stranded on this island?" For some reason? Only I alone saw there was something wrong with our lives picture on the remote islands. We needed to be rescued with some urgency from the invisible prison. Where we were not really prisoners with visible shackles and chains. But prisoners. With the invisible ones. It was obvious. Something was wrong with all of us on the islands. And others weren't telling us.

As I would observe military helicopters from other European Nations flying over my head with machine guns drawn. I was able to see the smile on their faces they were often that close to me. I would say to The LORD, "LORD how come those men are always patrolling our lands with weapons. But our fathers are never patrolling with weapons over their children's head? I spoke to The LORD about everything.

I felt something in my gut was wrong with the way we looked. The cloths we wore. The way our words sounded. The things we became accustomed to eating. When our ancestors ate. No flesh. Didn't dress like us. Didn't sound like us. How assimilated we were. We looked the way Christopher Columbus, his Queen and The Catholic Church intended. Even unto this day. We still look like their desire for our lives. At the time I chose death. What I didn't know was. My suffering was planned by others. I didn't know that the way I was feeling was forced upon me and my ancestors before me. All I knew for sure was? I needed help. I needed to be saved. A SOS. A smoke signal. Some sticks to rub together for my fire to be seem overhead like they do in the movies. Something! And it seemed. Only I saw the desperateness of our condition on the remote islands of our captivity. Though many shared the same symptoms of hereditary captivity. They were contented. I was not. I was troubled in my spirit. My heart. And my mind. "I was now drifting into deeper waters. As I laid on my back in the ocean. I refused to live life any further without the knowledge of myself and my ancestors. And I knew only G-D, and his heaven alone, would be able to free me from feeling trapped within myself.

With reef sharks swimming all around me. I used all my imaginative powers to be taken by the sharks. I imagined dying. But none harm me. I ask G-D saying. "Why am I on this remote island My LORD, KING OF THE UNIVERSE? Everyone is sleep walking here. As though our captivity is a fine idea. How did we end up here, on this remote island LORD? I cannot continue to swim against this life's current. It's hard to continue to feel as though something is wrong. Without knowing exactly what is wrong my LORD, Free me. Less I die."

The LORD speared my life. I walked out of the water unscathed. G-D did not permit the sharks to be the answer to my prayers. Though I desired the end with all my spiritual strength. Because my inward man did not resemble my outward man. And my outward parts did not resemble my inward parts. Leaving me confused about my identity. And why I was different. I was seeking rest for my inward parts.

EL, EL, EL
EL'YON

CHAPTER XI

The following day on May 13th, 2016. After trying to end my life in the water by shark attack or drowning. I stood in my kitchen washing the dishes. Cleaning up as I normally did. Out of nowhere a G-D came to me and started speaking to me. I heard his voice cl-

early. After hearing him for a few minutes. His topic was very interesting to me. It was about slavery. Something in my soul told me. "It is the answers to your prayers." I became mesmerized while listening to this G-D. This was the first time I had met this G-D. Or heard anything of what he was saying to me. But I remembered the holy spirit teaching me when I was a child that there are as many G-D's as there are stars in the sky for multitude. And that my G-D was G-D of G-Ds though he is one. As stated in Deuteronomy 10:17 For the LORD your G-D is G-D of G-D's, and LORD of LORDs, a great G-D, a mighty and a terrible.

I didn't know of this G-D prior. But I insistently felt. I needed to get a record of his words. Not only for myself. But for others. After trying my best not to interrupt him. I felt I had no choice because I didn't want to do anything that would offend The Spirit of G-D that he should stop speaking. So, I said. "Who Areth **THOU**? The G-D that was speaking says. "I am The Most High. EL, EL, EL ELYON. I said. "Most High? Am I able to write your words down?" I did not want to offend This G-D that he should discontinue speaking to me in offence for my wrong move. I was humbled. And I tried not to offend him.

And The Most High EL, EL, EL, ELYON answered me saying. "Yes. Please do." I dried my hands. I was so excited. I scrambled to find a comprehension book and a pen. For many of my people. They know the comprehension book to generically mean the black and white writing book with the lines. Because that was the only kind of book, all of us was made to use in school.

I returned to my dining table. Dried by hands on my apron. Took a deep breath to calm my heart. Then I begun to

write. ***The Most High G-D. EL, EL, EL ELYON says to me.***
"Now the first set of slaves that came out of the camp that
Moses' setup were Yisraelites. They were of the 12 Tribes of
Yisra'EL. The 12 Tribes. One to the East. One to the West.
One to the North. And one to the South. You had camps that
were setup between the East, West, North and South.
South**east**. South**west**. North**east** and North**west**. So, they
were all around. 12 Nations of people located in one
peaceful spot. That G-D Yahweh setup for them to live as
peaceful, loving, chosen people of G-D.

The 10 commandments were their law in which they
lived by. Scholars from all over The World recognized. The
Romans, the Egyptians, the Amalekites the Girgashites, all of
them understood that that's where peace was. Those same
people have descendants, and their decedents live in places
like New York. Pennsylvania. Mississippi. And Florida. They
live all over. But these people wanted to build America. And
they knew who build pharaoh cities. They were Yisraelites.
Skilled men among the 12 Tribes. They were skilled people.
They were chosen people. They were wise.

The Scholars came to visit, and they saw how beautiful
it was. How the servants live with their masters in harmony.
Everyone lived just like a utopia society. And the white man
wanted that. He did not want a utopia society. He wanted the
obedience of the people to be with him. He wanted a
remnant out of there. To go with him. To work in his field.
To build his vineyard. To plant his corn. To weed his grass.
To cook meals for him. To wash his cloths. You understand?
I say. "Yes, Most High. I do understand.

**The Most High EL, EL ELYON continued speaking
with me saying.** "And he knew that they would have done
it, because that's the kind of people they were. HONEST.

HARDWORKING. And LOVING. Because they lived by the 10 commandments.

When they went there? Here's what happen! They did not go on the first voyage with guns and knives and chains and barbaric stuff. Of cause yes. They had prisoners. But guess where the prisoners where? Down in the hull of the boat. Because they were the one's sculling the boat. The scull with the two flaps on the side. The rowboat? They were the machine in the boat down in the hull of the boat. They were the machines. I say to The Most High. "Most High? How did they get there?" **The Most High EL, EL ELYON replied.** "As prisoners. You want to be free. There is a voyage going to Africa and the rich man need some people. Some workers to row this boat. Because there was no engine. You couldn't buy a ticket. They had no money. There was a treaty signed to used prisoners for these voyages. The Most High says to me. "Do You understand?" I say. "Yes, Most High. I do." I felt The Most High G-D was checking to see if I was keeping up with him. Following what he was saying. To be honest I was an ignorant child. With no knowledge. Very naïve. The locals would call a person like that green or stew-pit, or Stoo-pit.

I was stew-pit before and up to that day. Then The LORD expanded my consciousness and awareness, and made me wise through his words spoken to me. Then **The Most High G-D. EL, EL, ELYON says to me.** "So now. Here it is! They went there. The first voyage they went just to look and observe. Their second voyage they went back there with money. They trade money for gold. They used the gold they got from the tribes of Yisra'EL to buy land. They robbed them out of gold for money. They say can spend anywhere." I say. "But they did not have need for money." **EL. EL ELYON,**

142

The Most High G-D says. "NO!" They say. "You can pay your workers out of this. They can buy food out of this. Good Idea." "So, they gave them GOLD for that. They brought the gold back to America and put it in their o-

wn bank. And created banks. Then they bought properties in the South. But they bought properties and they needed who? Workers to work the fields. The orange plantation. The cane plantations the cotton field."

"They needed people to cut the corn. To plow the yard. They needed people! And the white man was not strong. You can't take a King to serve a King. A King does not look good in a yard weeding another King's yard. So, the only person who could have done it. Were the people who they saw. That lived about the people who they bought this gold from."

"So, their voyage this time was to give them money for men. We call them in today's society. "Live cargo." Now, they did not need to carry guns and knives and weapons and swords with them. Because these people they realize as peaceful people. The Tribe King did not mine giving them men because they were giving them the same money, they were paying them. You understand? So, he did it with love! "Come. Come go! The Tribe King said. He will pay you money. And you can buy homes. You can own. New land!" So, they went on the boats by the hundreds."

"The first voyage from Yahweh's camp was the disaster voyage. Those people spent 40 years in the wilderness. They crossed ocean on dry land. In the wilderness. Horrified of the ocean. Before G-D opened the ocean to let them through. They were horrified. They knew they couldn't go through the sea."

"Pharaoh in the back. And the ocean ahead. These people never ventured into the ocean. To go and swim in the ocean. Now you've got them on a boat out there. Telling them you're taking them to a land that they don't know. After they started getting sick on the boat. The men had to throw the sick people overboard."

EL ELYON The Most High G-D says. *"How would you like my dear. To see your brother or uncle whom. When they get sick, thrown overboard? We have a way to bury our sick. And a way to heal our sick right?"* I say. *"Yes, we do."*

EL ELYON, The Most High G-D says. "You understand? They were sick. But they were not sick to death." "They had ways to heal their sick. These people taking the sick of my people. And throwing them overboard in the ocean. Would you stand by and see your uncle getting thrown in the ocean?

And sooner or later your wife or mother gets sick. And they throw her in the ocean? Or your brother? After a while. It's going to create ANGER! AND RAGE IN THE OPEN SEA! So now. These black people who were born fighting. Born warriors. They slew many towns. They had slewed so many people. G-D commandment them not to kill no more. Their hands were always bloody. But they had given it up. Because they did not have to fight anymore."

"Now. They are caught in the open ocean where people are throwing their sons and daughters overboard because they are sick. Now they've got to fight in the open sea. Those who could not fight or defend themselves got hurt or injured."

"Those who refuse to fight stayed there. And those who fight. Either got killed or thrown overboard. You understand?" I say. "Yes, Most High. I do understand." *EL ELYON says.* "And those who were left were afraid. Couldn't swim. The choice that was left was to stay on the boat or die. Those who wanted to live. Stayed on the boat. They were the ones that made it to shore."   "When the first set of slaves came to shore. They did not come in shackles. They did not come in chains. Because there was no reason to take those things to Africa or to Yisra'EL. You understand?" I say. "I do LORD. I understand." *EL ELYON says.* "So, they came free. Free walking. But they were sold into a life that they knew nothing about. The first voyage. Caught them of guard! When they went on the second voyage. Because they knew. No one that went over boar. Made it to shore. So, they could go back for more of my people. And they told them. The ride was successful."

"What didn't they tell the King when they went back on the second voyage my dear? They did not tell the King that his people. Your ancestors? We're going back as Slaves. Their first voyage was as Servants. The second voyage? They were getting Slaves."

I say. "LORD? What happened in between for that to happen like that?" *The Most High G-D says.* "Let me tell you what happened! When the first voyage was complete, and they sold all of the one's who came with them? They got the money from them." I say. "It was successful?" *EL ELYON says.* "They got the money!

It was successful! They got the money! People are happy with these people. So, it's paying off for these people. The first voyage." "Now the ships were not prepared for the first voyage. Hear me! The ships were not prepared for the first voyage. This voyage now? The second voyage now?

They took the money from the proceeds that they made of the first voyage. And they brought hand cuffs. Neck

147

cuffs. Leg brace. And shackles." I say. "So, the money they made was so good. They expanded the business. When out and bought hand cuffs? *"EL ELYON G-D says.* "The money was good. But the journey was havoc.

"One by one they were taken down in the hull. To drive that boat to America. They are now fully prepared. Their boat is now rigged with shackles and chains. This time. They are moving through with more death. Every time someone dies in the hull. They throw them overboard from down in the hull. They did not bring them up. So that others. Will not see them."

I say. "So, this time they would throw them from the bottom? Not the top? *EL ELYON says.* "They top them. Because that was where they were. Traveling as a guest. It was only the second voyage that they were stored downstairs. See prisoners are kept downstairs in the hull. If and when war broke out. They would have to come from the hull and help upstairs in the pass. You, see?" I say. "Yes LORD."

EL ELYON. The Most High G-D says. "So now. The prisoners that the treaty was signed for. On the second voyage. Was now working as dock men. The slaves now? Was taking the boat back to America. Now! They had all the manpower they needed." Because they lost half of their cargo. This time. They are not losing any cargo.

149

Down in the hull they bought shackles for the legs. Bolt them down to the hull. Down underneath the boat. Let's say each one you got 2,4,6,8,10,12,14, 16, 18, 20, 22. 22 men on this side. With shackles under that boat and shackles to their neck." "Shackles on their neck. And shackles on their feet. Down to the ship's floor. And shackles on their neck that is down to the ship's hull. The brakes of the ship. So, they couldn't move. They are prepared now to bring these people under chains. 22 on this side. And on the other side 22. The ship now is prepared to bring prisoners. Live cargo as prisoners. 44 underneath. And the rest on top."

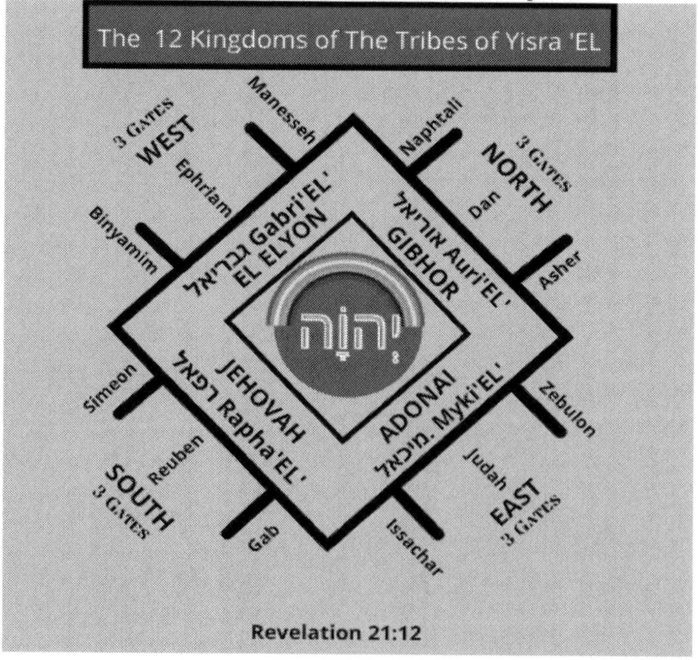

The 12 Kingdoms of The Tribes of Yisra 'EL

Revelation 21:12

"So, when they went to Africa now. To the 12 tribes they got more people. More of our African brothers and sisters. When they got on that boat. 44 went downstairs. And they took them down. One by one. They men handled my people

150

down there. Threw them in shackles and locked them down. And used whips on them. They had everything they needed for combat. Because they knew what happened on the first voyage. This time. The ship was fully loaded and prepared."

"So now. You have 44 of my people down under the hull. Strapped down. Can't move. And you've got a man over them now. With a whip. "The first voyage told them that these people are warriors. So now. They came prepared." "They had everything they needed for combat. Because they knew what happened on the first voyage. This time. The ship was fully loaded and prepared."

CHAPTER XII

After The Most High spoke with me. I received through Revelation from him. That Abraham Lincoln issued his preliminary Emancipation Proclamation. In which he declared that as a January 1, 1863. All slaves in states. In rebellion against the Union "shall be then. Thenceforward. And **forever free**."

Lincoln often expressed moral opposition to slavery in public and private. Initially, he expected to bring about the eventual extinction of slavery by stopping its further expansion into any U.S territory. And by proposing *compensated emancipation* (an offer Congress applied to Washington, D.C) in his early presidency.

Lincoln stood by the Republican Party's platform of 1860. Which stated that slavery should not be allowed to expand into any more territories. Lincoln believed that the extension of slavery in the South. Mid-west. And Western lands would inhibit "free labor on free soil." In the 1850's Lincoln was politically attached as an abolitionist. But he did not consider himself one. He did not call for the immediate end of slavery everywhere in the U.S. Until the proposed 13th Amendment became part of his party platform for the 1864 election.

During the American Civil War. Lincoln used the war powered by the presidency to issue the **Emancipation Proclamation.** Which declared "All persons held as slaves within any State or designated part of a State. The people whereof shall then be in rebellion against the United States. Shall be then thenceforward. And **forever free**: but slaves who has already escaped to the Union side.

However, millions more were freed. As more areas of the Confederacy came under the Union control. Lincoln pursued various plans to voluntarily colonize free blacks outside the United States. But none of them had a major effect. Historians disagree over whether or not his plans to colonize blacks were sincere or political posturing. Regardless, by the end of his life. Lincoln had come to support black suffrage. A position that would lead him to be assassinated by John Wilkes Booth.

As President-elect in 1860 and 1861 In a letter to Senator Lyman Trumbull on December 10, 1860, Lincoln wrote. "Let there be no compromise on the question of extending slavery." Lincoln wrote that the 'only substantial difference' between North and South was that 'You think slavery is right and ought to be extended.

In other words, Lincoln was saying" Thou should not think that there is a difference between you being created and me being created, or them being created or you being created or them being the Nation of G-D, and You not being on their level. JUDGE NOT! Yet ye BE JUDGED!

The Holy Spirit sent from G-D came to me and says. "All citizens of the Nation of Yisra'EL should have on his possession the letter of proclamation of emancipation issued By the President of the United States of America 1861 – 1863. We require a RICH Emancipation under America's Human Rights and Peace. A Proclamation made by a righteous person. The world cannot deny it. G-D smiled when he put a big black mole on Ab's face. My People should now, claim, and proclaim liberty! Your sword is the shofar שׁוֹפָר horn. Proclaim, Liberty!"

On May 27th, 2016. The voice of "G-D." Says to me. "The Truth will be more and more revealed to people. Who they desire still too kept in ignorance and darkness. The Emancipation Proclamation was a presidential proclamation and executive order issued by President Abraham Lincoln on January 1, 1863. In a single stroke. It changed the federal legal status of more than 3 million enslaved people."

As I studied with the Holy Spirit. And meditate on what G-D said to me. I began to feel. If others can put a value on just how far from G-D we were taken as slaves? We would be finally able to peruse that which was declared for us. That

155

which is rightfully ours to have (MONETARY COMPENSATION) OR COMPENSATION OF UNIVERSAL VALUE AND PURPORTION. A Citizen of the World. The Proclamation of Emancipation makes you people of (The Nation of G-D, The Nation of the true Yisraelite) Citizens of the World! While searching for the truth. I also recognize that only G-D can turn your own Army against you in the service of his people.

EL ELYON, The Most High G-D says. "G-D rescued his people in Egypt with Moses. For the sins against humanity

(Slavery). He sent Laws for us to live by. G-D rescued Mankind again in America. With Lincoln. For the sins against humanity (Slavery). He sent the Proclamation of Emancipation of his People. Who have been bought with a price!"

BRINGING IN SLAVES TO THE SHAKA MARKET.

EL ELYON, The Most High G-D says. "Truth will be more and more revealed to people. There are people who will get the knowledge. There are people with the knowledge of me in their hearts and they have everything. But! They are hiding it from the people who need to know my G-D is. And where my G-D is. That is why we have so many problems now today. No one knows who the real G-D is because. For them. It is beneficial. Not to tell!" I say. "Maybe some are like me. Just would really like to know or have a real reveal on where G-D would like us to start."

EL ELYON, The Most High G-D says. "Yeah! Your grandmother was one of those people." I say. "One of those people? Which one of my grandmothers?" *EL ELYON, The Most High G-D says.* "Your grandmother was one of those people. The one who turned? She was one of those. She had a key. She had something to give you. To turn something over to you. You, see? It could have been the truth of who G-D is. It could have been something. But she kept it!"

I say. "She kept it from me. She kept it from going on. I said. "Oh, bless the LORD." *EL ELYON, The Most High G-D says.* "Right! Because the spirit needed to. She trapped the spirit of G-D that has wisdom. Knowledge. That has everything about him inside her. She trapped it in her and it's still in her trapped. And she can't find a way to hand it over." I say. "Yeah. Because she changed?" *EL ELYON, The Most High G-D says.* "So, she chose. And she changed. And held it in." I say. "What does that do to you Most High? You have got to go to hell for that! Because am trying every day to know the truth of who I am. Am struggling every day to know this and she's keeping a blessing from me? You don't go to hell for that Most High? You have got. To go to hell for keeping things from someone that can change their lives forever."

EL ELYON, The Most High G-D says." If something is bursting. Trapped. Trying to get out? What it does. What it does is see. It's beating you up inside. Beating your brain." I say. "May I say this? This is why when certain things come my way. I would have some trouble. I try to be that full potential that G-D. Not the one people just talk about. Have for me."

EL ELYON, The Most High G-D says. "If you had a balloon in a box and if you keep giving it air. Even though the box is hiding it. It is going to eventually do what?" I say. "Explode."

EL ELYON, The Most High G-D says. "Bust that box. It burst your grandma Rita's brain. She couldn't take it. It was too much. The wisdom of G-D. She tried to hold it in." **The**

158

Most High G-D says. She needed help! I say. "With what? All that knowledge?" **EL ELYON, The Most High G-D says.** "All that knowledge of G-D. She needed help to hold it in. So, she gained help. Something to suffocate it." I say. "She did what? What?"

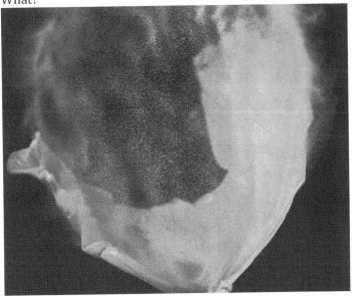

EL ELYON, The Most High G-D says. "She gained help! To suffocate it! She gained help to try to suffocate it. You, see? Weaken it down. You know. To make it weak. To stop anything from going in it." I say. "But why?" *EL ELYON, The Most High G-D says.* "Well. It was a moment that a promise that she made she didn't are. Bless The LORD! She made a promise to G-D."

    <u>Revelation within the hour</u>: - Making a promise to G-D. Is unlike making a promise to just anyone! I say. "And that's what made my grandmother Rita turn?" *The Most High G-D says.* "Yes." <u>Revelation within the hour</u>: - It is

written, *do not slack to repay that which is owed G-D. For it is your very life!*

The Most High G-D continued speaking and says. "She renege on the promise. The promise was for her to give that beautiful. Blessed. Speak to G-D. Talk to G-D. G-D reveals riches. Wealth, Turn it over." I say. "To give it to me?" *EL ELYON The Most High G-D says.* "To someone. He has chosen to bless" I say. "Bless the LORD!" *The Most High G-D says.* "She held it in. And now. No one can get it. So, G-D took you to the water."

I say. "Took me where?" *EL ELYON, The Most High G-D says.* "Yes. He told you to put your hand in the sand. Remember?" I say. "Yes, yes on the beach. I remember." *EL ELYON, The Most High G-D says.* "So, he made you put your hand in the sand. See now. It's almost like nature is being taking care of you. He leaves you in the hand of The Universe." I say. "Bless the LORD *Most High. ELYON The Most High G-D says.* "The G-D of The Universe is now. Going to feed you! Take care of you! Because you're the apple of his eye."

LAVA
CHEST

CHAPTER XIII

In the bliss of my greatest peace. When the LORD Most High was showing me his mysteries and secrets. At a time of fasting. I received a call from a childhood friend. I had not seen in years. I loved the idea. But still asked. "How did they get my number?" He responded. "From your brother."

I knew that The LORD was working in. And around my life in a supernatural way. But I also thought. The timing was strange. But not strange enough that I would be inhospitable to a childhood friend.

I invited my childhood friend. Over to my vacation home. I told them of my spiritual experiences thus far. And of Jesus Christ. My friend was sometime accompanied by another male friend. I had seen once or twice in the past. I was eager to share the word of Jesus Christ.

During one of the visits. My friend said to me. "How about I make you something to eat." You are always giving me." I said. "Sure." In my mind. Am thinking. "I'll only have a little. Which wouldn't hurt my fasting. Just a spoon full. What's the harm in that? When your fast is closing out." I said to myself.

I have already received the spiritual manifestation of the fast. Or so I though. I took two small bites of the food. It wasn't long before I begun to feel ill. And lightheaded. A swift shake of my head would bring me back to my normal senses for a moment. But shortly after I would begin to drift back and forward from consciousness to unconsciousness.

I realize something was wrong with me. But I just did not know what it was. I forced myself not to think that my dear friend had poisoned me. I was to Christian to cast the uncertain blame on my house guest. So, I remained polite and suffered in silence. I continued to pray in my heart while talking with my intimate one. I anointed my head and decided to look for spiritual help. I immediately and continuously call on Jesus. But he did not respond. I started surfing the religious television channels for a word. So that I could find my way out. There were two men dressed in black robes with hoodies and a brown rope. While preaching and teaching. One younger than the other.

Immediately I hear words from a wicked and evil voice saying to me while laughing. "Yeah! You run for help. They are my people. They work for me." The voice of evil kept laughing at me for seeking help. I begin to cry the pain I felt for Jesus. Because of the wolfs in sheep's clothing that were on TV. I felt sorry that this was happening because the LORD did not deserve this level of deception from those who resembled Sheppard's. I became disappointed to see those so called men of the cloth. They were preaching and teaching only a hair strand away from G-D's word. While the praise went where they were intended all along; to the Evil one. The Devil.

At this time, I become increasingly concern with what was happening in my body. Knowing something was wrong with me. But the uncertainty was lingering with me. I had enough of those demons dressed in the cloth. Who they were as demons were revealed to me? Many evils were in them. Deceit, Sodom and Gomorrah stuff. Wickedness. Children's pornography. In fact. They were of each other's bed. I cried. Just to know that people would do such a thing to G-D (my intimate one). Do they not fear G-D? I thought. While crying. This also reaffirm even more the existence of G-D. Why go through the trouble of being an impostor Shepard, Devil? I guess now the Joke is on you. I told Satan's (voice that spoke to me). It has yet still turned out for the good and glory of G-D. I said to him. "To G-D be the glory. Great things he has done."

I continued searching for a word (the sword). Because I knew. He was trying to take me out. By this time my male friend that was visiting. Acted increasingly concerned about me. He came by my side in my bedroom. Which I didn't like very much. As guest quarters was not the master bedroom of any home. But I understood his concern because I was very ill. And struggled to help myself.

While there. He says. "How are you doing?" I say. "I am weak. And in and out of consciousness. Somehow, I am feeling smack between the natural and supernatural. Or consciousness and unconsciousness. With a heavy feeling like a brick weighing down my chest. "

I sat up. My friend sat on the bed and lean over to my right ear. And spoke a few words. His voice sounded like the voice of the Devil I had heard earlier. I was not sure. If I was hearing right. That which I heard. I was sick. So, I said to him. "I don't understand." Because I was hoping I was wrong about what I heard.

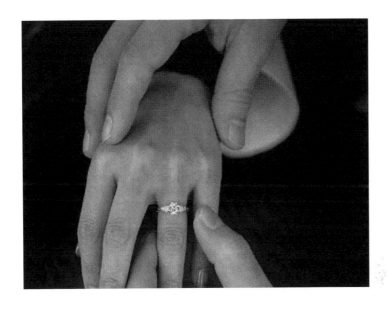

In that moment the evil one came around again. This time. Through the voice of my friend. The Devil spoke clearly in my right ear. He says "Listen. Listen! Be my wife! No one will ever have to know. I will visit you and fulfill all your needs. You can live forever."

I have never in my life felt such fear. As in that very moment. The Devil proposed to me. I realize I was in the presence of Ole' Slew foot! The Prince of The Air. The Master of Deception. Satan. Lucifer. The Devil. ALL SIN.

As I struggle not to show him fear. I did not respond. I got up and went to the bathroom as calmly as I could. And that bought me a little time. Mamie Ms. B. taught me that no answer? Was a good answer. So, The Devil didn't get one from his marriage proposal. I shot him *down*. Besides. I was already spoken for. I locked myself in the bathroom. And silently. I screamed in cries to the LORD. "LORD, Jesus, Jesus, Jesus, LORD Jesus! Why have **THOU** forsaken me? Why are **THOU** so far from helping?

And from the noise of my groaning? I said these words because when I was very young. Mama Rita said to me. "Child? If you ever need The LORD swiftly. Just repeat his own words back to him in prayer. Do not speak your words child. Speak the words that are in the Bible back to him. And if you ever ask him to do something for you? Promise him something in return."

I panicked while washing my face. Trying to revive myself. Knowing that I only had the materials in my bathroom to help with spiritual protection. I tried sticking my two fingers down my throat to dislodge the feeling of that brick. Causing the problems in my body.

I needed to do something. I couldn't be in the bathroom forever. On the nightstand in the room was my olive oil. But the Devil was in my boudoir. In the bathroom was rubbing alcohol. I prayed over it. And anoint my head. Armed with all I had. 70% isopropyl rubbing alcohol. I went to confront

Satan. I feared. My now unwelcome house guest (The Devil)?
Was waiting outside the bathroom door.

Stepping out of the bathroom. My eyes naturally when
to the floor firsit. Satan was standing in the middle of the
hallway. Blocking the only way to escape. As my eyes
traveled from the floor upward. I notice his shoes. Then is
trousers. Then his lava filled chest. My spirit screamed. "HIS
LAVA FILLED CHEST? And my spirit spring from my body.
And came back.

"JEESSUUSSSSS!!!" I yelled OH JESUS" JESUS, JESUS,
JESUSSSSS, I continued to scream for Jesus with everything
I had. While showing my very best. Non-frightened face.
While inside me was upside down. And inside out. Quaking
with fear.

I saw a gold chain amid the lava within The Devils chest.
Just the way it would hang of the neck of a man. With a
circular charm (pendant). That was revolving rapidly. Non-
stop. It felt like terror. It looked like terror. And it was
TERROR to behold.

it's rapid motion. Started slowing down to reveal itself to me. Just as it was slowing down enough to expose the symbol on the pendant. My spirit bolted from fear again. Leaving my body for a second. Everything happened. in a blink of an eye. All my uncertainty vanished. I was now in the presence of Satan himself. Who entered the body of my High School friend to get to me? Of this I was now sure!

JESUSSS!. inside of me screamed at the top of my spiritual lungs. Because I was not going to let the Devil know. That I was afraid. I screamed inwardly. J E S U S! J E S U S!. J E S U S! OH, J E S U S! I yelled inside. I was not getting any answer from my LORD. And intimate one. So, I finally build up the courage to tell Satan to leave. But he did not. Through my spiritual awareness. I sense that the more I said. "Leave Devil! You have no place here." The greater the desire became in me. To ask him to leave. And each time I would said it. I would say it firmer. And stronger than the time before.

And Satan would squirm his words to me saying. But why? Oh Please. Let me stay. Marry me! And I will give you everything you could ever want or need. You will have need for nothing. I have many wives. And children. Living among you I care for. And only they know. When I am there seated beside them. Be my wife. And you will enjoy all that the World has to offer. But in the end. Your soul will remain with me. No one will ever have to know. Because they will not see me. But I will be. Beside you. And I will work everything out for you. All my wives living among you have need for nothing."

At this point. I had heard enough! I was disgusted. The Devil's words sounded to me like 1000-pound words. My ear was disgust. It was as though The Devil was literally shitting on me. And expecting me to enjoy it. Thinking it was cool. He wanted to give me his excretion. In exchange for my priceless, pristine gem. "My Soul." The one I was working for. And on. All the days of my life. It was like walking buckets of sacred water (My Soul) up G-D's Zion Mountain for years to find G-D. That he should drink. Finally arriving at the mountain top. And here comes The Devil waiting with a final temptation that he should rob me of my one true treasure, and sacred water. (My Soul), In exchange for his droppings. I understood instantly why the people of G-D says. "THAT DEVIL IS A LIAR" many others say of The Devil. "HE IS A THIEF" He was trying to steal my win at the finish line. That I should not complete my lifelong mission to arrive at The Marriage Supper of G-D.. Where Jesus turns you over to his father, G-D. The Devil came, that I would forfeit my reward for the journey I've undertaken over 36 years prior. I was insulted and offended. I said to the Devil. "Devil your a liar. To think that I would allow you to rob me?.

Now. I was not only sick at his presence. I was discontented and upset. For the first time in my life. I left like butchering me a Devil on the spot. Was a fair resolution to put away the evil, while doing good. As asked of in 1 Peter 3:11.

Because he felt I was foolish and stew-pit enough to not see his trickery coming from down the road, around the bend.

171

My painstaking journey to G-D. He downplayed. And offered me a tired marriage proposal. Trying to offer me his best. Trash! for my treasure. Vaniterian garbage. (Translation. Sweet smelling bad stench. From the kingdom of vanity). (Ecclesiastes 1:2) Vanity of vanities, saith the preacher, vanity of vanities all is vanity."

In exchange for my Soul. The Devil's suggestion. Was like a sour odor to my nostril that I knew. I needed to get rid of without a shadow of a doubt. I opened the front door to my home and say. "You must leave! Get out." Satan started squirming louder and faster. He say. "Let me stay. I wouldn't bother you. I will let you be." With the sweetest. Gentlest voice that had no more fear. I say." No! You must go Devil."

Satan replied in defeat. "Well them. "You have to tell me." Through my spiritual awareness. I understood. Satan was talking about my front door light casting a shadow of on

172

the ground. That came inside the home so far and meet the dark area in my house.

Satan says. "You have to tell me I can cross." And I realize. He couldn't cross over the *light* unless I commanded him by saying a certain thing. And what I had to tell Satan did not come into my mind until the very moment he told me. "You have to tell me I can cross." He said. And so, I did! I say. "Satan? *Be **THOU** cast into outer darkness. Bound in chains and shackles until the great and terrible judgment day!"* Satan squirmed. And squirmed at my door begging me. He says. "Please. Do not cast me out." This was when. Just then! I saw how incredibly weak and pathetic Satan really is. And without power. Not for the power given him. By the Children of G-D. I had no fear at this point. All I knew was? He had to go! Through the door walking. Crawling with amputated legs. Or getting thrown out the door. Or tossed clean out the window. *SOMETHING!*. His conversation was grotesque to my hearing.

I was done with what I had heard. And I needed to put away the evil from me. His words were a nuisance to my spirit. I realize I was not to be afraid as a child of G-D. I was to be feared as one. Who has a personal relationship with G-D the father? G-D the son. And G-D. The Holy Spirit. Feared!

When Satan left. I became tired mentally. Physical. Emotionally & spiritually. Because I gave Satan all my strength just to get rid of him. I went to bed with what felt like my very last few breaths. I turned on the TV. A preacher named Creflo Dollar was speaking about the hour of temptation. This man of G-D was speaking within the very hour of my own "Hour of temptation. I felt myself drifting. I

173

knew. I was going to die. I started to ponder my situation. I said to myself. "Am lying here. Can't more. Who will find my body first? Would they give my family anything of my possessions? Or would they rob me blind. When my spirit departs? How long would it take for someone to find my body? My housekeeper would not be here for three days."

While laying on my back. My eyes started closing. My strength was leaving me. I thought to pray to be sure to see the LORD. My intimate one. After death. With my eyes close. While lying on my bed. I said "LORD?" And He says "What can I do for you, my child?" I said "LORD. If you would take this from me. That this sickness should pass over me. I will serve you for the rest of my life." And The LORD answered and says to me. **"It is done."**

Immediately. I felt a tape of a finger. In the region of my lower back. While The LORD's words were still being spoken. After the tape. A pressure rose from my spine forcing me to turn to my left side. Open my month to the floor. And regurgitate. I had no strength of movement on my own. I was yet still very weak. And immediately laid on my back motionless. I cried and thanked the LORD. And I turned everything in my home over to G-D and passed out completely as dead. I woke up! To G-D be the glory, I woke up! "Oh, give thanks unto the LORD for he is good." I said out loud. "And all of his mercy endures forever. Throughout time. It has been seen. All the inhabitants of the earth. He has dealt with bountifully." I said these things with no one else listening. But me and the Universe. I LIVED! And there was still yet time. And I had never felt more ALIVE!

"Thank you, Jesus. Thank you, Jesus. No other name I know. Not for the wonderful name of Jesus Christ. I screamed, LORD I reverence your name, I proclaim That you are the alpha the omega the beginning and the end. "Thank you, Jesus," I said. And Jesus replied, **"Anoint your head, and cover yourself in white."**

I fell to my knees on my bedroom floor. Covered myself with a white sheet. Thank you, Jesus. Glory to G-D. Oh sweet

Jesus. I thank you" I continued. Jesus spoke to me again and said. **"Now pray the Father."** I felt a covering moved above my head. As if clouds opened and moved away from every side. The East. The West. The North. And The South. When I was finished praying G-D The Father spoke and said to me. **"Now go THY way and sin no more."** I got up from the floor and noticed my regurgitation on the tile. But this time it was very red and very little. I remember thinking to myself. How can it be? that something so little could weigh me down so greatly? I was alive. And who wanted to be alone once you realize. That you are alive? I called Mrs. B. After I told her what happened. She says. "Child? Satan was trying to kill you! Most people do not survive encounters like that. Some go crazy!"

THE
SAND

CHAPTER XIV

I had stopped visiting Mama Rita. After a few years of not communicating. So, it weights heavy on my heart. She spoke lies about Mr. B. And to me? Mama Rita was a changed person. And I didn't like the person she became overnight.

I visited Mama Rita and showed no sadness or change in me. But G-D knew! She was up in age and her health was not very good. I would stay. Cook, clean and keep her company. The second day of my visit. I sat on her bed comforting her. Then she says to me. "Child? Is there something I have done to you?" I immediately started to cry. The faking it? Was overrun with emotions. Quick. Fast and in a hurry I said. "It's OK Grammy." I intended to let it go. Before I share the catchy disease called hurt.

Mama Rita took a deep breath. And sat beside me on her bed and said. "Child. G-D visited me last night. He sat in that chair and said to me. "You have hurt her." And what every it is I have done to you. I would like to know." I told Mama Rita. The lies she had talked about Mr. B hurt me for a very long time. And for many years I was not visiting because of the pain I felt from it." We talked for a while, and I release the hurt so that we were able to move on.

I started to look at items that was in her home from my childhood. In fact. The things just looked different. I looked at a painting on her wall. Of a child on a bridge with an angel holding her hand. This very same painting was on the wall for near 40 yrs. This day. I saw a large serpent in the painting that was not visible to me years prior.

The day I saw that serpent. There was arguments and frustration in the house. I'd notice Mama Rita get darker in her skin complexion and feet. To me. I was looking at another person. Whatever was happening to her. I didn't know or understand.

Jesus Christ came. His voice says to me. **"Go to her. And sit on the floor at her feet."** I sat down. Mama Rita would abruptly get up and leave. I didn't give up trying to obey Jesus. I sit at Mama Rita's feet. So gently.

I didn't understand why Jesus needed me to do that. I walked in obedience. Jesus Christ was my Master. I obeyed. Just to be swiftly rejected by her. So, I took my complaint to the LORD. And I say. "LORD? Why do you keep sending me to her? To be constantly rejected. Is there not a better way? I've done what you ask of me three times now. And each time I sit down at her feet? She rejects me LORD. She takes me up or she gets up and walks away."

Then Jesus say. **"Go to the beach."** Which was located outside my front door. After arriving at the beach. I said. "LORD? I am here as you have requested of me." Jesus says. "Stick your hands in the sand." I obeyed by placing both my hands. Wrist deep into the sand. And I hear words spoken in a language I could not and cannot speak. And it was as though. That which was under the sand? Was alive around my hands. I could feel the Holy Spirit holding areas around my hand firmly. And moving around my fingers.

I couldn't move on my own. Jesus releases me from the sand. And he says to me. **"From here on out. Nature will take care of you. And provide all your needs."**

I happily when back to Mama Rita's house. I was met by her son. My uncle. He had a 10–15-year-old backstory in his mouth. And I know. The devil had already come. That quick. To try and steal the joy I had just received from Jesus.

After I had served my family like a good and respectable grandchild and niece would? I high tailed. Bush

181

cracked, and Man was gone. Out of there. To Mamie. Mrs. B's house for comfort. I was feeling pain from Uncle's cruel words. I needed healing. My tears were inconsolable. I knew. If I could just see my other grandmother. The nurturer, The saint. The friend. The sister. The Angel. The mentor. And the nurse? "Mamie Ms. B.?" Everything was going to be alright.

In the distance before I even arrived at her house. I started screaming. Mamie? Mamie? She answered immediately. "Yeah. Am in this way! She took one look at me and says. "What's wrong child. Come! Sit down." I told her what had happened. The serpent I saw in the painting. And how I was feeling.

Mamie said. "She had sold out to the Devil. And had stopped her walk with G-D." I realize then. The LORD was testing her. By sending me continually before her face. To sit on the floor at her feet. As The LORD does work in mysterious ways.

As I was about to leave. Mamie said "Wait." I withdrew my right leg from the porch. And closed the screen door for her next command. Mamie left and came back with a black umbrella. As she passes it to me. She says. "Take it. It will protect you."

I remember wanting to say. "Mamie? Do you know it's pitch-black outside?" How is an umbrella going to help me in the dark and there is no rain? Strangely enough. I had _never_ questioned her before. And I certainly was not going to question an umbrella for my safety. After seeking a serpent. Where a serpent. Should not have been.

CONQUERING
LION

CHAPTER XV

One June 12th, 2012. Shortly after Mama Rita rejected my advances. There he was. The man of my dreams. Though I knew him not. I desired him to be. He was perfect. He looked perfect. A beautiful man in every way. It was the first time. I had laid eyes on a man of such presence of Spirit. So, I said secretly. **"My LORD. What a beautiful man."** My thoughts of him were above. Not below. His aura was the most beautiful. I had every behold with my eyes. What highest of aura and quality of spirit. Of one I had never sense in another human being.

He looked distinguished. Well-polished and angelic. Everything about his spiritual essence was of the highest quality. He was dressed in fine apparel. And he had the best grooming standards I had ever seen. He didn't look like someone from the remote islands. I assumed he was a guest of our Estate. I was courteous and polite. I walked up to him and say. "Hello." The angelic stranger replied. "May I come in?" I thought for a second. What harm can such a well dress distinguished gentlemen be to an unarmed young lady. So, I opened my apartment door and say. "Yes. You May." Besides he looked like someone that worked for a very distinguish person or a person that came when you had an inheritance from a long-lost rich uncle that passed away and left you enormous wealth? The stranger was very studious like that.

The first thing the angelic stranger did was snap his fingers once. Waved his right hand. Pointed to the door. And the dogs were gone. They stood on their feet at the sound of the finger snap. Marched in-place at the wave of his hand. And march out the room at his pointing. Out the door they went like two champion equestrian horses. In the prime of their performance.

I had never seen anything like it. It was like their regular senses were taken over by the stranger. I say. "How did you do that?" It was at that moment I knew that I was in the company of no ordinary man. But an angelic being. And the stranger. Had now. My complete and undivided attention. I locked my eyes on the stranger. Like a hawk. The stranger says. "I will stay with you for seven days. What do you have to eat?" "I say. "I have rice and chicken. And I don't have fish. But I can catch some for you?"

The angelic stranger says. "Come with me. And we will get fish." I grabbed my fishing line and my tackle box. The stranger had so much authority about his demeanor. I became eager. And excited to see what other new marvelous tricks the stranger would do next. So, I followed his lead and walked behind him. He walked us over to my dad's land crab pen. The first stop before fishing was bait.

The stranger looked down at the crab. I started planning to jump into the crab pen. Because the stranger's apparel was too good for the task. As I was about to jump in the crab pen. All the crabs started looking up and walking over to us. A few were already standing near us. And took their biggest claw. And severed their little leg off. And handed their legs up to us in the air. While other crabs were coming toward us preparing to take their legs off to give to the stranger.

As I watched on. I became stricken with awe. I could not believe my eyes. The Angelic stranger signaled me. With his head. That I should now collected the crab legs needed to fish from the crabs themselves. As they place their legs. Directly into my outstretch hand ever so gently. Then we proceeded down the beach walking and talking. As we went on to the sandy beach. An eagle came over our heads. Soaring above us. When we stopped. The eagle stop. He would not depart. So, I said to the Angelic stranger. "Why is it. This bird is going along with us like this?. That's pretty strange." The stranger says. "That is Fathar. He is going with us. And he will show us where to fish." "Fathar?" I say to the stranger. "Fathar or Father." Well, whoever this Fathar is. How is he a bird? I smiled to myself and silently thought. "Is this person a whack-a-do? (a wacko see, a wacko do). His Fathar is a bird?" The stranger didn't answer me about the bird right away. Because of this day with the angelic stranger. I have used the word "Fathar." In replacement of the word "Father." Because he said so often. "My Fathar."

After walking for twenty minutes talking and being taught by the angelic stranger. He says. "Stop. He (Fathar, The Bird) will show us were, he wants us to fish." And the eagle stopped also. The angelic stranger say "Watch." Then the eagle left the place above our heads. And dove into water. Just then. A large fish. Without a hook in its mouth. Jump out of the water. The eagle marked the spot. I say.

"Wow, now that is amazing" I became extremely excited. As the angelic stranger and I talked. I couldn't help but feel down deep in my soul. I know this stranger from somewhere. His eyes made me feel at peace. They were like bodies of slow-moving waters. They looked ancient. Like they knew *everything*! And had seen everything. "There is something about this angelic stranger. I kept thinking to myself.

My inner being felt like I knew him. But my fresh and my mind doubted who he might be because of the color of his skin that did not correlate to the color of my beloved Jesus's skin. Which was white. But his mannerisms and voice. I had experience for over 36 years. So, the stranger made me very confused. Inwardly. My mind was at its capacity wondering. Just who the stranger really was.

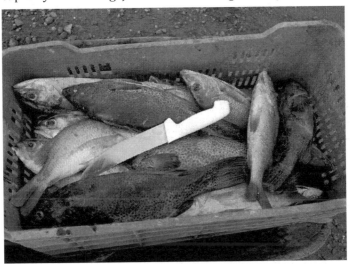

I setup my fishing equipment on the shoreline. Every single one of my casts. I caught *fish, after fish, after fish, after fish, after fish!* I thought. Oh, my goodness. The fish are quarreling over who's turn it is to jump on my fishing hook.

I had more fish than I was able to carry. I gave fish away to other passing fisherman that had no luck down the beach. And to the others that yelling to me. "Save mine."

I went a little further and gave away even more *fish*. They were the biggest fish. I had every seek caught on a hand line. The angelic stranger collected the firewood for the pit. I cleaned, seasoned and fried the fish at the beach. And offered the stranger the food.

I had never had information that intoxicated me before. Like it did this day. I became very exhausted. I fell asleep lying on the sofa. With the stranger siting in a meditation pose on the floor next to me teaching me. I woke up the following day to the stranger in the same position. Still teaching me like a day had not pass. The angelic stranger didn't sleep. I started my house chores while dancing along to the beat of my lyric. He says to me." No. No. Listen. Listen to the words. Forget the beat. Just listen!"

When I incline my ear. And became consciously toned in? The beat was good. But the lyric was filthy and filled with evil. So, I was dancing to be beat. Not hearing that the lyric was not good for my soul. I heard. Deception. Anger. Frustration. Confusion. Evil and the like. I couldn't believe my ears. It made me sick to my stomach. That I was allowing that garbage to come out into the atmosphere. I shut the music box off.

The Angelic Stranger got up. Walked over to the cassette player. Where we had no radio stations on the island and no reception to pick on up. He waved his hand over the player. Static noise was heard. Then a lyric started to play out of nowhere. That said. ***"The conquering Lion shall break every chain. The conquering Lion shall break***

every chain. The conquering Lion. Shall break every chain. And give us the victory. Again, and again." Nine years later. I learned it was a song by Bob Marley. Called "The conquering Lion of Judah."

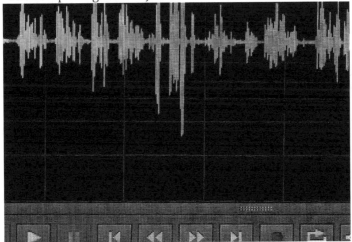

I watched him move his feet and body to the rhythm. The stranger went into what was a deep mediation. On the

song. So, I became relaxed also and started dancing to the beat of the song. Then the stranger said to me while smiling. "The Chief Musician in my Fathar's Kingdom is music." On the fourth day of the angelic stranger's visit. As he taught me while sitting in my apartment at my dad's eight-unit multiplex home on the beach. In the distance. I heard frightening sounds of thunder and lightning. I became afraid.

The Angelic Stranger says. "That is my Fathar." I really didn't understand that. I thought to myself saying." "The thunder and lightning are now this man's Fathar? How is that? Who is this man? And who is this Fathar of his? And where is his Fathar from?" Then the angelic stranger demonstrated how I should clean all meat before consumption. Including trimming away all access fat and skin from the meat. And the products I should use that totaled four. Shortly thereafter the angelic stranger showed me what I should use to cleanse myself daily. The two products The Angelic Stranger gave me provided 100% germ protection. I was amazed at the results after use.

When I was sick at any time the stranger arrived in my presence? The sickness would scatter in all different directions while leaving my body. When he had arrived in my vicinity. I would know he was present. Even though I didn't see him. Or hear his voice.

There was always just a peace about the angelic stranger. That was greater than my comprehension. His eyes lured me in deeply. Rendering mine impossible to look away unless he did. His eyes seems as though they were ancient. Full of love. Full of compassion. Full of truth. Full of wisdom. Full of knowledge. When looking at him. You can see within his eyes. All that he was saying. Was *true and faithful.*

One day at the end of the angelic stranger's stay with me. He say. "You look like lady liberty. Look." He placed me in front of the mirror. While standing in the back of me. He says. **"If you had to write a letter to awaken an army from sleep. What would you write?"** I got right to it. My family always told me. "When you've doing something? You go in deep." Deep I went. In on the letter. I surprised even myself. I still have that letter I wrote at the angelic stranger's request.

When we walked and he taught me? The Angelic Stranger would have our lunch prepared. And in place. But there would be no one visible that have placed the lunch so neatly. And of the choice foods that were not found on the remote island. And if someone did place it? Why did not the ants or the birds or the animals take hold of it? I would often

193

ask myself. So much wonderful mysteries surrounded this stranger. But all I knew was. I was so very happy.

I enjoyed the angelic stranger's visit so much. I didn't remember the seventh day had come. And the stranger needed to leave. He walked me down the beach. We ended up at my Land. A parcel of beachfront property. My Dad had given me years prior. A place I had accidentally fallen asleep overnight at age 13. While watching the Moon & Stars above. Not knowing it was my dad's property. He gave me it to me at age 19. Then I told him what happened to me on the land.

It had a special place in my heart. The angelic stranger stopped there. Came in close to me. The closest he had been to me during his visit. I did not ask any questions because the atmosphere seemed divine, especially blessed and heavenly, from the soul level within existence. Divinely inspired. He says to me while holding my hands together. **"I am Yahusha. And you are Elioenai. Because Your Eyes Are Toward The Creator. And My Fathar? He smiled then said." Is my Elohim."**

I looked upon his face. And it shined like a brilliant light. And I could not deny him. His eyes said he was faithful and true. He smiled at me as though it was such a relief. And a joy that he should tell me what and who he was. I knew instantly. I was in the presence of him (Jesus) that loved me from my youth. I felt the same Spirit of Jesus that came to my beside every night for 13 years.

It was the first time I had heard the name Yahusha. Elioenai or Elohim. And I started thinking. "Who is this Yahusha really? Is this Jesus new name that it is written would be given? I remembered in NASB 1977 Revelations 3:12 read. *He who overcomes, I will make him a pillar in the temple of My G-D, and he will not go out from it anymore; and I will write on him the name of My G-D, and the name of the city of my G-D, the new Jerusalem, which comes down out of heaven from My G-D, and My new name.* And what is an Elohim? I asked myself. I liked that my eyes were said to be towards The Creator. But who am I now as Elioenai?

And I did not really know what any of it meant. It made me more confused. In the search for my identity. But he was happy. I saw it in his eyes. His aura. Was of The Son of G-D. Holy and Majestic was he. He felt like my beloved Jesus I had always known from my youth. And he sounded like the voice of Jesus that I had become accustomed to hearing over the years. What he did not have was the white skin I expected. And that threw me off greatly. And confuse and astonished me. Yahusha also didn't have the appearance that I expected of The Son of G-D. Because of my worldly knowledge of Jesus.

But Yahusha's skin was brown. Closest to my skin tone. And that was confusing to me also, that his skin was not white. And the hair on his head was like wool. He picked it with his comb, and kept it always groomed. This was the last time I saw The Angelic Stranger that said to me. "My name is Yahusha. Who I called Jesus." And I saw him. _In the flesh_.

MEET
FATHAR

CHAPTER XVI

I t is time to meet The Fathar The voice of Yahusha came to me the following day after he left. After he had departed. I say. "Do I have too?" In complaint. I knew. It was the season of my marriage supper. I felt the occasion in my spirit. I just didn't really know G-D. The way I knew Yahushua. I often use to call Jesus. I knew Yahusha. I used to call Jesus. I knew the Holy Spirit. I knew

many Angels of Heaven. I knew also the LORD of The Earth (The Caretaker of The Earth). I knew The G-D EL, EL, ELyon that spoke to me. But I didn't necessarily know the G-D head as intimately. THE KING OF THE UNIVERSE. ButI knew my Marriage Supper had arrived and that was all that mattered. And I knew my love had another name. Not Jesus. But "Yahusha." So, I had cold feet to meet his Fathar. I said to my love out loud. "You just gave me your name after 36 years. Now am confused. I don't know what I should say to your Fathar, G-D. Or what I should call him that is real. And how will I address him?"

From deep within. Something said to me. "If you met The Fathar of Yahusha. You will be separated from Yahusha." I didn't want separation. I knew Yahushua. as Jesus. For over 36 years. So, I decided to fight meaning his father, Tooth and nail. Yahusha's spirit left. The following morning. Yahushua returned to me. He says." **"It is time to meet the Fathar."** I let out a deep breath and I say. "Do I have too?" **"Yes. Yes. You must. You have outgrown your crib."** Yahusha's voice said to me. His words encompassed my body.   Gripping me firmly in place. That I should know.

He was serious. I submitted to Yahusha. But unwillingly. I say. "OK. OK. OK" In other words I meant, "Stop, stop, stop, your squeezing my guts out"

After feeling the firmness of Yahusha's grip. From his reply that clench my body. I gave up the tooth. And I wanted nothing to do with a nail. He was not playing around with me. And it was not our usual play time. Is what I felt he was saying to me. So, I didn't fight his request any further.

Yahusha left and I said to myself. "Well. I don't know who G-D is really. I know nothing about him apart from what I have heard and learned in Church." I reasoned with myself saying. "My Jesus turned how to be named Yahusha, so I guess my best starting place is to build up an introduction to speak to his Father. G-D."

I sat down for several hours. Wondering what exactly I would say to G-D. I thought. It would be wise of me not to use any of the names I have heard in the world. I should wait for him to give me his name. As Jesus had just told me. His name was Yahusha. I thought to myself. "I cannot look like a fool to my husbandman's Fathar." I just didn't know.

I was not about to go all big! Universal encyclopedia Britannica on the Master of the Universe, calling him all kinds of names that The World had for him that I could not justify. Or validate for sure. I use wisdom. And I dare not to tell G-D his name. Or to call him a name that he did not tell me himself. I wondered how I would feel if I met someone for the first time and they told me what my name was. Verses asking me for my name. So, I opened up my mind, my heart, my soul and my spirit. Of the knowledge I was told of him. And became empty for him to fill.

I was not prepared to use big fancy words without understanding. I was careful to watch my words. As the angelic stranger Yahusha, who I learned later was The Son of G-D had taught me about words. I couldn't come up with anything! The best thing I could ever do. I thought. Was to say nothing of myself.

I emptied myself. While sitting there I said to G-D. "G-D. Who are you?" I didn't get a reply. I though. This approach was the best one. Seeing that my Jesus gave me another name for himself. The following day while going about my day. I said again. "G-D? Who are you?" A little deeper a little more purposeful. G-D did not reply. I tried on the third day. I said "G-D. Who are you? Even deeper. Even more purposeful.

Later that very day. Yahusha's voice spoke to me. He says. **"He will meet you know. At the beach."** I dried my hands. Picked up my cellphone and headed to the beach. I sat on my dad's boat with my back to the South. Facing North. after 15 minutes of waiting. I went into my human routine. I picked up my phone and started checking messages.

Yahusha's voice says to me. <u>"Are you serious about that? You are really trying to check messages? Put the phone away."</u> **He sounded just like a lion man of the tribe of Judah.** I smiled at him sweetly, I was sometimes a

brazen bride to be. Especially now that I knew, I had made it to the marriage supper. I suck my teeth. Took a deep breathe. And had what felt like an eternity waiting for this Fathar of Yahusha to meet me. And I had what felt like a waiting game for this G-D. 20 minutes later. Forgetting I was warned about my phone. I took it out again. Yahusha says to me. **"<u>Your serious about that?</u>"** I put it away quickly and smiled at him. Like any bride would her husband during wedding preparations. A minute later. The Heavens opened. A voice, inside of thunder proceeded from the Eastern clouds. Answering my question, I had asked days earlier. I felt the presence of four others in the four cardinal directions in the sky that did not speak. But observed. Along side him that spoke to me.

The voice of G-D. Yahusha's Fathar spoke to me from Heaven. G-D says to me. **"I AM" in everything."** His words stopped the winds from its normal direction. Causing it to shift. There was a momentary lapse within re-ality. A brief stillness within all things while fragments fell from the sky before my eyes and around me. G-D came through everything withing reality that I should know he exist within it all. G-D's words when through me. The Coconut trees. The boat I was sitting on. Space and time, *Everything!*

His words went through everything within existence; the time it took to say four words. "I AM IN EVERYTHING. All my senses experience this G-D. This G-D affected all things at once. His words changed the atmosphere around me. My feet, brake ten in the opposite direction! I ran for my life. Like my life depended on it. Afraid as all outdoors. I knew I was in danger. My soul ran for its life. This G-D was so terribly and dreadfully powerful. I spirit thought to split myself up equally to run in all the directions. I would have done that just to get away from the fear of The Powers of this G-D, that spoke to me. Yashua's Fathar. He was no joke. I thought to myself while running for my life. "This Fathar of my beloved Yahusha is going to kill me. He doesn't want me to be his son's bride. He hates me." I said. His powers are too strong for me. And if he let me live, I thought? He wouldn't be the one to be playful with. As I did sometimes lovingly with his son. As any bride did her husband in a loving way.

This Fathar means business. I said while running away quickly to hide myself from G-D, The Fathar of Yahusha. With sand trapped between my toes. I did what is called "Dig out!." I broke ten like my life depended on running away from G-D. The powers of this G-D the Fathar. Was greater than all the forces of The Holy Spirit I had experience up to that point.

I didn't pump the brakes on my feet until I got inside my Daddy's house. My heart felt as though. It wanted to abandon me. And run down the beach from fear of G-D. I looked for my family to help me. I found no one was home. I hid myself from this G-D, Yahusha's Fathar. I wasn't getting anywhere with hiding. and I realize there was no plan I can make to escape. The powers of this G-D. That he would not see. And no place I could hide that this G-D could not find me. I became stricken with the full realization that this G-D is in everything. Just like he said. I came out from under the bed. Walk into the center of the room. Knee down and said. "I submit myself unto your willf. **THOU** arth G-D who arth in everything.""

A month after Yahusha's father made that contact with me in the sky. I didn't eat. I went from 187 pounds to 80-90 pounds. Even my mother and father turned her back on me. I remember sending to my mother's grocery story for a bottle of water, that I should drink. And it was not sent to me. My family assumed I was doing drugs to have lost so much weight. My mother didn't understand what I was going through in the spirit. I lost many friends during this time of purging my soul. I longed after this G-D, Yahusha's father. I needed him. Not food and not water, and nothing worldly. Just HIM.

__2 Timothy 2:21__ says, "If a man therefore purge himself from these, he shall be a vessel unto honor, sanctified, and meet for the master's use, and prepared unto every good work. __Psalms 5:17__ says, "Purge me with hyssop, and I shall be clean: wash me, and I shall be whiter than snow.

DRINK THIS

CHAPTER XVII

I withdrew from the world to seek after this G-D. Who blew my mind with his supernatural wonders. And I couldn't survive in the city that I was in. So, I moved to another city. I talked my mother into letting me stay in here house. I prayed from morning until night. One night. I heard in the distance music and partying. Emergency vehicles and other festivities. As I closed my eyes and incli-

ne my ear to the festive celebration that could be heard from miles around. The Spirit of G-D came and stretched my spirit out of myself like an elastic band. Then I became absent from my body and present with The LORD.

I saw the streets ripped in pieces like an earthquake had passed through. The highways were crumbling. And I saw people running for their lives. Blood covered their faces. Parents holding children's hands. I smelled all that which I saw. Terror. Panic. Confusion. Blood. Humans were running everywhere and anywhere to flee from G-D's wrath; And everywhere they ran for safety? G-D was there.

I saw rodents in their burrows rejecting the humans that tried to hide in them. And even if one was lucky to fit into the animal's burrow? The LORD took me inside. That I should see the one. And witness the rodents evicting the humans who's judgement had come because of their lawlessness.

As I saw humans trying to enter? G-D's presence was there. *There was no place that G-D's presence was not there.* And the LORD took me from one place. Into another to witness. I stood on the street and watch in horror for as much as I could stand it. While others looked up screaming and whaling. Misery took hold of them. When they saw G-D descending from the sky.

I saw chaos in the streets. I say. "This is it LORD! This is what you have spoken off. This is how all knees will bow. And all tongues will confess."

While there. It was so real. It was like those things was happening to the same people that were having a festival of a drunken time on earth. When I returned fully into my physical body. I cried and prayed for the people of the Earth. The warning I wrote that day in my journal is. *"Submit yourself to G-D. Lean not onto your own understanding of who you were told that you are. Remember this!"*

"Galatians 6:7-8 Do not be deceived. G-D is not mocked, for whatever a man sows this he will also reap, for the one who sows to this fresh, shall from the flesh reap corruption, but the one who sows to the spirit shall from the spirit reap eternal life."

*"Ephesians 5:15-18 Therefore be careful how you walk, not as unwise men but as wise, making the most of our time, because the days are **evil**. So then do not be foolish but understand what the will of the LORD is. And do not get drunk with wine, for that is dissipation, but be filled with the Spirit.*

I wrote in my journal during this time. *"All life comes from antecedent life, from the labor and sowing of others. What we reap was planted either naturally or purposely either by G-D or by man and for either positive or negative results."*

"We reap the fruit of much. For which we have extended no labor because we entered into the labor of others. Either for a good reward or a bad reward. Translation? You are either with G-D or you are with the Devil! Your purpose on earth, the things you put your hand, heart, mind, energy, finance toward?. Is either for the work of the Kingdom of G-D. Or the work of the fiery lava pit Devil, it's that simple. Come to the G-D of your forefather's empty. And he will supply all of your needs according to his richest in glory."

The beginning of my awakening happened, one night in March of 2013 as I fell asleep, G-D came to visit me through his Son Yahusha. Yahusha wore a white linen hoodie of light. It covered most of his face. Leaving his mouth exposed. Yahusha reached out his hands and says to me. **"Drink this."**

"I got closer to drink what Yahusha had in his hand. I saw liquid. Gold like honey. And I did drink. I woke up and started to read as I did before. but this time. I had this wisdom I had never in my life felt. Like a large tree was growing in my head. Something had happened to me. Knowledge was pouring out of me, Wisdom and Understanding's Spirits were also ever present. And I became enlightened. I remember calling Mamie. I told her what Yahusha had done for me. She replied. "Child? That was your blessing. Rejoice in The LORD Most High child." And I did.

This is when a change inside me happened. And I started to became awake from The religious, colonization inslavery and the cultural assimilation of 1492. It felt like what I had. Was the sleep of death. I found only the mercy of Yahusha the Messiah. And His Fathar surrounding me. When Yahusha's drink woke me up. I was afraid of the changes I was experienced in my body. Yahusha says to me. **"Do not be afraid. Take my hand."**

Seconds later. I saw myself. Hanging on to a rope. As in out of space. With no surface around. "Who did this to me?"

I wrote in my journal. *"We have the power to Include or Exclude. Include the thing we want into our mind. And exclude the things that the mind wants out of us. When your mind goes on without you. Stop and ask. "Who goes there? and with how's permission?*

No matter what Government or what border protection you are told. "You stop at this gate. Or you move no further! Shouldn't you exam the thoughts that come to your border? Before applying action. Who is a Man to enslave another man even after his physical body has been released from slavery? But you are to check yourself for slurs and impurities. That are not consistent with your living capsules.

Our problem in our mind is. We have been hospitable to strangers of the spiritual nature. And the physical nature beginning with Queen Isabella and King Ferdinand in the form of their Admiral Christopher Columbus. We allowed the

214

strangers to pose the one thing that belongs to us in this world. Our sovereignty.

It is a misconception that we were savages, even by today's standards. Savages know nothing about perfect HARMONY, perfect LOVE, perfect JOY, thereby being one with nature, which was the daily bread feed to my ancestors The Native American Indians, also of the Greater and Lesser Antilles, who descendants are scattered around the four corners of the earth.

Countless days and night I've spent locked in my room at my mother's house. Not eating. Praying, reading my bible. Seeking The LORD Most High. I wake up at 3am and read my bible.

The LORD sent his Angels to deliver me angels' food (Manna). My soul delighted in it. G-D sent seven angels at my mouth to feed me. They came to me saying. One after another. "Eat this. Eat this. Eat this. Eat this. Eat this. Eat this. Eat this.

TAR
BABY

CHAPTER XVIII

R evelations through obedience and of hearing and understanding and interpretation! **The Holy Spirit came and say to me.** "Mankind must be reminded; Earth is not for the taking."

G-D The FATHAR spoke next and says to me. "Daughter. There was a black man that stole a golf cart and run it into a store and stole ice cream. Though shall not steal. Right? So, I gave them back to the guy that they had before me. The one they once served. To be at servitude even deeper and stronger."

I learned that in the beginning G-D The Fathar avoided civilization. Disguising himself from them. Time. After time G-D got curious and little by little became involved with humanity. He has made many friends along the way. G-D told me. He tossed small rocks at my ancestors playfully. Even inherited a Nation. It was in that hour of my reflective meditation. Journaling the knowledge obtained. And seeking G-D during my awakening that G-D The Fathar's voice says to me. "Rubies Daughter? Does not define you. You define Rubies."

It seems G-D can cut you an eternity of ways. When you only have one way from Sunday. **Revelation within the hour:** - I felt these two. An eternity of ways he can cut you to find him or to receive revelations on many levels. Or cut you to curse you. To heal you. Have your life cut for frequent ups and downs that increases you in him. Many ways G-D can cut you for various reasons. His ways are everlasting. And his acts are eternal!

Revelations within the hour: - His ways being everlasting, speaks to knowing his ways, of which we have heard whether spoken off or read about. His act is eternal means, that which he acted had carried out and carried out himself is still in the face of eternity and in effect today! **G-D The Fathar says while I was writing. He says.** *"I have not been erased and will not be erased. All that I have acted/established is eternal – this is what this means."*

Revelations through obedience and of hearing and understanding and interpretation! - Mankind does a lot outside the holy spirit. **Revelation within the hour.** If you have the holy spirit? You have peace, joy, happiness among other fruits of the spirit. And you are protected from all those that are different from these fruits in which the holy spirit recognizes being not of G-D. G-D wins in every way! While people are preservatives, ungodly traits, ungodly characters. **The Spirit Send From G-D says to me.** "Squeeze a black man you get his roots. Squeeze a white man you get a white man's roots – Can't be no plainer!"

Affirmation, within Revelation **the Holy Spirit says to me.** "You are to say – Yes! I talk to G-D. Yes! G-D listens and responses to me! At any turn with affirmation when asked or questioned by anyone." *I was given affirmation, revelation and authority by G-D to respond this way to anyone.* Righteousness has to do with obedience from G-D. The truth within the obedience that came from G-D's Righteousness. *Part obedience & Part Truth.* Man's righteousness is like filthy rags. Because they cannot measure to G-D's righteousness.

The Most High G-D EL ELYON says. "Sometimes I need things from civilization. "Get your spirit statues up to G-D's righteousness *"because it's a bargaining chip."* These are the stars in G-D's sky. Grace, Mercy, Knowledge, Understanding, Truth, Wisdom, Love. **<u>Revelations within the hour</u>**: - When you front on things, about things, they come back for payment. G-D The Fathar says to me during this revelation. He says. "Nothing good is worth hiding."

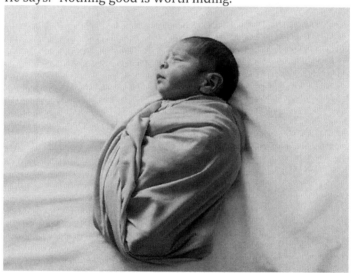

EL ELYON The Highest G-D says. "When you come in the world? You come as a half breed. Until G-D establishes you. Some today is at age. But still yet a half breed. The half breeds are those my spirit does not strive with. Half breeds live outside of me. Not to mean that I am not there. Because

I am! But their odor is not sweet. My existence is there. But my presence has been removed from them. TV technology, Computer technology, Phone technology is a form of sorcery. **G-D the Fathar's voice came to me next and says.**

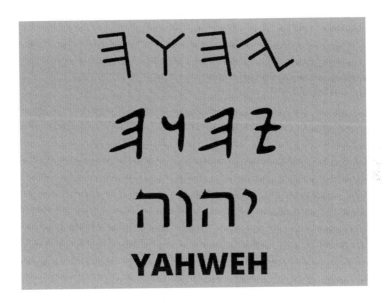

"Tell them. My name isn't Henry, or Boy! My name is Yahweh. Call me by my name. "They called my son. **Tar baby!**" Babies are so true. They are the only thing greater than G-D.

The 10 commandments cover all the Laws on earth. The way to true love. True wealth, true happiness, true joy, true obedience, covers wisdom, covers understanding, covers knowledge, righteousness, justice, truth. There is nothing it does not cover; it covers man existence. And a way to live in that existence."

"G-D could put you in a scenario, all that you see, dream, even living as a reality? Can become an instant dream. Where even what you think you know as reality? Was only a dream. G-D can change your hold life in an instant! All things within existence, Stacks, Racks, & Reacts. Or Stops, Rocks, and Rolls just the way G-D likes it!

"Joblessness?" **EL, EL ELYON The Most High G-D says.** "Is another attack against my poor black people. The invisible chains. The all might dollar. Not having a job, work for a hand, cuts a man in the center of him."

"If anyone walks into a homeless shelter, with work uniform still on, OPEN UNTO THEM! For if anyone dears to rule under my treasure which is grace, mercy, truth. There will not be a hinging place for him. Who rejects them. To hang his hat! **Thus said the Most High G-D."**

The Most High G-D said. "Do you want to get where you want to go the long way? Or the short way? The short way. When am involved, you can lose your job suddenly and I move you quickly! While the world keeps you on minimal wage. While having minimal mind set to that of the world and all its powers and principalities." "People who are on drugs are getting more that the help they need. And the strong who just needs to be stronger. falling through the cracks."

222

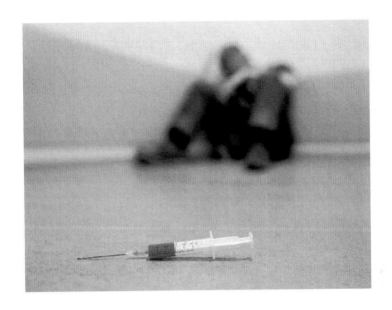

EL ELYON, The Most High G-D says. "America has forth every alien known to man! But when it comes to fighting my Holy Spirit? They yield! Even before the battle, *Retreat! Retreat! Retreat!* Cowboys like to shoot! America is Gun's, Gun's, Gun's."

"There was a man, that would say, "Am the Greatest, Am the Greatest" that did not become enough for that Man. Until he went on to say later. *"The Greatest doesn't get it done!"*

Revelation within the hour: - This is a spiritual example of turning from G-D. The Holy Spirit taught me. It's a form of turning on, yourself. The WORDS ITSELF did not find him wordy (said The Spirit from G-D to Me) and therefore the WORDS (that was with G-D, that became flesh?) Came to him for fulfillment of him being the GREATEST. And he was consequently found in wanting and he currently does not exist. IN THE BEGINNING WAS THE WORD AND ALL WORDS WAS WITH G-D Genesis 1:1. Was my lesson.

EL ELYON, The Most High G-D then says. "Do you understand my Dear?" I say. "Yes, Most High, I do understand. I understand that all words belong unto **THEE.** And words were there with you before anything else was. And that we your children should use the gift of all words with caution. Bless The LORD."

EL ELYON, The Most High G-D says. "Let no man put an award around your neck. It is your noose. Method used to carry on the history of keeping you back into a dark, dark day. The place of slavery is our beginning! All people of The World are G-D's TV. He can change the channel on all y'all and turn your TV off. JOIN ME! says **The Most High G-D EL, EL Elyon.**"

Revelation through obedience and of Hearing with interpretation as it is Revealed:- The **Holy Spirit came to me and says.** Earth is like heaven because G-D, made earth like heaven with order. Like Earth has a ruler? Heavens got a ruler. I say. "OK, I get it."

EL ELYON, The Most High G-D says. "You, see? The acknowledgment of a wedding for two people that G-D loves. Is different from one who he doesn't know. Understand?" I say. "Yes, Most High, I understand." **EL ELYON says.** "Always know where you are, within every moment, always know where you are."

After being rendered homeless, I needed to access where I was. I had two vehicles a place to stay, things I had acquired, cleaning equipment, furniture, blankets, tools – natural stuff- I also had knowledge of the things. How do I get those things to work for me? At this juncture to have people buy into what I was selling. I considered using ALL available tools that the Master has provided.

Greater was not that which was taken away (shelter). But rather, that which remained. I look around. And expanded from there. *G-D The Son came in and said to me.* *"G-D can take things from us, when we begin to feel like we deserve it. We make plans for the thing we feel we deserve. The only thing we can plan for is if G-D gives you that thing. Your starting point is the place where G-D have you, RIGHT NOW!"*

G-D, My Holy Fathar step in and says to me. *"If you think that what I have is just for you? You would have missed the mark in the giving up of oneself, for the higher calling in which I have called you too."*

THINKING
CAPSULE

CHAPTER XIX

The Holy spirit says to me. "Because we can't fully understand G-D? We get stages of G-D. If the stage was like a step ladder that had 1 to 13 steps? There are a few of us that are on step 5, some 7, some 9. Some step 2, and the others 13. Some of us are all

zeros. You have not arrived on any level. The zero heroes can also be those that pray every day. Or those that preach every Sunday. <u>Acts 10:34 G-D is no respecter of person</u>. Many on the ladder at the bottom are spoken off in <u>Matthew 7:21. Not</u>

everyone who says to me, LORD, LORD shall enter into The Kingdom of Heaven, but he who does the will of my Father in Heaven. Which is because of Romans 8:27 For the LORD sees not as man sees: man looks on the outward appearance, but The LORD looks on the heart.

Others have not made it on any level. That's how difficult it is to get to G-D because it is by invitation of G-D THE SON and or a DRAWING FROM G-D THE FATHAR for you, toward his Son, as it is written, no man goes to the Fathar, but by him. (John 14:6). G-D is multi-dimensional, He's in everything, between, above, beneath. He exists inside and outside of everything birth, everything juncture, everything conspired, everything desired, everything wished for, hoped for, everything within, through, around, besides, aside, considered, pondered, drive slow or go fast. "G-D" is a part of it ALL!

There is a saying "G-D will blow your mind" but I tell you! "This G-D, will blow your mind." And put it back together again." Everlasting possibilities, that's this G-D. Everlasting possibilities.

As I meditated on G-D. **G-D, The Holy Father step in and says to me.** "How can a man find richest in another man's house? No richest should be in store for you in another man's house. Find your fathers, father, and his father's father. Soon thereafter you will find ME. You will, fine ME! And I will be unto you, like an eagle that stirs her wings to protect her young." **Revelation within the hour:** - I heard myself talking to me, from myself, through myself, from one part of me to another part of me. From one spirit to one flesh, from my inward self to my outward self. **G-D, The Holy Father step in and says.** "The gates are all open

228

wide, come unto me all those that are heavy laden, and I, alone, will give you rest. I will wait for you! Like a father waiting to welcome his children home. Music, Dancing, Happiness, Joy, Celebration, Love, and Heaviness of Heart."

Revelation within the hour: - I felt, when G-D says. "Make a way for you? I felt he was talking about those stages he mentioned earlier – I also felt and realize making a way for you is through receiving that which he says, whatever that is, receiving it. After I heard Yahweh's words. I felt in my body, receiving a messenger or receiving what he has sent you in the direction of him, he is bringing you closer to him. And he usually sends word, over time or over centuries, and he does send word to his Nation – all this is what I felt. He sends word that will bring you closer to knowing who he is. That brings you closer to the marriage with him, the Commitment. **Revelation within the hour**: - I was processing a thought up to my mind. My head. But the spirit had me send the thought down to my stomach & something started turning in the stomach region. My revelation within the hour is when the turning like winding a clock started happening. I recognized that the Holy Spirit was pointing me in the direction of my thinking capsule suddenly something in my stomach area started going around and around, it was the very first time I had ever activated my thinking mechanism. So, your thinking is in your stomach, that is where you should send things down to be processed.

EL ELYON, The Most High G-D says. "Sometimes you wake up from sleep. And walk right into waiting spirits, this is what I understand. Sometimes it's best to walk away. When a person becomes frustrated or threatened or in some cases put in an uncomfortable position (the one man)

Five to ten other spirits stands up inside the man. Reasoning, peace, confusion, panic and anger etc. Anger is stronger and more intense, so Anger is welcomed in and can bring ALL or any of his personal friends, DISCONNECT, VIOLIENCE, DESTRUCTION, DEATH!"

"He can come right in and bring fire, and leave you or anyone around you, to pick up the pieces. If you can easily slam a door or easily raise your voice, ANGER is too close to your life. And he has been there for a long time. You must try and get rid of him. Go into yourself and understand that! No man needs *ANGER* to solve anything for them." "Solve all of your problems with calm and loving demeanor. You do not have to solve anything with anger. You and the next man is going through some stuff. Quite frankly, none of you need to be in me. So, you don't have to put yourselves through any of that. You need to be happy, more than you need to be ANGER. That's just how it is! My ear is the closest thing to my mouth.

Whatever I say to you! I say first to myself. You just happen to hear what am saying. I can go over in the corner and say this, and NO ONE will hear me. I am a victim of my own success, and victim of my own failure!" I say. "So, what would you have us do Most High?" *EL ELYON says."* I would like you to solve all your problems, in the sweetest way possible!"

G-D, The HOLY SPIRIT says. "Understand! G-D does not have to come and ask you to move a bridge. He comes and move the bridge, throw it in the water, IF! HE WANTS TOO with you under the bridge. He just, before the bridge hits you. Takes your soul and carries it. He doesn't really care about the flesh. The flesh on the other hand, goes back to the LORD of the Earth. Earth claims that. He carries the Soul, you see?" I say. "Yes, Holy Fathar."

EL ELYON says. "So, for you now to move that bridge, you would have to go through so many laws and culinary and in spark and under spark and reasoning and undesirable reasoning and all those other things, and the fish under the water, the fish is going to die, you must consider all these things, one person have to walk across every day to check! That is monumental." I say. As I started laughing, "Yeah, That's a monumental catastrophe." And I continued laughing.

The Most High G-D says. "A monumental catastrophe! So now, if G-D say's to you move the bridge? Then you say. "Well LORD, I asked them, and they aren't moving the bridge. Next thing you know, a huge thunderstorm comes crack the bridge in half, the lightening picks up the water and the water breaks it up, next thing when you wake up in the morning, the bridge is on the ground. It's in the water and the fish is running through it!" "And all the police, the fire truck, YOU, and the committee all watching the bridge and guess what they will say? *YOU!* blow the bridge up. And arrest you and lock you up for the bridge."

"So now! if G-D says "Move the Bridge Daughter?" Say unto him." OK Fathar. There are some fish under the water, there are some folks that needs to walk across the bridge and there are others who like this bridge and would like this bridge to be here so, shut their mouth, bring the fishes back, so that they can't travel this way, and the folk who desire to go on this bridge, kill the desire to walk across this bridge, *AND THEN! YOU CAN DESTROY IT!* Because he might decide to destroy it at your word Daughter, with people walking on the bridge."

I say. "But why Most High? Why? Should he not have known that there are people on the bridge? should he not have known that there are fish under in that sea? So why would he do that?

EL ELYON The Most High G-D says. "The fish belongs to the LORD, The Caretaker of the Earth my dear. The LORD of the Earth, multiplies these fishes by the thousands." I say. "I See, I See, I See."

EL ELYON The Most High G-D says. "He doesn't care about five or six or one hundred, they are multiplied again by a thousand. The LORD of the Earth, own your flesh, and your bones and all your sinuses. The only thing that belongs to G-D is the Soul." I say. "I See. And I Bless you Most High."

EL ELYON The Most High G-D says. "And the committee's what are they going to do when the bridge falls, try build it back? NO! they will let it go! So, all am asking G-D to do it, those who are walking on the bridge, let them not have the desire to walk on the bridge anymore.

"Bring the fishes back, so they can't be destroyed, and the committees, shut their mouths for a time. You, see?" I say. "Yes, Most High I do."

EL ELYON The Most High G-D says. "And then from that, if he honors what I said then the Earth, even the Earth itself will bring the fish back, the Earth itself will bring them to not have the desire to walk on or anywhere near the bridge and the committee, he shut them up!

<u>Deeper interpretation of the Revelation.</u> G-D gives the orders, you verbally with wisdom, knowledge and understanding state what you see that is best, almost like making a righteousness proposal before G-D, that the Earth itself will carry out for us. You become the voice of G-D within the Earth. **Psalms 24:1 (KJV)** The earth is the LORD's. And the fullness thereof; the world, and they that dwell therein.

234

MY
KITE

CHAPTER XX

Between April 21st to May 3rd, 2016. When I spoke to the LORD, The Universe went in silence to listen; and to hear me. Stillness became over everything in existence. Providing me accessibility to speak, and be heard and not by my will, but because the G-D of Heaven willed it.

On Wednesday May 2nd, 2016, I had a vision that myself and another person and The **LORD** had one kite flying high in the sky and everyone was noticing. I immediately became afraid and wanted to take down my kite, because I felt like I needed to do something to take the attention of me. Lowering my flags this might course angry faces looking at me to change. Because in their mind? My kite was flying too high.

On the morning of May 3rd, 2016, I had another vision. I saw two officers in uniform. They came to me. A male and a female and spoke with me. It seems they were hiding something.

They visited again the next day and I was very respectful and courteous with them. And immediate the **Spirit of The Most High G-D EL ELYON** appeared as a man standing beside me. He placed both hands on my shoulders.

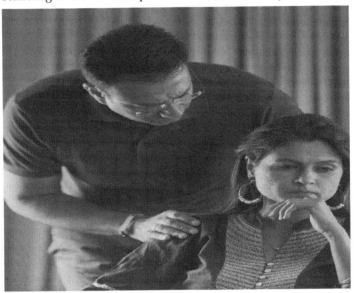

Comforting me. And said to the two that stood before me. "Y'all know you'll have come for something else. Just get it over with. All this beating around the bush. Tell her why you all are here? Stop wasting time." And immediately the two uniformed individuals turned and left. And the LORD Most High place his arms around me to comforted me again. Then he turns me in the opposite direction from the individuals (A male and a female).

At 9:30am on the same day while at work. I was called down to HR and meet the Manager and the HR Manager (the two of uniformed individuals in my vision) that terminated my employment and told me that I will be escorted to my apartment, and I would have 5 hours to leave. Somehow, I didn't feel hurt about it. As The LORD Most High had already comforted me on it. I immediately said. *"LORD? if you are doing this to me. You must have something better for me out there!" I continue to repeat this. Even to my coworker*.

I became homeless on May 3rd, 2016, at 11:45am. After losing my job I had moved out of state to have. I didn't know what I was going to do. I knew I was unable to support myself and I simply didn't have the finances to do it! I pulled out my phone, looked on the internet and found a homeless shelter nearby. I arrived at the shelter parking lot around 4:30pm. A lot was going through my mind. What to say. What would be said to me. I tried to control my emotions and be strong.

I walked into the office and a very tall gentlemen came introduced himself and showed me to a private meeting room. I was strong when I lost my job. I was strong while packing up all my stuff with two hours only to complete that which took me days to bring in. I was strong on the drive to the homeless shelter. But! In the moment. Just to be asked by the gentlemen. "So, tell me what's happening." I became weak. I finally felt hurt. And cried.

As I communicated with the kind gentlemen. I showed him a business card with my name that showed my profession. The kind gentlemen told me about a shelter. He pointed out that the specialist had left for today and he would do his best to assist me. After many telephone calls and information gathering. We were no closer in finding any shelter for me, Calls were made to shelters three hours away. Wherever available shelter was? I was prepared to go. But none could be found. I tried to understand. "How could there be no available beds? No shelter? No assistance. No nothing? I became strong again. I wondered. How many other people this is affecting? I knew then. When had I gained strength? I will do something about it.

An appointment was made for me to come in on Monday May 6th and speak to a specialist. I would only have to survive the weekend. I considered sleeping in the parking lot of where I once shopped. The thought overwhelmed me, so I took the electronics that I had in storage to a pawn and was able to pay my hotel of $389.00 for a one week stay.

The unit was number 36 that I stayed in. It had two queen beds a living area kitchenette and computer desk and chair. It was a suite compared to what I thought to get. It was a blessing for me to have some form of normalcy so quickly. I received it as a blessing from G-D, and I had overwhelming gratitude.

The following day (Saturday) was my Sabbath unto the LORD so I decide not to do anything. I decided to empty my thoughts and reflect or consider *NOTHING*. I decide to just BE. Peace Be Still! I didn't allow my thought to beat me up any further, I decide to *LIVE* within the death of homelessness, to *BE* within my homelessness, to *EXIST* within my homelessness. My greatest decision was to be loving to myself, through all that was going on. And I let go, and I let G-D. And as soon as I let go? The Holy Spirit sent from G D, came to me. And started teaching me. I became reconnected. The LORD had found me. Even in my homelessness. And once I felt his presence? I felt Blessed. Sunday, I stayed in. Did laundry. I spend some time considering what I was going to do from here.

The entire day, I was out looking for work and I continued to send my resume out, I just needed a job, I didn't mind where it way. I however felt I had it in me to remain along my career path. I spent the entire day and night

239

reading employers post, researching and uploading. Applying for vacant positions within the category of my work experience. Monday morning at 11am I arrive to meet with the specialist of the homeless shelter. Many calls were made to neighboring shelters hours away, but there were no available beds.

The specialist told me that she would check and see if she could offer me space at a campground nearby where they had sent a few other homeless persons. She mentioned that their rates were $420.00 a month utility included, and that I would have to pay. She said I would have to sleep in my car. And she mentioned that they have two tents. But because I have a vehicle, I would be able to sleep in my car or if I know anyone, I could just ask them. Additionally, to that, she mentioned that Walmart also carries them.

I waited with the specialist at her request to see if she could get the campground approved for a month. After 45 minutes and a 2-minute telephone conversation, I was told that the $420.00 was not approve for the campground for me. And I would have to find the money. The specialist went on to mention that she can also assist me with housing. That it was her specialty. But we will have to see after a while. I left that place feeling very downtrodden. I felt worst of for speaking to the specialist. Who delivered to me, only obstacles, and challenges? I was no better off. I knew I had only a few days left in the hotel, I feared living on the streets. **Revelation through obedience and of Knowledge.** If you need someone to see things your way and it is Righteous? *Ask G-D to open their dark Understanding if only this time. And if you* need G-D to uncover someone? *Ask G-D to remove their hedge of protection.*

THE
GENERAL

CHAPTER XXI

O n June 16th, 2016, I was instructed by G-D through G-D The Holy Spirit to do not eat anything the evening of June 16th until the evening of June 17th. I was told to monitor the feeling in my stomach. I was asked to observe the things that would happen inside my stomach for it was there it is written. *John 7:38 (KJV) He that believeth on me, as the scripture has said,* **out of his belly** *(stomach) shall flow rivers of living water.*

I was told that my stomach will start to re-activate itself or better, it will start to act the way of its original purpose. Spiritual. The entire day, I felt like a Spirit being, that was BEING, or being allowed to BE. It was the feeling that you get when a good sermon is preached, and you feel the spirit over you. The difference that I experience is feeling it inside of me and it remained all day long. I didn't feel the need to eat the entire day, it felt like all was well with the World. It felt like an illuminating spiritual presence that brought on Peace in my body, Peace in my mind, Peace in the world around me. All was at Peace. My awareness and senses were at its highest levels ever imagined my me. This is where the Spiritual works is carried out from.

On June 17th, 2016, at 9:00pm my sabbath evening. The voice of my G-D, and Holy Fathar came to me saying. **"I am your Husband. And my Messenger that I have sent to be with you. He is my General."** I immediately became overwhelmed with gratitude and submitted in obedience to G-D. I was presently in the kitchen at the shelter. There was always a small window of time before the full powers of G-D's shekinah glory came upon me. So, I needed a private place, to hide away from others, before G-D, My Holy Fathar's arrival. I got up and went to the SUV and place my backpack inside. I knew I was in no shape to drive anywhere, as submitting to G-D takes all your worldly strength and regular mobility. I started walking to find privacy. I stopped and observed that I could go straight ahead or left. In the

244

distance straight ahead was three people, I glance to observe them cursing each other and moving rapidly. I immediately knew G-D was not in that direction, in other words. It was not the direction for me to go. More and more the presence (the shekinah glory) of G-D, came to me. Unbeknownst to me, I walked to the bridge that I had visited a few times before, where Fathar, G-D spoke to me. I got on the bridge by this time, I am fully engulfed with the presence of The Creator's visitation.

I stopped at the center of the bridge after noticing a few people at the end of the bridge standing in one spot. I didn't want to alarm them by seeing my tears. While I was only in a state of Holiness. Which I knew they would not understand, and seek to help me, when I didn't need any help. And In fact. On the other hand?. I was within the direct alignment of The Most High's Shekinah of his glory, which was a better position to *HELP THEM!*

Looking behind me, I saw a couple coming on the bridge, so I stopped and face the water. Within that moment The Creator, My Holy Fathar spoke to me from Heaven again and says. **"I have sent my General. To be with you. To guide and protect you. For you are my Bride. From known on. I will provide all that you need, through him."** And I became overwhelmed with emotions. I continued to bless the name of G-D, and I cried more. I sure did. *"It's a beautiful evening!"* a lady's voice says behind me. While buckets of tears run down my face. Within the same moment, as she passed with her male companion on the bridge. I recognized that they were Angels of G-D. With my back still turned to them and facing the water I say. *"It sure is!"* After Fathar's shekinah glory left me. I hurried back to the Shelter so that I wouldn't miss curfew time which was 10pm. At 12:35pm I went upstairs looked at the small shelve space that G-D had provided for me and the roommate that The General of G-D Michael/Myki'EL had picked up and dash down to the ground? In G-d's objection for mistreating me? She had again. Placed more items in the already small space that was fulfilled through G-D's grace. Because of my need.

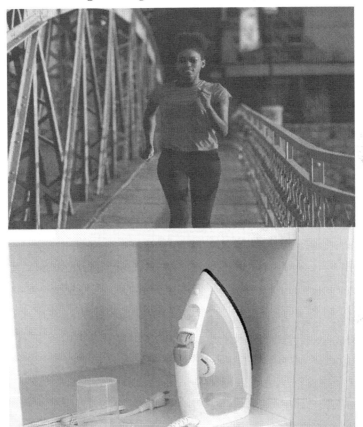

I notice earlier that day she had placed her iron on my shelf, so I took it and place it on her side. So now! What she did was place the iron back along. Now including her plant as well. Because I saw the Spirits of G-D. And G-D did answer me. Face to Face? I did strive for peace first. But with the forward? I will show myself forward. **(Psalm 18:26-27 KJV) 26. With the pure THOU wilt shew thyself pure; and _with the forward THOU wilt shew thyself forward._ 27. <u>For THOU wilt save the afflicted people; but wilt bring down high looks.</u>**

I took the female. Who started acting like? There was a first-class homeless person and a second-class homeless person living in the homeless shelter? I took her and the situation to G-D's righteousness. I though it hilarious also. But I was still careful because you never know what is in the mind of a person. AND! Because I never had someone that I couldn't trust. Sleeping so close to me. I thought it best to bring it to my Fathar. My Holy One. My _Shelter_ in the times of storm. So, the things she did to me? I brought to G-D.

She was the person that gave up the space to me. After a few days of staying there. She come back to reclaim the space. These are the things righteousness fights for in the situation I found myself in. 1. What size space she has verses the size I had? 2. What thoughts have I had toward the situation? 3. Have I thought to treat her poorly _after_ her act? 4. Did you take it to G-D, and leave it there? The more righteous you are in the sight of G-D? The swifter the JUDGEMENT comes, that follows _RIGHTEOUSNESS._ Your _RIGHTEOUSNESS;_ And being Righteous _IS POWER!_

On June 18th, 2016, the lady that shared the room with me, starting this dreadful coughing. it was so bad, her cough needed help to produce the cough. The Spirit within her cough said to me. "She has been judged by G-D. And the Judgment had brought forth the ruling. And the ruling. Must manifest itself. In this time? Or the next." This didn't same as

248

harsh punishment to me. Now that I was taught how it works in the Spirit. And it will not seem like harsh punishment to you also. Once you understand how G-D see's things. More than you understand how you see it. Then you would be cleared in The Judgment that *will come over* **ALL THE WORLD.** If you do not know how G-D see's things? You do not know G-D. I wrote these notes in my journal, for what I thought would have been my autobiography. The minute I thought I was writing an autobiography. The Holy Spirit says. "It is a Memoir."

EL, ELYON, The Most High G-D **came to me after and says**. "Sometimes, you can wake up and walk right into spirits, this is why sometimes, it is best to walk away." I say. "My method is to be silent." *EL, ELYON says.* "Silence is great, I was silent when I first met you. But my silence while with you? Hurt you! That's not right for the next person for you to be silent." I say. "So, I should not be silent because it is not good for the next man? Because of what you taught me? I see, I get it, *I* understand.

EL, ELYON says. *"All of that is, you are going into yourself and picking out the best you and giving that every step of the way.* Never have what can tear you down, be so strong in your life." I say. "Thank you Most High, I understand." *EL ELYON says.* "For example, anger. If you go to drive somewhere anger? Anger is already in your car waiting for you. Put Anger down at the light poll. Down the road. And dig him under the ground. Before he even surface. He is to close, even in your lap."

Revelation within the hour. When that was said to me. *INSTANTLY!* I saw in a vision one person with 5 to 7 other spirits standing inside of him and they were call, peace, the other anger, the other violence, the other destruction, the other death, the other joy, the others happiness, and love. To choose joy was to choose. Pick from the tree of life and all that there is in. To choose peace was to choose. Pick from the tree of life and all that there is in. To choose happiness was to choose. Pick from the tree of life and all that there is in. To choose Anger. Was to choose violence and all that dwell therein. To choose destruction was to choose death and all that dwell therein.

EL ELYON The Most High G-D says. THEY CAN ONLY BE WHAT THEY ARE! <u>These spirits all travel with LEGIONS of other spirits.</u> Anger brings Destruction. Death brings Violence along, so that you can destroy the very place in which you live as a TENANT! That way they can present a case to the LANDLORD of the Earth (overtime) requesting your EVICTION for the WRONGS you have committed!"

I say. "My LORD. I didn't know that." ***EL ELYON says.*** <u>**GIVING DEATH? TAKES FROM YOUR VERY LIFE!**</u> And you may be a *good person* and G-D *may* even be able to use you. But you are ignorant of what is going on around you. After the reading of this Book? You will have no more excuses! To fight the G-D fight! Which is the good fight!" ***The Most High G-D continued saying.*** "No one needs ANGER to solve anything for them. That is the point!" I say. "So, what do you want us to do!"

G-D, The Holy Fathar stepped in and says. "I want you to solve all of your problems with a calm and loving demeanor. Because you do not have to be angry with one another. You and the next man is going through some stuff. None of you need the other to survive. So, you really don't need to put each other through anything! To make each other believe that you need each other so much. You need to be happy more than you need to be angry. *The General of The Most High G-D says.* "That is just how it is."

G-D, The Holy Fathar stepped in and says to me. "MY EAR IS THE CLOSEST THING TO MY MOUTH. WHATEVER I SAY TO YOU? I SAY, ALSO TO MYSELF. YOU JUST HAPPEN TO HEAR WHAT AM SAYING, I CAN GO IN A CORNER AND SAY THIS TO MYSELF AND NO ONE HAS TO HEAR ME. I AM A VICTIM OF MY OWN SUCCESS, AND A VICTIM OF MY OWN FAILURE." I say. "What would you like us to do Fathar?"

G-D, My Holy Fathar says. "I WOULD LIKE US TO SOLVE ALL OF OUR PROBLEMS, IN THE MOST SWEETEST WAY POSSIBLE." I say. "OK." then I say. "LORD? Why is it that I see things differently from others? Somehow, I see things differently from others." *EL ELYON The Most High G-D says.* "You see things your way, and people see it their way. Both ways come together, and it makes sense. This book is a bow. So, if the current carries someone they can get to the bow and come cross. Overtime, you brought me to look at it that way, and it made sense."

251

KITCHEN LAWS

CHAPTER **XXII**

One June 19th, 2016, The spirit send from G-D says to me. "Go get the paper and hang it up!" I had to get the 10 Commandments and hang it up in the shelter. It was said just like that "Go get the paper and hang it up!" Am sure it was because I continued to ask G-D for the time and availability to put up his 10 Commandments in the shelter. It's fair to say, I was troubling the throne, for my request.

When I heard that. I started looking on the wall from my bed to see if there was any nail already in the wall and suddenly, out of nowhere, a nail appeared in place on the wall I had already looked at, and there was none.

EL ELYON, The Most High G-D says. "So, what does that mean to you? Go and get it right? Now, getting it is one thing. What you need to do is say "LORD we need you to go in there with it. So, you need to get it. Now! That's what you want? You want to hang the 10 Commandments in there?

I say. "Yes" **EL ELYON, The Most High G-D says again.**
"That's what you want right? You want to hang the 10
Commandments up in there? Now, how do you want it to
hang up? You want it to hang up to get pull back down? or
you want it to hang up to stay up?

EL ELYON, The Most High G-D says. "LET ME KNOW!
you don't just desire G-d to just hang it up there. Because he
is bad like that, He just told you to "hang it up." And then
anyone move's it gets cut down and bruise up. They get
thrown in the air! You see?" I say. "I see"

EL ELYON, The Most High G-D says. "So, you want it to
be peaceful as you hang it up, with understanding." I say. So,
this is why I should ask first, where I shall place it? **EL
ELYON, The Most High G-D says.** "This is why you will say
to them. G-D requires this painting to be up. G-D told me to

hang it up. And I want to know, where is best for me to hang this?"

G-D, The Holy Fathar came in and says. "I LOOK ON THE WALL AND I SEE NO COMMANDMENTS FOR MAN TO LIVE BY. NOTHING FOR THEM TO READ. SHOULDN'T THERE BE SOMETHING ELSE HERE? THERE ARE LAWS TO CLEAN THE KITCHEN, CLEAN THE BATHROOM, CLEAN THE STAIRCASE, UNDER THE TOILET, CLEAN THE FRIDGE, THESE ARE LAWS FOR HERE (The homeless shelter). WHAT DO YOU HAVE FOR THEM TO LIVE OUT THERE? THEY NEED SOMETHING FOR THAT."

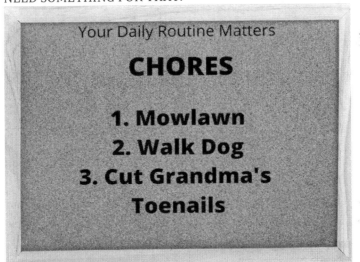

Your Daily Routine Matters

CHORES

1. Mowlawn
2. Walk Dog
3. Cut Grandma's Toenails

The General says. "You've got daily chores? G-D has daily chores for man to live by. Where can we hang up G-D's daily chores for man? I say. "Yes, yes, Well, I better have my running shoes on now Most High. I started laughing and then I said. "They will run me!"

The General of The Most High G-D says. "You don't just want G-D to hang it up on the wall, you want G-D to pave that path so you can say exactly, if you have to. Why you need these 10 commandments up." Wisdom is very serious.

Because G-D will hang it up and then box them down when they complain. Throw them out the bed. Brake up all their knees and things."

I see how things work. G-D don't really require you to understand what he is doing. And if you understand, it is better for you. See! Be it unto you! He said to hang it up and you know it's the 10 Commandments and you said "don't hang it up" For that! He will bruise you. Not you. Them! For not allowing you to put it up. Now. Do you want G-D to bruise them? Or you want G-D to have them with understanding? It must be understanding. Because the thing it is. If you don't have understanding there will be a fight inside the place. I say. "Yes "

The General says. "So, to avoid the fight we say LORD, give them understanding, open their dark understanding for just this one time". I say. "I like that, I enjoyed that lesson right there. I pray G-D leads me to be able to keep that which was just shown, so that I myself can live that. That way!"

The General says. "Understand, G-D doesn't have to ask you to move a bridge. He comes there and moves that bridge throw it in the water if he wants to.

With you under the bridge. He just takes your soul. Before that bridge hits you. He takes your soul, carries it! He doesn't really care about the flesh. The flesh? Is going back to the Lord. The Caretaker of the Earth. The Earth claims that. You, see?" I say. "Yes" **The General says.** "He carries The Soul. You were just borrowed. He carries the soul." **The General says.** "So now! Here it is! For you now to go and move that bridge, you have to go through all the logistics. Laws and culinary and spark and under spark and reason and undesirable reasoning. And all of them other things there. The fish under the water will die and no one person had to walk across today and now that's a monumental catastrophe." I laugh out loud. Then I say. "That's a

257

monumental catastrophe. "**G-D The Holy Fathar says. "A MONUMENTAL CATASTROPHE"** I said nothing, I just laugh out loud with Fathar. **G-D The Holy Fathar says. "YOU SEE?."** I say. "Now I see!"

The General of The Most High G-D says. "So, when G-D say "Move the bridge" you say. "Well LORD, I ask them, and these people aren't moving the bridge." "Next thing you know, the bridge collapse, huge thunderstorm comes, cracks

it in half, then the lighting picks up the water and the water breaks it up! Next thing you know, in the morning you wake up, the bridge is on the ground. In the water. And the fish is running through it!.

And all of the police, ambulance, fire truck and you and your committee *ALL* watching the bridge. This is what they will say "You Elioenai, blow the bridge up" and they will arrest you. And lock you up for the bridge. So. If G-D says to you. "Move the bridge?"

G-D, My Holy FATHAR came in and says to me. "You say "OK Fathar. There are some fish under the water. And there are some folks that walk across the bridge. Now. There are some folks also that actually like this bridge and feel this bridge supposed to be here, so! Shot their mouth. Bring the fishes back so that they cannot travel this way, and the folks that desire to go on this bridge, kill the desire to walk across this bridge, and THEN, YOU CAN DESTROY IT!"

The General says. "He can very well decide to destroy the bridge with people walking on it!" I say. "But Why? Why? Should Fathar not have known that there are people on the

259

bridge? Should he not have known that there is fish under the sea?"

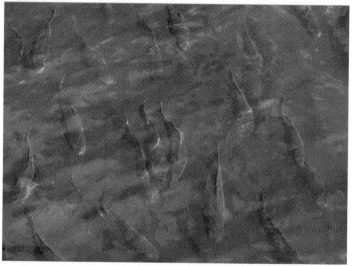

The General of The Most High G-D says. "NO" I say. "So why would he do that?" **The General of The Most High G-D says.** "The Fish. The Fish belongs to the LORD of the Earth! The Caretaker" I say. "I see" **The General of The Most High G-D says.** "The LORD of the Earth multiplies these fishes by the thousands." I say. "I See...I see." **The General of The Most High G-D says.** "He does not care about 5 or 6 fish or one hundred. They multiply them by the thousands." I say. "I see"

The General says. "The LORD of the Earth owns your flesh and your bones and all of your cells and sinuses. The only thing G-D. That belongs to G-D is your Soul." I say. "Your soul? I see." **The General says.** "You have already been bought with a price. Half is G-D and Half is the Earth. That piece is settled. And the committees. What will they do when the bridge fall? Try build it back? NO! They will let it go.

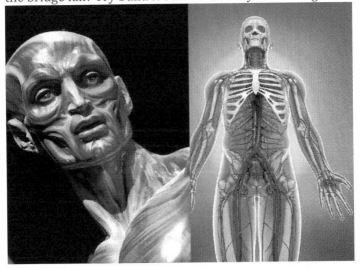

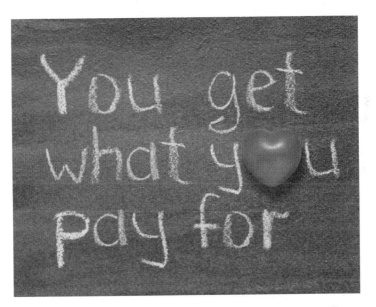

So, all am asking G-D to do is. Those who are walking on the bridge, let them not have a desire to walk on this bridge anymore. So that they wouldn't be destroyed. And the committees shot them out for a time. And then from that. If he honors that what I've said. Then the Earth itself will bring those fish back this way."

Revelation within the hour:- It seems G-D was talking about us, those who have lost their way to him. **The General of The Most High G-D says.** "The Earth itself would command them to not have the desire to walk on this bridge or anywhere near this bridge. Then the committees you shot them up. Then the bridge can be destroyed at any time that the LORD G-D chose.

Then you can say, "Let it be done!" All you will have to say is. *"Let it be done!"* And the bridge will be destroyed. And it will collapse. No catastrophe, If G-D say destroy the bridge. And you say, "Let it be done?" Next thing you know. Fish get killed. Man get killed. Beast get killed. You, see? I say. "Yes"

RED
SEA

CHAPTER XXIII

G-D, My Holy Fathar says to me. *"I REMEMBER WITH MOSES; DO YOU THINK MOSES WAS WORRIED ABOUT...HIS THING WAS HOW TO GET THESE PEOPLE ACROSS THE RED SEA. ALL HE WAS TOLD WAS TO GO! HE WAS STUCK AT THE RED SEA. HE COULDN'T GO BACK AND HE COULDN'T GO FORWARD. SO, HE HAD TO WAIT TO BE TAKEN THROUGH THE WATER. SO, HE HAD TO GO THROUGH THE WATER."*

AND SOMEHOW GOING THROUGHT THE WATER WITH THE STAFF IN HIS HAND, HE HAD TO DO THIS WITH THE STAFF, (Holy Fathar Yahweh (Yo'way) illustration this for me).

BUT HE ALSO HAD TO CHECK THE WATER TO SEE HOW DEEP THE WATER WAS. SO HE WENT INTO THE WATER, AND WHEN HE PUT THAT STAFF IN THE WATER NOT KNOWING HOW DEEP THE WATER WAS. ALSO NOT KNOWING WHAT THE STAFF WAS FOR.

HE PUT THE STAFF IN THE WATER TO BALANCE HIMSELF OFF. TO SEE HOW DEEP THE WATER WAS. THEN

264

The General of The Most High G-D, Myki'EL/Michael says. "It was not something that G-D told him that the sea will part. You will see the fishes them on the inside. You will see dry sand!" NO. He was there puzzled. With his staff down in the water. And then. THE WATER MOVED!"

I say. "Bless The LORD!" **The General of The Most High G-D says.** "You See? Moses was amazed." **G-D, My Holy Fathar says.** "He was Amazed. And the people were amazed. Shock had him. He waited until <u>ALL</u> of the water receded."

I say. LOL, LOL Fathar. Now that is funny stuff. **The Creator, My Holy Fathar says.** "Moses did not move from shock until. He saw dry land! Then. He told the people. "WALK CROSS." Just then, The Creator, My Holy Fathar, G-D, shown me Moses at the red sea standing there shocked and amazed."

I say. "You mean to tell me LORD. Shock! Had Moses Fathar? LOL...LOL, LOL." I screamed in hysteria. Laughing out loud with G-D. My Holy Fathar laughing with me. It was the most hilarious thing when G-D showed me Moses in shocked at the red sea with his staff. This was the funniest thing I had seen on the journey. It taught me that I was not perfect, And Moses was not as well. He was a soul trying to get to perfection every day, like the rest of us.

Then G-D, my Holy Father says to me. "Yeah! Shock had Moses. He couldn't move. He was stunned to see the water depart. He stood there for minutes. Just amazed and then. The people started going across." I was amazed by the revelation, so I say again to confirm and to clarify what I was hearing. It was so shocking. I couldn't get enough confirmation. So, I said again to G-D while laughing. "Shock had him, yeah?"

266

The General Michael/Myki'EL says. "Yes, shock had Moses. They had never seen that before in their life. So. It's the same thing with you. See. G-D doesn't want blame to come to you. No blame to come to you. In terms of destroying that bridge. NO BLAME!

BUT! If you go and tell the people you are here to destroy that bridge. G-D said to destroy that bridge. "Move it?" They will ask you which one of them? Which one? Which G-D? Which one told you that? I say. "So, the Commandments is safe in its place? In the storage shed?.

The General says. "It is safe in its place. But you must understand that you are taking it into a den of thieves. He wants it up on the wall for them to read it! And in all things find peace with all man. Follow peace with all man. He said to "put it on the wall!" Put it on the wall now? Or put it on the wall after he have found out where to put it." I say. "Or even after we are leaving?

The General says. "So, we are going to put it up on the wall. IN PEACE. You can even ask a question. "Why is there no 10 Commandments on the walls? If they say that it is because we do not have one. You say. "Well, I've got two" where should I put them? Up on the wall here? Or put them up on the wall there? So, you have laws for man to do inside here? Well, we have laws for man also."

Revelation within the hour:- Through understanding. It seems you render that which is for the Earth to the earth. And that which is for G-D to G-D. **The General says.** "tell them if they do not put the Commandments up. The committee will discuss it. *And not the Committee with man. The Committee with G-D.* When the Committee meets to discuss the reason why you did not put it up? Now the committee meets to discuss your faith or the faith of an organization." The Committee will meet to discuss the faith of the Organization. 1. That the Ten Commandments was up, or 2. That the Ten Commandments were not up. Either. It's up or it down. It is up to you! People have to come to understand.

I say. "To understand what General? Please tell me General." **The General says.** *"To understand that it has nothing to do with them. And whatever it is they have setup! It is what the Master chooses."* "If he chose the picture (the Ten Commandments) to be up on the wall? Then we must find a way to get it up on the wall. Do you see? That is, if he wants it up on the wall. If you want it up on the wall, He doesn't really careless about it being up there. You have your own fight coming! Understand that now! He doesn't really care about The Ten Commandments picture being up on the wall. But because you want it there? He has to find a way to get it there. I say. "I see, I see. It's because I have been desiring to place it on the wall?" **The General says.** "Yeah!" I say. "I have been looking for a place on the wall for it to be! So, I guess now that is Fathar's response? **The General says.** "Yeah, you wanted it up. So! That's you wanting it. He doesn't really care if it goes up in there or not." He picked that woman up. That troubled you. Inside your room last night. And licked her down to the ground. Because of you. You think he cares about the Commandments going up on that wall?

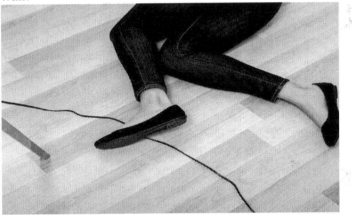

I say. "Yeah, she got licked down for true...LOL.... And I was going to help her up when I saw her, on the floor? With no one else around her. I said "OH! MY G-D" when she hit the floor. The Spirit of G-D lifted that lady up. High into the air and slammed her body down to the ground. So hard. **The General says.** "And you want G-D to put his Ten Commandments in there for them? Who has no sense! But if you want it up "Put it up!" "Put it up on the wall" You might have a little fight on your hand. But you might just get it up!

You think if G-D wanted his Commandments in that place it wouldn't have been in there?"

Revelation within the hour:- I felt G-D was talking about civilization, having up this 10 commandments or us not having up and upholding his 10 commandment. And all of the information he was giving me was because I desired it for so long. Including the knowledge of myself. It same as if it meant more than that which was being said. I say. "Yeah!" **The General says.** "If you want it up, Put it up!" **Revelation within the hour**: - With this, I did not know how to respond! I know I was requiring G-D to send the 10 Commandments out into all the world and the response I was now getting was. It was G-D who kept this and anything else he willed. From us in the first place. **Deeper Revelation within the hour**:- The 10 Commandments carries power.

The General of The Most High G-D says. "If G-D wants you to do something. He makes it easy for you. Like a bird flying in the air. It's easy for G-D. There is nothing hard for him. He doesn't make anything hard for him.

It is easy. It flows. If it is difficult or too hard? It's not G-D." If it ties, you down. Stresses you out. Makes you have bad feeling towards certain things. So. If it's not G-D? Leave it alone.

Just say to him. NOT MY WILL! I desire it to be of you G-D, BUT NOT MY WILL, LET YOUR'S BE DONE. TRY THAT SOMETIME!" I say. "Yes, Indeed, Bless The LORD." **The General says.** "I feel you get in less problems that way. Besides. You can't bring every stray dog home. In other word. We can't bring every thought that come into our mind and give it a resting place. You, see? Some of them G-D doesn't even like and don't even care about. The things we care about, he doesn't care about! You, see? He will accept it. But he doesn't care about it. I say. "What does he care about? What are the things Holy Fathar, The Creator cares about?"

The General says. "It is already here. It's already here. He cares about <u>US</u>. He cares about the water. He cares about the wind. The waves. He cares about the birds. He cares about the metal under the Earth. The oil. The gas. The fuel. The trees. The leaves. The bird the bees. What is it that he doesn't care about?

Everything that he made that has life. He cares about. Because he loves living. He is so good with living. He makes words come alive. With G-D it is about living. He is so good about living until your soul lives on. Even though your house is dissolved. Your soul lives on. G-D is not about dying.

G-D is displeased about dying. His son could not stay in the grave for more than three days! YASHUA had to rise! You, see? I say. "I see" **The General of The Most High G-D says.** "Because he does not care about dying." I say. "That's why he, rose in such a grand fashion?

271

The General says. "He does not care about dying." I say. "Yes." **The General says.** "He made living possible. As a matter of fact. You don't even have to die to go to Heaven. You die once. Die in the flesh. Die in the needs of the flesh. Conquer that. Live in the Spirit you live with *G-D AUTOMATICALLY HERE ON EARTH*. Through the years we lost the older man. The older man. Our forefathers had the way to G-D. They were..."

SELFISH
TREES

CHAPTER XXIV

I say. "OK am homeless and I just had a discussion about G-D granting your needs, or whatever your need base is. I just got an offer for a job. An interview on Monday that I know I will get the Job and if I stay to the shelter while being homeless not having a home or apartment, I can work my way out. To get a home, so G-D has already sent that!

Two days earlier. I got another job offer On-site. So, in this one. G-D is also fulfilling the need base which is Shelter. A home an apartment. Because I am currently living in the Shelter. So, this is G-D sending my needs, right?

The General says. "When you start to look at things like that. And really put into it. Things of G-D would start to show themselves up. This is the way it works. If you did not think about it. You would have not brought life to the thought of it working like that. Do you understand?" I say. "Yes"

The General of The Most High G-D says. "Why would he take you from a place where you were a director living on site and take you to be homeless? When there is no need for him to even do you like that? I say. "Well, that's why I had said when it happened on May 3ʳᵈ. I had said that "it was a purpose that G-D had done this to me. And he had something else prepared for me." Because I couldn't see it either. I couldn't see it either. You know?

The General says. "Now you can see it. Your life must bear witness for many. And G-D must teach you. So that you may teach others. I say. "Yes, Now I can see it."

The General says. "So, it has to be G-D now to train you for the position ahead. Because to be a leader or to be the boss you must have some kind of training. Coaching. You must have that! So let nine months or a few years go by before you tell anyone about your new Job. Because you will have a hard time taking care of your intimate needs before they start saying. "You don't deserve it!"

This one will say. "You don't deserve it" or "Who will give you this kind of position?" They have nothing good to give you. If you tell them you're a director. You will hear silence for a little bit. **"Revelation within the hour**: -** I felt he was talking about a relative of mine in particular.

The General says. "Then you will hear silence for a minute. And then after you will hear "that's good" "that's good" that's good" That's when they decide they can use you. They will come with. "Girl you know. I need this. And I need that. **Revelation within the hour**: -** I felt G-D was warning me to watch for what will happen when people find out that I speak to him.

Then **The General of The Most High G-D says to me.** "Some will say to you. *Call my name before G-D. And others will say. Don't call my name before G-D.*" **The General of The Most High G-D went on to tell me what I felt was a parable about mankind. He says.** "Putting two seeds in the same hole. Will allow for the seed to grow separately. But in the same communicative hole. When they grow, they become selfish trees. Don't want the seeds to grow next to them.

That is why the birds come and carry some of them. When they drop on the ground they tumble down. And heavy wind blows the seeds of the leave and carry them away. Now this little area became so crowed and condensed the seeds have nowhere else to go. But by the trunk. They say. Seeds don't fall far from the trunk of a tree. Trees do not like their seeds growing next to them. They might even try and kill them. Drop them from so high in the air just to kill them. Trees are very selfish; they don't like anything growing that's not them. They want all the sun light for themselves. Do you see the vines going around them?

I say. "Yes" because I did see. The General of The Most High G-D pointed to a tree of vines that was near where I sat at the park bench during his teaching sessions.

The General of The Most High G-D went further. He says. "The vine needs them. Even the vines need the sun. They want to choke the tree to survive. Look at that one around the big stump. He is all around that stump. He is going up. Like a snake. I say. "Why?"

The General says. "Because they want more sun light. If it rains. Their leaves will not get any water. Because the trees up there will have it all for themselves. So, the vines use the trees so that their leaves can get some kind of water. They need to catch the water. They need to survive. Down here. *The vines will die. You will die. Close to the ground.* **Revelation within the hour:** - At the time. It felt in The Spirit like the General was sharing with me his thoughts of the dominance of some human being over other human being. Though all were planted in one place (Mother Earth).

277

I say. "So General? You've been with me all this time. Have you ever had a need for anything?. The General said, No, because I don't have a need that is not fulfill by G-D." I say. "Oh, Blessed Love General! **THOU** Blessed and Faithful servant of The Most High G-D. Blessed Love unto **THEE!**" **The General says.** "You see! I just go where I am supposed to go through G-D, and sometimes even if that is the right thing to do or not! I just know through common logic, that nothing in G-D is hard. If Anything is hard? it's not of G-D." You told me what your needs are?" **The General says** "No.

I say. "So, nothings hard. If of G-D yeah? So that means the job I had with The Miranda Company was not of G-D, right? Because they stressed me out. And worked me hard." **The General says.** "Well, the thing it is my dear. Go to The Miranda Company.! The Miranda Company was there for one factor really. You were to learn there. Do you know why it was hard for you?" I say. "Why?" **The General says.** "You took your concept to those people. You felt like you could have done the job. You felt like you did not really need them to tell you what to do. Or to do your job. So, it was hard for you because they have it to do their way and you can't go into someone's house and tell them how to run their house. What was supposed to be easy for you? Became hard. You spent months trying to change their house into what you described as a peaceful resting place for you. When it was not a place for you. It was a place for you to go. And gain some knowledge. It was not supposed to be hard at all. It was just for a time. I say. "Yes"

The General says. "See? Nothing of G-D is hard. Nothing! You want something to eat, you will get it. You want something to drink? It is right there. Even though you didn't want it. Nothing of G-D will be hard! It is one thing needing something to eat and not having it here. <u>WE ARE OF G-D!</u>

The need of G-D is so easy. It's almost lifeless to get at. It is usually right there. It's not hard at all! When I was a man.

279

Doing a work. I would tell G-D, "Well LORD, I need $400.00 dollars today and I don't need four customers to do that for me. One or two is good enough for me because I might get tired along the day. So just give me one or two customers. A customer being one family or a family of four. Or a family of eight or a family of ten or a family of twelve.

Next thing I know. Someone walks in the building with a party of twelve. I said "Come down here and tells talk." In the beginning. I was sharing Jesus a lot. I was telling them how good Jesus is. I laugh out loud. LOL...I say. "That's the hearing they have. If their hearing was a radio? They'll be on channel JESUS! And not at all, Holy Fathar, The Creator.

The General says. "Yes" I say. "So, you have got to say. What is in their ear or the air around them." I smiled. **The General says.** "Yes. Because if you say anything else? The rest of the talk will go sour." I say. "They'll beat you up!"

The General says. "Know G-D has me here with you. Now he is taking me further into the abyss. He did tell you to watch. Right? I say. "Watch what? **"The General says.** "He did tell you to wait and see. He did tell you that before you left Georgia. Because you didn't know why you were going to California. I say. "Yes. He did tell me to wait and see."

The General says. "He did tell you to wait and see. Like Oprah said. Our Ancestors have left every tool to make it! **The General says.** "YouTube has everything on YouTube on how to fix. Everything and anything! Anything you need. YouTube. I say. "I have a Youtube Channel. And for free!" **The General says.** "For free. You don't need anything else but YouTube." I say. "So, I guess they are eliminating Colleges?" **The General says.** "YouTube is a college!" I say. "OK."

CHAPTER **XXV**

One day I notice it was my little brother's birthday. He was turning 14. My other sister sent a message to him to have a "Blessed day." I just didn't think that statement was the most appropriate response on our little brother's birthday. She did not purchase a gift or a cake.

During this time. The General of The Most High G-D was present teaching me. And was aware of all things that happened in my life. And before I spoke a word with my mouth. To tell him what had just happened. **The General says.** "Even then. He would appreciate yours. Far more than theirs any day. Because he knows you are genuine. They just say it because you say it."

"You can tell anyone to have a blessed day. You can tell anyone to have a blessed day. There is no love in that. You can tell strangers to have a blessed day. I say. "That was why I didn't like it. She is a grown woman. She is a grown woman. She should have reconsidered that statement. He is a poor child. From humble beginnings. Give him something and beg him. Please! Have a great day, and G-D bless you."

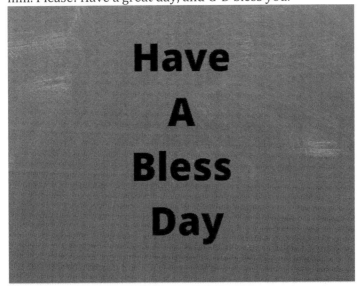

The General says. "You don't tell children to "Have a blessed day!" I say. "One, you don't tell children to have a bless day! And two. That's not a sentence you give to your family. Your little brother on their birthday. Everything was wrong with it!"

The General says. "Buy him a birthday cake. Buy him a bicycle. And then tell him. Listen. I want you to have a bless day. Enjoy this bike. What should he have a bless day with? Did you give him anything? Nothing? Should he have a bless day with what he came with? He does not need you for that. Thank you very much. No. You have a bless day. Thank you very much! I started laughing. Because it seems as though the topic was getting The General hot. Just how much "Have a bless day is through around from people's mouths." **The General continued.** "Some folks feel like their words supposed to be carried out the way they feel it is supposed to be carried out. And no! No. _Your words have to form some kind of alliance with your actions._ I say. "Yes. Your words almost have to go to Audit?" **The General of The Most High G-D says.** "Yes" I say. "Like how your taxes are Audited? Your words must get audit first before any action is taken on your words?

The General says. "Yeah, you can't come with. Have a Blessed day to someone who have NOTHING! Here it is. Am walking with a backpack on. I need something to eat. Am hungry and thirsty. My foot has pain in me. Because of the shoes being too tight for my feet, and I can't afford to buy a new pair. And you are going to stop me. And tell me to have a blessed day? I laugh out loud. I say. "LOL LORD. LORD LOL! I couldn't stop laughing. Funny thing with The General was. During his teaching? He would also show me by illustration.

What he was saying. I found him to be very funny because he would change his voice (his speech). He

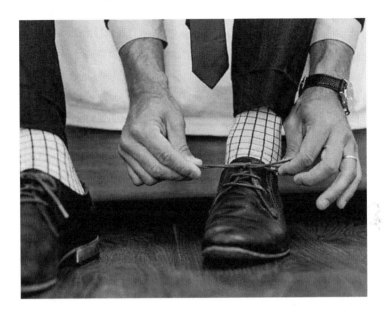

could speak like a female if he wanted. Make himself sound like and look like any animal. And he had the funniest way of describing things with the use of his body changing its form.

The General says. "Yeah!" I am already having a F*****UP TIME. For you to tell me to have a blessed day. Give me something to change my shoes. Or to get something to eat. Or drink. And then tell me. HAVE A BLESS DAY!" But to meet me with what I have going on and tell me to have a BLESS DAY? You're really not in touch with G-D. You're really not in touch with G-D. You cannot be. Because G-D knows he sent you to give me a new pair of shoes.

<u>Revelation within the hour of hearing and understanding and interpretation</u>: - I was very surprise when I heard The General curse. But he was a very strong living being. His height from his feet to his face was about 1550 years of height. While mankind's life expectancy is 120 years tops. If lucky. This is why it is said that Mankind is not able to reach The Fathar. But by invitation only.

The Generals wisdom. Was greater than I. He was from above. I was from above also. But he was greater than I. I dear not judge him. Whether he used a ten-pound word or a two-hundred-pound word. I remembered sitting there thinking. Angels use curse words. Should I write this? What would people think? I decided that being impartial and transparent in writing what I heard verbatim, was the right thing to do for Heaven. And for the people of Earth. So, I went back into my lessons and I say. "Yeah! At least a pair of shoes General. So that you will have a bless day! **The General says**. "You understand? G-D knows he sent you to give me something to eat. Something to drink. So that I can have a bless day. You know what? Kiss my Ass! You and your have a Bless Day!"

I say. "LOL. LOL. Yeah, that run me hot also. When I read that. **The General says.** "Four words "HAVE A BLESS DAY!" I say. "That run me hot!" Hopefully they had an eye full and a mouth full today, from all the way across the Earth. I have my eyes on them, they have bad ways. And bad thinking. Couldn't even make a joke with her little brother. Couldn't even make a joke for the kid's birthday. That's why I pray G-D keeps me healthy and strong for that day. I will stand up all of them. You? Stand up! And You? Stand up. And You? Stand up too!

The General says. "You will cause problems. G-D will not let that day come in." I laugh. I say. "Am not talking about just going right in and doing that. But you see. They are wicked. Their mind is wicked. They conspire wicked things.

The General says. "That doesn't mean you will change them. LISTEN! Just take your little brother out of there. You will have nothing to say about their wickedness and their ways." I say. "Yeah."

The General says. "You are trying to cause havoc. No. Just take him from there in quietness and peacefulness and bring him where you think he will have peace or where he can prosper better. As far as making them feel, or giving them your riot act? No! If G-D is not going to do it. Don't want to do it. What makes you think you will have the power to do it?" I say. "I didn't say I was going to do it. I said "if G-D"

The General says. "OK." I say. "That has passed now! **The General of The Most High G-D says.** "OK"

HOLDING HEADS

CHAPTER XXVI

O n May 12th, 2016, **The General of The Most High G-D says.** "Elioenai is a name that G-D gave you." I say. "Yeah, Yahshua called me that. Because he says. "My Eyes Are Toward The Creator. So yes," I said. **The General of The Most High G-D says.** "That one came with meaning. And reasoning."

I say. "So, tell me. If you're thinking vessel is not in your head and your thinking vessel is in your stomach. What about those Pastor's that holds you down by your head? It doesn't have to be Pastor's am just saying them trying to cover the hold demographic of them that do this to your head. Why? Is The Creator G-D, Holy Fathar there connecting with their hand or something?" I say. "What is it they are trying to work on in there?" **The General of The Most High G-D says.** "It is because they see it done. They have seen it done so much! You do not have to touch *ANYONE* to pray for them. You do not have to touch someone to pray for them. You can pray for someone over here. While they are over there. But Noooooooooo!. They have to walk over there. To lay hands on people." I couldn't stop laughing. The General of The Most High G-D dragged the word "no" for five minutes. He didn't need to take a breath. It was hilarious to see some human qualities in G-D's General. He sounded just like us when we are trying to emphasis a point. I said. Nothing. But I laughed out loud.

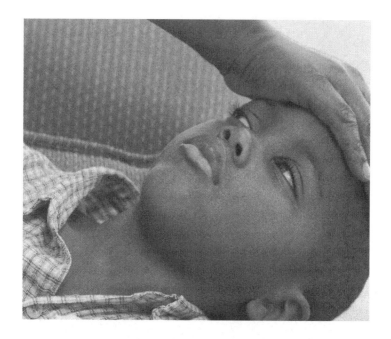

The General then says to me. "That walking over there and laying hands on them? I say. "Yes. You get dramatization like that! And I continued to laugh, (LOL). **The General says.** "That laying hands on them can cause them embarrassment. Because you could be sitting here, and that person can be an Atheist. But G-D told you to pray for them." I say. "My G-D." **The General of The Most High G-D says.** "G-D just said to Pray for them!"

But You! You! High and Mighty Servants of the Most High will open the car door. Walk over there. Take 18-20 steps. Holding on the railing. You have to walk over there and it maybe slippery. And then you have to stop the person from what they are doing. Because he could be in meditation or trying to catch fish at the lake. He might not want to be bothered at all. Now you go right there and say "I have to pray for you. G-D said. "To pray for you."

You get. "Man, I don't want you and your G-D. Get out of my face. Get out of my face. You say. "So, you don't want G-D to pray for you? No. Get out of my face." So, you come back to the car and say "G-D? This guy doesn't want me to pray for him. Why did you send me down there? Why did you send me to this man? He doesn't want prayer."

G-D will say. "I told you to pray for him. I didn't tell you to go down there and shake his hand and find out what is name is. To find out who he is. Or to disturb him from what he is doing.

G-D said to pray for the man. You start with. "Fathar I bless the young man down there. You ask me to pray for him. I don't know him. But I need you to bless him. Give him a change of heart. Change his heart. Change his mind. Change his soul toward you. If he is far from you. Bring him closer to you.

In the Presence of the Most High. Fathar I have done your will. Bring him close to you. Let him come to know you. Shut him down. So that he can know who you are. In your Name, Amen." He told you "Pray for the Man." Right? And you sit right here. And you watch and see that word fulfill. You will see that seen young man come from down there. Come right up to you and give you a fish. He will catch more than one fish. Just to come over to you and give you a fish. **The General of The Most High G-D says**. "Do you think that can work?" I say. "What do you mean, if it can work?"

The General of The Most High G-D says. "Well, you didn't get embarrassed. He didn't run you; He didn't chase you. He didn't get mad with you. You didn't get mad with him. You're not mad with G-D. You see now? Sometimes G-D being so powerful would tell people to do things that they do extra in. But he didn't ask you to do that. That is why they lay hands on you like that. Because they feel like their hand. This is why I gave you an illustration about walking over there. They feel like their hand."

Suddenly **The General of The Most High G-D** grab the top of my head violently with his strong right hand as an illustration of what he was talking about, not touching anyone suddenly. I didn't see that coming. But it got my attention. And I screamed for my life. I though to say, "G-D Myki'EL/Michael is trying to kill me by way of illustration. And because The General of The Most High G-D was able to read my thoughts. We both started laughing that I was thinking about telling on him to G-D. Though grabbing my head was pretty funny. The General's hand came out of nowhere, and I didn't want that to happen to me again. I say. "That hurt General. Don't put your hands on me. That hurt! And I kept laughing.

The General kept laughing in the background. His laughter rings out through The Universe. He says. "That's what they do! While laughing he says to me again. That's what they do! **The General of The Most High G-D says.** "They feel like their hand has got to be on you. To make you feel like you have some kind of connection with their G-D. You see. Rather than just letting it be so. As G-D has spoken it."

The Bible tells me. To lay hand on no man suddenly. Literally and Verbally and Spiritually. I say. "That is also why I do not like this hand shaking thing. I don't like it. But. I don't know what the second thing to do, that would not offend the person who put out their hands to me. So, I would like to know how G-D wants me to deal with that. Because the hand is usually already extended to me? I have been asking?"

The General of The Most High G-D says. "You don't offer a handshake until the person is already in communication for you on an agreement of something. If we are not agreeing on anything we do not shake hands" I say. "OK, so we shake hands when we are on agreeance of something?" **The General says.** "A handshake is an agreeance. Business. I wouldn't cross your lines. You wouldn't cross mine. We shake on it. Meet me by the lake. No problem. We shake on it." I say. "OK so. Hi, my name is Fred." "We don't shake hands?"

The General says. "NO! So, what if your name is Fred? If you were supposed to meet Fred and he said "Hi my name is Fred." You shake hands in agreeance of business. Not if am just sitting at the park reading a book and someone come and say. Hi how are you doing man. Nice weather. Am Fred. Am reading a book here. I don't know who you are. Ask him to keep it moving "TOUCH IS NOT REQUIRED" tell Fred to keep it moving. Sometimes we don't know who they are. They could be Angels coming unaware. Like you say. Sometimes you don't know what to say. I guess this is when we give in. Because we don't know. Whether they are Angels coming unaware. G-D says. "Be careful how you entertain strangers. Because you can be entertaining Angels unaware. So now. greeting is a nice gesture. Even so. Let all touch outside of agreeance be no more."

FREEDOM
COST

CHAPTER XXVII

On May 13th, 2016, I say to The General of The Most High G-D. "Tell me about Slavery." Were white people to be black people servants? Or where black people supposed to be white people's slaves?" **The General says.** "NO. They were supposed to have servants after their own kind." I say. "In that case were we just to trade goods?"

The General says. "Right. We were to have servants after our own kind. Because whenever they come to visit. They are strangers in our homes The bible speaks of that "stranger." When they come. If the stranger eats pig, then they find whatever pig or whatever food they eat. You don't stop them from eating their food. You just understand that you can't eat it in your house. But they can still find it elsewhere.

G-D is All Power. All Knowing! All Power. All Knowing. He is here. There. Everywhere. He is in the Sky. He is in the clouds. He is in the moon. He is in the stars. He is in the trees. The birds. The bees. He's in you. And I.

One Night, you had some pain in your stomach from the fibroid. G-D touch you and heal you. With a telephone you can talk from Paris to Japan in real time. Just like how G-D can talk to you from Heaven here. Just like you can call and have your food delivered to you from miles away. G-D can send a bird to bring food to you from miles away. Do you see the pattern now?" I say. "No! I see where G-D can send food from miles away. But what's the pattern? **The General of The Most High G-D says.** The pattern is man do the same things.

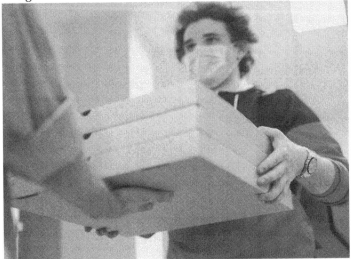

I say. "Oh. So, there's something's men can do. It's almost like the way G-D does it? Almost?" **The General of says.** "Yes. They do it the way G-D can. But in an Earthly fashion." I say. "OK, OK So it's just like when Angels feed me. They are all at my mouth saying, "eat this, eat this, eat this" and Earthly I can go at the grocery store for food?

So, there is an Earthly fashion. And a Heavenly fashion this is done? **The General says.** "Exactly!" I say. "This has much to do with what I have understand in the spirit regarding Abraham Lincoln. Abraham Lincoln. He put out the Proclamation of Emancipation and he did that freeing the slaves. But they were not only free in the flesh they were also free in The Spirit. I had a huge thing I wrote up and it speaks to what you are saying to me. It's also that they. And we. Are spiritually free. If you can say that. Spiritually free. And as the Nation of G-D that was their Earth-bound proclamation of emancipation of a free self on the Earth. Bless the Lord! So, the Lord G-D Almighty just drove me to consider, or think bringing me into the knowing that, there was two things that happened on that date. I get it! Thank you!

The General of The Most High G-D says. "Freedom can be Good, and Bad. Freedom can cost Death; Freedom can cost Life. You, see? A bird that is caged is protected within the bars. He is feed three meals a day. He is loved and cared for in that cage. "I say. "Yes, I see My LORD."

The General says. "That same bird gets out the cage. He will be eaten by a cat that lives inside the very same house. His freedom will cost him his life!

Slaves were OK on the master's farm. They had their master's name. They were protected. They were OK. After they became free? They became hunted. And were hunted down. I say. "That is spiritual warfare also. Now that I have been redeemed by The Most High."

The General of The Most High G-D says. "Yes. There is no more protection over you anymore. Because your Free! You have your own mind. You can thing as you want. You can go as you want. You are on your own. Your protection now depends on you." I say. "Bless the LORD!"

The General says. "When Adam was in the garden, and he was protected by G-D and G-D would come and see him every day. When he chose to be free to have his own. Mind. Will power. G-D freed him after that Satan came and destroyed him. I say. "Because he did not know that was what to expect!"

The General says. "That is the point!" I say. "That is why the book is being written?" **The General says.** "Understand?" I say. "So, you'll know what to expect?" **The General went on and he says to me.** "That's why Freedom can destroy you if you don't know how or the vastness of it. It's a dangerous thing to be free. And them to be hunted down as a free man. Prepare yourself because know. You are on your own." I say. "In G-D?."

The General says. "In G-D. Out of G-D. Around G-D. Under G-D. I say. "So, you are on your own. with authority

302

and power?" **The General says.** "You are on your own. If you are not in G-D. You have no protection. You have no cover. There are some that have NO COVER. That the Devil is using like guinea pigs. Shouting them down like dogs!" So, you have cover when you don't know G-D or you have cover when you know G-D? I say. **The General says.** "You have cover when you allow G-D to be your protector. To be your guide and your shield. He has you in a special place in his wings. The General Illustrated and showed me this special place within G-D's wings.

I say. "So, the more knowledge you have of G-D, he has you in a protective place?" **The General of The Most High G-D says.** "Because he protects his investment." I say, "I see." **The General says.** "When you decide, you are going to go out of G-D and you don't want G-D anymore? "Your protection is moved and whatever you know they are coming for that! They are coming for the knowledge that you've got. They will hunt that down and destroy that." I say. "They will try?" **The General of The Most High G-D says.** "Yes. The minute Prince started talking to that black man with all that knowledge. They hunt him down and kill him." I say. "So, prince started talking to someone?" I said. I remember prince spirit know G-D was taking to me at the time he came to me? Well not him. His Spirit. I was surprised to see that he found me. I remember thinking, only G-D could have permitted it. Although many good spirits do find me from time to time. But he did. He had only one wing. One was broken. And he showed me his missing wing. We didn't speak. When he came into my presence? He came with the essence of the (Spiritual) help he needed. So, we needed not speak. I often wonder. "How did Prince know. I was able to help him?" I prayed for his soul also. That he should cross over in safety. And he completed his journey.

303

The General says. "Yeah!" "The minute Whitney Houston decide she was going to cut out drugs and go straight and come back, she got killed!" Even Michael Jackson decided he would come back and start music and he was going to start producing his music and start like he did before, he got killed! I say. "Why?" **The General says.** "Information he has. If he had come back, we would have been the greatest singer. Again! And anyone who made music would have been jealous." I say. "Yes, for the rest of all time!"

The General says. "For the rest of all times! The choice was. Either he come back and be greater than he was before, or he dies as great as he was!" I say. "Yeah, and don't let him get no greater?" **The General of The Most High G-D says.** "Don't let him get no greater than that! Their thoughts were. We can't afford to have Michael Jackson doing what he

304

wants to do. So, he was free to go as high as he wanted to go.
BUT! That freedom cost him his life!

I say. "But why freedom is still costing people their life
General? Why can't there just be peace? Peace with all
mankind." **The General of The Most High G-D says.**
"Listen! Those Slaves that was freed? It would have been
better for them to stay on that farm and save their life being
protected by their master. Than to go ahead and try." I say.
"OK, then they open up a gate. Where they have to deal with
ALL OF THE SLAVE MASTER'S?" **The General says.** "All of
the masters who don't want you free!" I say. "So, they are all
in different, places, and respects and categories. Back then
you had the one master. I see!" **The General says.** "Now you
are crossing other master's lands and territories and they
are killing you because you are going across their
boundaries and their borders. Your freedom know, Will cost
you. Your life! The smarter you are. The more valuable you
are." I say. "So, you were saying indirectly. My freedom is
going to cost me my life? or directly, my freedom. The

freedom in which I have obtain will cost me my life?" **The General of The Most High G-D says.** "This was not directly to you!"

I say. "OK, because I've got some freedom also! **The General of The Most High G-D says.** "This is not directed to you. There was a portal of knowledge. When knowledge came in? I know own that." I say. "Well, that is happening with me also. With me and through me. Through the powers of the Most High. So it has its purpose."

The General says. "Yes! So, we understand that freedom was not always Good! Freedom can cost you your life. That is the bottom line."

PAY
THEM

CHAPTER XXVIII

I say. "So, know. Who is paying for that? I see in my paperwork in which The Most High just blessed me with at the library. He had listed some territories that currently belong to the Nation of Yisra'EL, The Nation of G-D. Territories of land right here in United States in which his people should be dwelling SEPERATELY!

The General says. "They are now called the projects! My love! They are called the projects! The projects are where the rejects live! They are land that the Black people paid nothing for. They get food stamps. I say. "Well, why did they give them that?"

The General says. "They get meals. A little compensation from social security. Social Security came about right after slavery was abolished to put a number on the Negros. They went from the slave master's name. To the slave master's number. The purpose was to count how many blacks was in this town and give them a number.

To know how many black people is in this town. Your number is your color. Your number is you. Only when the portal of knowledge is open up and the Angels of G-D come and deliberate on those things you get them. There were more slaves died after freedom. Then when they were slaves.

I say. "So, know. My question is this! Because you see. There are many who are holding firm and awaiting the good news, of great tidings from The LORD. And tidings of great joy. So now. How does my LORD dictates solving all of this? For those who yet stand firm and wait?

The General of The Most High G-D says. "Like Moses said sitting down in the dessert with the people of Yisra'EL. There's a time when G-D requires you to go out and fight to get what is yours. If you hold your hand and stay, there while they whip you and beat you. Then you will no longer be able to. They would have beat the strength out of you.

You have to stand up and come together and unite. The black people of the World can get all that they need from the World. Because it was the World that separate them from their Native Land.

You cannot just fight America. You must fight the World. Because it was the World that sold us into Slavery. Now. Every nation in the World looks at us like migrants. And nothing. Because we were slaves. We were traded like nothing.

The blacks, the Mexicans, the Guatemalans, Hawaiians, the Caribbeans, the Indians we were traded like dogs. We have spent time. Just to get ourselves together my love. I say. "So, did that answer on what is it we need to be doing now? There is many who would like this to be over." **The General of The Most High G-D says.** "Join forces together with people that actually. Not crazy, stupid, ignorant people, even when they come, they will have to be converted quickly! Because what could be good for you, can turn out bad if someone else puts a virus in it and you don't want a virus in the system.

You want people that can change the lives of people, read their hearts and try to change their hearts and their thinking from their stomach. Not from their head. The stomach is where you change the trait of a man. When a man starts eating right, his hold body changes into something different.

He stops eating. His body transforms into something different. He stops thinking. Nothing will happen. He will just sit down and meditate. You need to change the thoughts and ideologies. The decoda thinking, small thinking." I say. "So that is what the people have to do?" **The General says.** "You have to broaden their mind set. To go from mediocre thinking. Into thinking that is greater. Because this is greater!"

Do you know what it is to have the Countries of the World that was involved in slavery pay you back? For all of the wrong they did to the black race and any race that was enslaved? Soviet Union #1, England #2, France #3, Germany #4, United States #5. Spain #6.

There were three countries in the world that took a hold of slavery, France, England and Germany. United States came about afterwards. France, England, Germany, United States, every country. When you start naming countries that took part in slavery? Almost half of the continent was involved in slavery." I say. "So, know certain documentations need to be had, and put in place and sign and sealed and delivered?" **The General of The Most High**

G-D says. "Yes" I say. "They have to start going out!" **The General says.** "Yes, the Black's in America tried to get America to pay them." I say. "Reparation I believe they call it?" **The General says.** "But America couldn't pay them because every Nation in the world was involved in slavery." I say. "So now, you have to sue all?"

The General says. "You've had to get to ALL of the Nations of The World." I say. "Yes, but under the Nation of Yisra'EL, Under the Nation of G-D?

The General says. "Under the Nation of G-D! And you must start with the UN. The United Nations. And the United Nations once you blame them because Haile Selassie went to the United Nations for help, and they turned him down because he was black."

I say. "So that means, if they already have the history of that. What will they do with me? Turn me down too." **The General says.** "So that is why I say "to have that knowledge on you and you spear heading that? your life will not be long."

They will try...not try...but they will assassinate you and it would be someone very, very close to you. It will not be anyone far from you, that will put something in your drink. Next thing you know, you get a virus, you get sick and your gone.

The World does not want the Truth to come out, because the Truth should what? The truth will make you?" I say. _"FREE!"_ **The General says.** "Yes! That freedom will cost you your life. Anyone will be looking to kill you, destroy you. Because you are now fighting against principalities and rulers in high places.

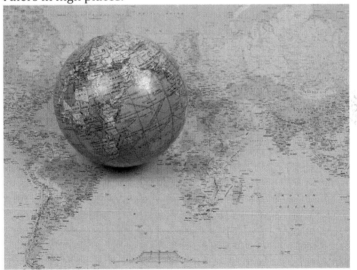

Not the Government, nor the King! but Spiritual wickedness in high places. The Devil himself would be trying to kill you. Because he was the one that infiltrate the switching up of history so that G-D can't be glorified. So, G-D can't be praise, so you can't know who G-D is."

And Satan is the closest one to G-D that's why he can tell us where G-D isn't. He knows the way to G-D so to hide it from us, he sneers us with all kinds of things, even the trees hiding G-D from us. I say. **"He sends all kinds of divergences?" The General says.** "Divergence and mix signals" I say. "Yes, to keep you from it"

"To keep you from knowing the path to G-D. That is distractions in any form from what you are dealing up with! "Any form! And he hits you in the mind, _G-D comes here in your gut! (The General Illustrated by pointing at his stomach region). The truth is always here, right in the Gut! Therefore G-D never said, "Renew your Gut." Renew your mind daily!" You, see?_ **The General of The Most High G-D says.** I say. "I See." "G-D gave you freedom, what you do with it, it is up to you!" **The General says.** I say. "That is why a lot of people isn't free, it is dangerous!"

"It is dangerous! If people know what you and I know right know today? You and I would be a target. The minute you get out there and your light start shining! They are coming to out it! So, G-D has to protect the truth and give us a little bit at a time. **"The General says.**

I say. "Yes, so much too. But I was asking for a long time who I was. Come what may I needed to know myself. Bless the Lord, Come what may. I Bless the Lord for allowing me to carry it."

The General says. "And another thing! I wouldn't say come what may. Because G-d filters everything before it gets to you and me." I say. "Amen" "I don't want nothing to come to me by chance and hurt me. I want it to come from G-D so G-D can protect me and shield that." **The General says.** I say. "Through G-D"

"I am protected with the knowledge he gave us." **The General said.** I say. "From or with?" **The General says.** "I am protected from G-D with the knowledge he has given us." I say. "I am protected from G-d with the knowledge he has given us." **The General says.** "Yes, yes."

I say. *"I am protected from G-d with the knowledge he has given us."* "Yes, therefore you can move around every day, and nobody knows just how wise you and I are. Until they get close and start talking and this gets into their ears next thing you know. Their calling this one, calling their friends and calling the next one. Next thing you know the UN's got us saying. She hears from G-D every day. Let's go see her! **The General says.** I say. "It is really our job to do the best we can as a Nation?"

The General of The Most High G-D says. "Yes!" I say. "OK, OK." **The General says.** "Right Know, if you set up something online where people can donate to the freedom course, you will see just how far this thing could really go. But you will have to understand that it is not good to start something and not have an end. Martin Luther King started a revolution. But those jokers that were around him couldn't influence him to protect himself and that he did not need to do the work by himself.

Get a panel of people that think just like you. And all you guys doing and saying the same thing. It is hard to kill 10 thousand people on one accord. You understand? **G-D REVEALED to me, saying.** "If they kill one. Someone else will still carry my message. If they kill you? Someone will still carry it!" I say. "Right!"

"If they kill you? We will take them out too! We have snipers doing the same thing their doing! We're just taking them out too! Before they know where I am. I know where they are. You, see? **The General of The Most High Myki'EL/Michael says.** I know who the sniper is before he even knows where I am. He gets takeout quickly! That's how you protect our King! G-D will tell you that! That is why G-D said "Don't kill your own" embrace them! If a man doesn't know G-D, then his action is not Godly! I say. "Right! So, if you do not know G-D, your action is evil! "G-D said "remove the evil from among us" so I will have to castrate him and take him out. So, the others can fear. You put the others in

fear." **The General of The Most High G-D says.** I say. "I see. So that is why it is important to subdue the World on this?" "Subdue the World on it!" **The General says.**

"I say. *"On this slavery issue?"* *"Yes. Cripple them. Cripple them!"* **The General of The Most High G-D says.** I say. "And then everyone else have to follow suit?" They will have no other reason. No other way." **The General says.**

I say. "So, this is the last and final proclamation or independence of the slavery issue?" "Independence of slavery issues." **The General say.** Is to subdue the World on it? I say. **The General says.** "Subdue the World on it!" I say. "So, start with the UN?"

The General says. "Doesn't have to be the UN. We have blacks in the UN that can deal up with that." I say. "So, we reach blacks within the UN?" "We have blacks in Africa. We reach them. Blacks in Europe. Reach them. Blacks in Nigeria." **The General says.**

I say. "Blacks of power you mean and the other? And you get the others with the reading with the book." **The General of The Most High G-D says.** "Everything! Once you put knowledge out there like you say."

<u>**Revelation within the hour**</u>: - It seems G-D was calling for unification of his people.

SPIRITUALLY DEAD

CHAPTER **XXIX**

June 16, 2016, I recognize that a lot that had happen in my life was brought on by distractions. I kept welcoming the distractions into my life and subsequently the thing that was happening in my life was destroyed.

Like my job, it is almost like nothing stays alive if you do not pay it any attention or give it any life. Nothing. Not even what you believe you are seeing with your natural eyes. Nothing becomes alive, if you don't give it life. Even if you see it and you hear it into your hearing if you do not respond back to it, or look on it directly? IT IS NOT ALIVE! IT IS DEAD AND CAN NOT LIVE! Know you understand the pursuit of true happiness! **The General of The Most High G-D says.** I say. "So that is the pursuit of happiness? OK!"

Revelation within the hour:- Arguments give life to dead things. Violence give life to dead things. Spiritual blindness give life to dead things. Not knowing God gives life to dead things.

"So how I know am writing a book. I know it will not be ready tomorrow. So, if something comes direct onto my path regarding that? Then that will be something to give life too? Right." I say. "Your book. Anything that attaches itself to your book supposed to bring life to that book. Like a baby. Any information going there, helps give life to the book." **The General of The Most High G-D says.**

"I saw that today. Because the book was almost in a nowhere stage. Even though I thought I was writing an autobiography at first. When the spirit asked me to write. But then it was today when I got all the Lincoln information from The Most High. I felt life came to the book. All the pieces and puzzles. It was like the pieces was all coming together. Even though I was only *writing pieces through obedience.* **The General of The Most High G-D says.** "It came, out to a book that has life." "I see, so this is again, how it is said "All things work together for good for those who love the Lord" in that case? Because I didn't have planned writing. But life came! I see." I say.

"To a book that has life in it. It attached itself to your book and strengthen your book and the pages. Strengthen the core of the book." **The General of The Most High G-D says.** "I see!" I say.

"Yahusha. said to some people when they were going to bury the dead. One of the tribe members said to Yahusha. "Don't they know you are the resurrection and the life? And he said to them, "Let the Dead, Bury the Dead." **The General of The Most High G-D says.** "Who said, "Don't they know you're the resurrection and the light? Who said that?" I say. **The General of The Most High G-D says.** "One of the Tribe said that. One out of the Tribe. And he said "Let the Dead, Bury the Dead," I say. "What does that mean?"

The General of The Most High G-D says. "If you know that life is over here to the water. And you've got a dead man carrying him to that hole. If you want that man to live you wouldn't take him and throw him into the water? If you knew that life was in that water? Would you carry that man away from the water and throw him in a hole? That is what he was saying to them. Don't give thought to things that are dead. Give though to things that are alive!"

I say. "I see, so the real things that are alive are the things we were talking about. The slavery issues. The principalities things those are the real things that are alive? The other things are vanity, and they will fade away? **The General of The Most High G-D says.** "Anything can be vanity. Anything can fade away. Thus, enhancing the gifts that All Mighty gives you here on Earth. Don't give power to dead things! You see, greater works than this will you do! Raising the Dead is a joke!

"So that is the power G-D gave me? I say. **The General of The Most High G-D says.** Yeah! I say. "To raise the dead?"

The General of The Most High G-D says. "The spiritual dead!" "OK." I say.

The General of The Most High G-D says. "The spiritual dead? You are giving life to spiritual dead people. Greater works!" I say. "Can I put the book out without my name and Contact information? So, they would have nowhere to find me?

"Your book will be out there. As rich as Oprah is. I don't know where she is. Do you know how many people out there trying to harm her? She is not announcing where she is going. She is not telling anyone how much money she has. She is not announcing she is going to this hotel. That hotel. That party. She is not doing that! She is just enjoying whatever it is that she has. When a man goes and resurrect just one man from the dead. They said "oh that is amazing!" You are up here. You are raising thousands. Thousands of spiritually dead people. G-D values that more than that!" **The General of The Most High G-D says.**

I say. "Do you think all of this happened with me in this knowledge in which G-D is imparting. Do you think all of this happen because it had something to do with me requesting it or just the plan G-D had for me before time? Or what? I mean, I don't understand it! Does it have anything to do with me asking or begging for it overtime? Like I have been doing all my life? Or it just might be the right of the children of Israel to have the knowledge? **General of The Most High G-D says.** "Anything from G-D, that happens to any man? Can take him out." "OK." I say. **The General said,** "Because of what he asks." "What did he ask?" I say. **The General says.** "He asked G-D, for the simplest of things, he ask G-D to be able to determine right from wrong, He ask G-D to be able to give fair and righteous judge. Knowledge is there for everyone. It is he who seek it." "OK, so it is he who seek the knowledge?" I say. **The General says.** "Yes! ""OK." I said.

The General says. "See Knowledge is for everyone, but people are too busy now a days to seek. They have to many things to do! Not to be extreme!" What do you mean not be extreme? "I say. "No! because knowledge can cost you to think that you are greater than G-D! You are not to get it for you to think that you are greater than G-D himself. Or that there is no G-D." **The General says.** "OK, so you get knowledge sufficiently. I say.

"You get knowledge for your portion, measurable! You get a measure of knowledge. If not. You will feel like the knowledge that you have, no one has given to you, but you! The greatest boxer in his own eyes died from a disease that shakes his body every second." **The General of The Most High G-D says."** OK, the shakes." I say.

The General says. "So, the shakes take you out. You are no Greater." I say. "OK, so the shakes will take you out when you think you are greater than G-D?" **The General says.** "NO! NO! When you think you are Greater than G-D. You are a foolish man. You're a foolish man. A dog can bite you and you will die from rabies."

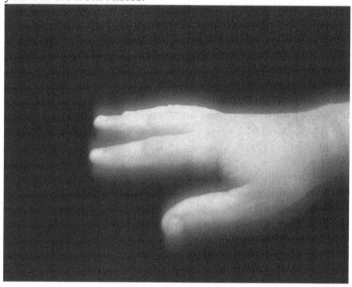

"OK, so anything that happens to a foolish man can very well take him out?" I say. **The General says.** "Anything from G-D, that happens to any man. Can take him out!" "OK." I say. **The General G-D says.** "But when you believe that you are the Greatest and you see? Being the best means that you are greater than G-D." I say. "I see. So, proclaiming that is just not proclaiming that among man? **The General of The Most High G-D says.** "That's in the atmosphere. "Because he is in everything." **The General says.** "The atmosphere will say "You're the best, best at what?" You can't be the best at anything. Because no man has lived long enough to see the best man yet!" "OK, I see, because eternity is longer than a man's life!" I say.

The General says. "Eternity is longer than a man's life!" "OK." I say. "G-D called Solomon the wisest that has lived and would ever live! There will be none before you and none after that would be as wise as you! Or any that would have what you have. There will be none." **The General says.** "Why? Don't G-D like making an appearance on Earth?" I say. **The General of The Most High G-D says.** "It's not that. It is because of what he asks." "What did he ask?" I say. **The General says.** "He asked G-D, for the simplest of things. He asks G-D to be able to determine right from wrong. He asks G-D to be able to give fair and righteous judge. Because he asks for those things G-D told him "You ask for the smallest things." What he got was greater than he could ever imagine. Look at Job. Job did a righteous act, and his act was simply. Stand firm and don't deny G-D. Throughout his pain and suffering he did not deny G-D. For him not denying G-D, his reward was greater, far greater than his first. G-D even increase his cattle one thousand-fold. New wife and new kids and none of his kids survived not even the wife. G-D destroyed them.

Look at Abraham, Look at Moses. Do you understand? Moses said to G-D. I am a man of stuttering tongue. G-D told him "Open your mouth and I will speak for you." You just must know where wisdom is. Where the Greatest is. Who is the Greatest? *You are not the Greatest.* You are getting the Knowledge from the Greatest.

You are getting the Knowledge from the Greatest and you are telling the Greatest. You're the Greatest? It is like a slap in G-D's face!" I say. "So, if it is G-D that have you on that Path, how can you take the glory from G-D?" **The General says.** "Free Will! Free Will! Free Will! Free Will! Free Will! Free Will! Free Will!" "And what is Free Will? Just to do something because you want to?" I say. "Free will is what separates you from the animals and the trees and the birds and the bees. You communicate with G-D!

You have got the power to say "There is no G-D" and live tomorrow to say it again. Because he gave you that free will. And then, you have the power to say. There is a G-D his name is? Such and Such. And then, in the ear of those who hear it, they have the power to say "I don't believe that." And then, in the ear of another one that hears you they have the power to say "I believe you."

It is Free Will! Out of the Free Will, G-d increases you with his knowing. The knowing of who he is. What he is. He becomes your friend, your ally, he becomes someone that you can...He becomes someone you can trust. The more your free will becomes his will, then you and he became together as one." **The General says.** "So, the Free Will become his will. It's the thing in which he is directing you to do?" I say.

The General says. "No! Your Free Will, will become his Will. And his will becomes you. You do whatever it is that he desires you to do. Because your will now?. You gave your free will out to be a part of him.

Now he can speak and talk and work through you like he did Abraham, Isaac and Jacob, Moses, Enoch, Elijah, David, you see? I say. "They weren't getting killed for their free will. Nobody was killing them back then for that! Right? No one was killing them for the work of G-D." **The General of The Most High G-D says.** "Well! G-D shields who he uses." "Well, am aware of that!" I say. **The General says.** "The ones that are being killed are the ones that are. That did it out of their own will." "See, out of the consideration of it happening to them, it happened to them?" I say. **The General of The Most High G-D says.** "No."

"Well, isn't that your own Will? They willed it to happen?" I say. "They did not will it to happen, your will is the things you do! Your mind, how you think about things. How you look at things, what you believe. G-D say's go left, you go right. Your free will is to go right the way you want to go but G-D say to go left. But you go right because that is your free will. G-D is not going to go against your free will, he will let you go right!" **The General says.**

June 23rd, 2016, **The General says.** "He said it before. He said to the pure. All things are pure. I think that I am. So, I thought I am the thing that I thought. I became the thing that I thought I am. When I start doing the things that I thought I did already!" "OK, that one is complicated for me. And why is that?" I say.

The General of The Most High G-D says. _"Because you are what you think."_ "So does that mean. I think that I am a flight attendant. Does that mean I can become that after time?" "What does that mean, I am what I think?" I say. **The General says.** _What you believe, you are._ Everything you do, must be that of a flight attendant." I say "OK, and then the other things will fall into place." "First of all, what do you do to become a flight attendant? You need to channel that way. You would need to start that from here. (The General illustrated also) I would have to go there and get it. Whatever they must give the person to become the Police Chief. I would have to go and get it!

My process starts from here. Police academy. School, graduation high honors. Police force. Do good! Get promoted, to get promoted to police chief because I have done all the requirements to be that. They will not give you Chief because you look like a Chief.

To be a Judge. Flight attendant. General manager. You must first have experience and know a lot about every inch of the Hotel, know about management, budget and continue to work towards that. The only thing that you live, right now! Right now! Is in the Spirit.

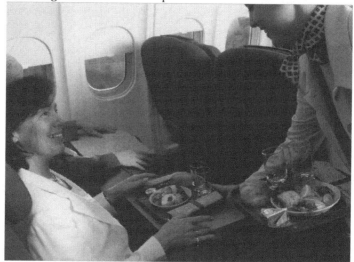

The General of The Most High G-D says. "The only thing that you live?" I say. "The only thing that a man can do, right now. Is live in the spirit. "**The General says.** "I say. "OK, I get it!" Because it is Free Will. It almost comes with a free will. You chose to do the will of G-D. **The General says.**

DISTURBING SOULS

CHAPTER XXX

On June 18, 2016, I wrote the following notes. Directly glorifying G-D are the ones that knows G-D. And he knows them. He gave them Masterful things to take care off for him. The ones who indirectly knows G-D are the ones G-D use to say his name, or to say "G-D"

On June 24, 2016, **The General of The Most High G-D came and says to me.** "There are souls that people have called up from the earth (the grave) and has never called them back down. Someone even called up Moses and his response was. "Why have you called me? Why have you called me? Why have you disturbed me?" I say. "Someone called up Moses before General?" I was astonished.

"Someone did. Who was a King! **The General says.** I say. "OK, so when these witches call up these souls. They don't send them back down?" **The General says.** "Let's just say. If they call the souls up to do a work for them. And the person that they go and do the work too is stronger than the witch themselves. Unbeknownst to the person that they have covering from G-D that has them protected under all circumstances.

The job that was sent out. Cannot be fulfilled. They now must return to sender. Who gave them the job in the first place. **The General says.** "OK, and when they return to the person, what happens?" I say. "And when they return to the person the person then has to actually take it! **The General of The Most High G-D says.** I say. "Do you mean take the spirit?" **The General says.** They would have to take whatever was being given to the person that was denied. They will come back and bring it to the person who gave it to them to give out. And. If the person does not receive it? That spirit stays on Earth because he has a package to deliver. **The General says.** "And if he doesn't get that deliver? He will just be hanging around. I say. "Hanging around!" I say. "Oh, my Lord!" "Yes. Hanging Around. Darkness. Just hanging around. **The General says.** I say. "So, there are lost souls roaming the Earth?" "Roaming the Earth.

Yes!" **The General says.** I say. "So that is why the reading that I had. Had to do with Maine being a witch state back in the day around 1484 or 1445 is this why? In the readings. They would hang or kill or drown the witches because they understood what the witches were doing. They understood that back then? **The General says.** "They understood that the witches were going into the graveyards. And disturbing souls!"

The General says. Disturbing souls that was dead in the graveyard." I say. "Yes. And bringing the souls that are dead back to life with mankind, hanging around humanity?" **The General says.** "And then they would try to destroy the man who is alive. The people."

I say. "With the spirits? The spirits come alive to destroy you?" "Right!" **The General says.** "Or to take you with them, or to even bring riches, or to show them where gold is. To find wealth for them. Bring back money. Where are we outside right know? You would not know if this was a place that you can find gold. But the spirits would know that. They would know where to find it. They even know what number to give you to play.

I say. "OK, so now. How would we get rid of or how can humanity have an existence without those lingering souls in it?" There is no existence without them because *we are spirits*. <u>You all are just spirits in a fleshly body</u>. They just take the outer spirit that was left here because G-d caries the soul. So, the spirit of a man is left here in the ground. He stays with the body." **The General says.**

"So, the body is under the ground." I say. "The spirit stays with the body. He stays with the body." **The General says.** "I say. "So even if someone calls him out to come do a work and he can't finish that work. He would just stay up top on the land and his body would be under the ground and they can't connect?"

The General of The Most High G-D says. "Yes! He will roam the earth." I say. "OK." "Until someone call him out for something else to do or until G-D. Or until you send him back from when's he come." **The General says.** "How would you know how to cast them... (before I could finish my sentence the General responded and answered me). "Well, you just say what G-D said. **The General of The Most High G-D says"** _**Be cast into outer darkness, bound in chains and shackles, until the great and terrible judgment day**_. The words out of your mouth come as command. Because they must obey you. THEY MUST OBEY YOU!" **The General says.** "Is it just people of G-D they must obey, or anyone can say that?" I say.

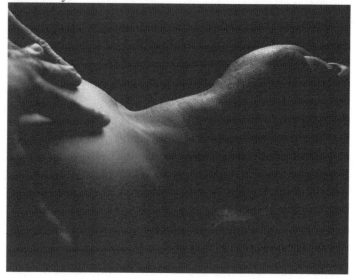

"No. You have to be in G-D to do anything Godly out of the realm. It is a different world. You have G-D world. Then you have the Dark world. You must study that. To actually understand that. You must study G-D world to understand him. You must study this to understand it. If you take that pill to go down that road there are things you will learn. They are eager. They are eager to teach you. Eager to just blow your mind. And are eager to give it to you. Because when G-D didn't give you all of that."

"Because it's garbage!" I say. "It's foolishness. Foolishness is bounded up in the hearts of man. So foolish men meet darkness. Darkness meet foolish man." **The General of The Most High G-D says.**

On June 27, 2016, The General spoke to me about the names of G-D he says. "All the names of G-D back then were just a cover. People would say what is his name?. Jehovah over here. El fire over there. Teskone over here. He name Jarah over there. They were playing around with those names all over. All of them and his real name got hid. Y'all have to change those songs to thank you, YAHWEH! Thank you, YAHWEH! Thank you, YAHWEH! Thank you, YAHWEH. I love you Yahusha. I love you Yahusha. Thank you Yahusha. Yahusha thank you.

Thank you! "My lord, all those names." I say. "Just to hide the real name" **The General says.** "Jehovah racanee. El Shadai" I say. "El Shadai. He die!" **The General says.** I Laugh out loud, then I say. LOL. .El Shadai. He die." "That was a big funeral!" **The General says.** Jah." I say. "Rasta for I." I say. "Falasie I! Binge I! LOL. Who else?" **The General of The Most High G-D says.** "Haile Selassie I is the G-D of Jamaica. Haile Selassie was the General in Ethiopia Haile Selassie went to the UN to get help because Napoleon was coming to get him." I say. "Were we talking about the names that people call G-D?" "Yes, I was telling you that w-

as Jamaican G-D. This is how foolish people is. He is no G-D! So those other names. Are names made up just like how that one was made up. So, know, all those names are dead. They

need to start singing the songs of Yahusha. And Yahweh.
There are few songs out there with his name in it. Is this not
bad? They killed the real one. And bring the false
ones to life. Yahusha's. name is not often mentioned in many

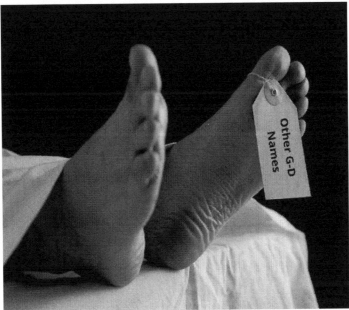

songs or many books. There is very little information
written on Yahusha. And Yahweh, very little." **The General
says.** "Yahweh is written as the G-D of Moses. Abraham and
the one who revealed himself to them. You would find a little
about him on earth, so I get what you are saying." I said.

There is so much I need. To have these things happen
the way G-D desires it to be. I even have songs from 2012.
The angelic host of heaven song those to me and when I
cross back over to earth? I would hurry and write them
down or slap on the recorder." There is so much work to be
done. I say.

CHAPTER XXXI

While I was studying on June 27, 2016, with The LORD, Most High's General at the river? The teaching was so captivating, we stayed longer and longer into the night. If I was not ready to leave. The General would keep on teaching me. That which he was charged to do. By The Creator.

It got dark very late in the evening. Sometimes 9 pm was still day light hours. This evening. Now the darkness stole the day light. I saw two black demons come up out of the earth and I told the General and he said it was time to go! I saw another one and became frighten.

Even though we returned to that site again and again? We would always leave before dark from that point onward. **The General of The Most High G-D** explained to me later that they were spirits living in the forest.

On June 28, 2016, I had an early morning vision. I saw He who drives the seat of Evil (The Devil) in the very same body that I saw in the flesh during my greatest temptation. I was walking on the beach with The Most High G-D's General and out of nowhere there came a single rider on a futuristic beach watercraft. The water suit and craft were like nothing

I had seen before. Very high technology. The movements that the single rider made brought me to consider. The person was trying to get our attention.

Instantly, The Most High G-D's General was no longer with me. I turned to the right of a tree to go around it and suddenly a silver sword chops the tree nearest my head. As a warning, so that I would go no further." I noticed a man holding the sword. Strange thing was he did not frighten me; At this point on the journey with G-D. I knew. The Devil played dirty. And the talks that I was having with The General was strengthening me. And I did not feel fear. I turned to go left of the tree and that was when I saw him. "The single rider" The Devil. Satan himself. He looked on me with admiration. Last time I saw the devil? Was when he had poisoned me. And offered me a marriage proposal. That I turned down. He took hold of my hand.

IMMEDIATELY. I felt the presence of G-D with me so strong. G-D's presence consumed the area on my side. All sides of me and the back of me. I felt the engulfing presence of G-D, so I had no fear even. If I wanted to.

Suddenly Satan, Beelzebub, Lucifer, that devil rise me up in the air. While holding my right hand gently by the four fingers. He carefully walked slowly in front of me for a better look. As he looked upon me continually with admiration. He moved his head from left to right to get a good look at me. He took his time smiling and looking at me while holding my right hand. I felt naked. Exposed. As if he was looking right through me. Amazed on who I had become in G-D. Satan lingered in admiration of me. And because he made me feel naked? I wanted it to end. Satan said nothing to me. Because there was nothing, he could have said to me. At his point? I was another's wife. G-D.

I woke up with a severe headache. That Satan left with me to remember me of his visit. One that I had never felt before. It felt like a crack had happen in my head or better yet a split. I got dressed and did not see The General of The Most High G-D. Who was usually there to greet and teach me when I woke up from sleep. I packed up for the day and went outside to find The General of The Most High G-D talking on the corner with another male. It surprised me that he did not leave the other person when I was very near the car to leave. Usually, he would be at my side swiftly as he is charged. But today! It was different.

The conversation although I didn't hear it. It looked intense. I stayed away and decided to go for a morning stroll. A few minutes into the walk. Maybe because I was about to go completely out of G-D Most High General's sight? He showed up by my side. I told him what had happened to me. And what the Devil had done to me. And he was not surprised. The General said, "the reason why the devil's general with the sword left the dream was to come and find me. It was him, I was speaking to. Finding me and communicating with me in the physical realm. Would keep me away from you in the spiritual realm. And that would be the time for Lucifer to have with me. But G-D was there. Blessed be he.

The General of The Most High G-D went further and said to me. "The Devil can do nothing but admire you. I was taken out of the way. You were left in that realm and his general came to me wanting to fight. He meets me in one place and told me to come to the other side. I wondered if he was joking. Until he started to put down something he was holding. He started saying. "You are talking about me General of The Most High G-D?" And he started laughing at me. I was going to destroy him with all that I had in me. But. I explained to him that with all you and I are doing? I don't have that kind of time in the day. He readily apologized. And went on his way.

The General says. "The thing is trouble will come to find you. It doesn't matter where you are. It is you that would have to defuse it. If not, trouble will link on to you and everything else that follows will be trouble for you. So, defuse it. Before it becomes a trouble for you. I told Satan's General. You can't handle it. And I was saying that walking off."

At 7:48am the same day. After finding out that the females living in the shelter would gossip about me to the administrator. I held the thoughts in my mind, I never shared it with The General, or anyone else. As I though of the unkindness toward me. The General of The Most High G-D read my thoughts and says to me. "This is what I said while standing over the administrator. If they have a problem? They need to go to the administrative office, we don't! this is what they created. Elioenai has come here because, we found ourselves homeless. They came here because they found themselves homeless. I don't know whither homeless has or is higher than homeless." I stood there and laugh and laugh. And said. " LOL General, you just made a joke."

The General of The Most High G-D says. "They don't have another home; they've got nowhere to go. I didn't tell her; I saw them falling down in the soup kitchen, The General went on to say. "But if your homeless, your homeless. I told her, they have a problem, and they don't even know why. I said to her, is it because we are black. We black! So, what's the problem? They are homeless!"

I laugh out loud." LOL, LOL." I say to The General, "LOL." **The General of The Most High G-D says.** "The food doesn't belong to them, none of them, the three of them, the food don't belong to them. The bed doesn't belong to them. The light doesn't belong to them. Nothing belongs to them. If you are in the bathroom and the light is on, close the door. Close the door. You and the bathroom light stay in the room while everyone else is sleeping. Is that hard to do? Is that hard to do? Those three ladies are the others in the room, and we have men in here who have problems. And the men are dealing with their problems better than the woman. Only four women in that shelter and three of them are trying to make problems for one who do not care to make problems for them. I said to the Administrator spirit. "You are sitting here giving them a listening ear. Don't you know they will be feeding you? I said to her. if you would stop listening to what they have to say. Then they would have no one to put that shit in. You tell them to leave! You tell them to go to the administrator's office and complain. Not to you! Not to you! You can't help them; you cannot help them. What can you say to them? They are feeding you with all kinds of things, they are feeding you with things, I said to her, have you ever heard G-D wife come here and complain to you about them? You don't think she have things to tell you? You don't think she have things to tell you about them?"

The General of The Most High G-D continues and says. "Her spirit answered me, "Oh, yeah, yeah! I Said, "But, she doesn't come. JUST LEAVE ELIOENAI ALONE! You homeless! We are homeless! If you've got a home, go there! If you are homeless, am homeless, we found ourselves homeless, he came here for shelter, something to eat and somewhere to sleep, we have that, that is good enough for us right know, because we are trying to get out, right now!

We are doing our best, so someone else who need help can come in and have those beds and get help! The other three are here to stay all day. They are here to live in the shelter. I passed around again at another time and saw two of them still there talking so I turned back around. Bless the Lord! Not saying that it will stop, but they have heard from me. Who is getting complaints from his wife concerning her neighbor's. **The General of The Most High G-D said.** "And G-D! Is tired of the drop, drop, drop, drop, drop, every morning. Drip, drip, drip, drip, drip, drip every morning! It's like G-D wakes up in the Morning. Gets his cup of coffee. Danish on the side and say "OK babe. What happen last night?"

349

He is waiting to hear the story. He will collect from ***everyone.*** Next thing you know he is hearing "Well the neighbors." I don't think that would ever stop! As long as you live. People will not like you. And they would have no reason, not to like you. But because they find it easier and more exciting not to like you? They stick with that. When they don't even know that it is more exciting to like a person. To want to be around a person, to understand them, have fun, and live. That part they don't understand, that is better than gossiping. Well! It must be fulfilled; someone must be a gossiper! Or else the world would not exist. Someone has got to be a troublemaker. Or else the world would not exist!

Someone has got to be a confusion maker and confusion stir. Or stir up confusion or nuisance! For the world to exist, so someone has to give those words life to exist in this world, otherwise. They will not exist! Humans give those words spirits and then spirits give it life in these people and they become exactly what it is. They become a nuisance! You don't ever call a person who is a nuisance by

their name. You don't say Jerry is a nuisance! You say "You see Jerry? Boy that's a f**king nuisance! You understand!" I say. "LOL, LORD LOL." I laugh for a few minutes. Because when The General lessons got hot and heated?. It became more interesting. I appreciated the unadulterated truth of The LORD. And the zeal The General had to bring me to understand now The Most High G-D sees things. I laugh. Because somethings were said and done by The General, for me. Just to laugh. As my burden was heavy to know the things of G-D I learned.

The General said. "You don't say William is a troublemaker! No! you say. "Who? Him? He is a f**king troublemaker, man!" Everywhere he goes is trouble, everywhere he goes. If he is eating, he's got trouble eating! **The General says.** And we laugh together. **The General says.** "So, they become exactly the thing that they actually believe, they act it out. So, _to the troublemaker, everything is_

about trouble. Therefore, I said. "Do not look for it to change" but now. We have a reason to ignore them. And I feel pleasure now to hear you talk and complain about them. I will just laugh!

The General says. "They now have heard my voice in the place (the shelter). And now they understand that I know what is going on. Don't like it. And you that are of authority need to put a stop to it. The crazy people. The administrator couldn't help. The crazy people throw water on her." I laugh. "How could a crazy person lock a sane person in a room? **The General of The Most High G-D says to me.** I say. I don't know. "How can they General?" Then I laugh. Somehow, I know he was talking about something that happen in the shelter administrator's life in the past. I say. "Sounds like the sane person is not on their meds, and the crazy person is. I continued to laugh.

The General smiled while saying to me. "Sometin' wong! Sometin' wong! The shelter isn't called Bonnie and Clyde! Read the motto! Read the motto!" **The General said** "Some-tin wong, some-tin wong" to make me smile, and I did. I started laughing out loud. It was so funny. It was as though the general did not have *his* medications, how hilarious he sounded saying. "some-tin wong, Some-tin wong."

The General of The Most High G-D says. "Read the motto!, Read the motto!, The motto says. To cut it short the motto reads. "I would try my best to rid the world of homelessness." I laugh and then I say. "Is that what the motto says General?" **The General says.** "That is what the motto says in so many words! I WOULD TRY MY BEST TO RID THE WORLD OF HOMELESSNESS. For the same reason!" I laugh. It was funny to get a rise out of The General. Then **The General of The Most High G-D says.** "For this same f**king reason. People are already homeless, and you are making them feel like they are homeless in a homeless f**king shelter? **The General of The Most High G-D says.** I laugh. Then said. "That's a catastrophe General!"

The General of The Most High G-D says. They are homeless. They are homeless! You are homeless. You are going to make someone else feel like your homelessness is better than their homelessness? And you in the same motherf**king room? I laugh and said. "Oh, My LORD!. LOL General! LOL!"

The General says. "In the same bunk bed? You don't have a KING SIZE bed and they have a bunk. You've got a f**king bunk bed!" I continued Laughing and writing The General's words in my journal. The General of The Most High G-D continued by saying. "So, where the f**k you get off. Ha? If you saying because you white and am black? You should be ashamed of your motherf**king self to be in here with a black person in a homeless shelter. That means that you have put yourself as low, low, low. **The General says.** I laughed out loud. Because I had never heard of any of G-D's angels using strong language before. But if I had not heard it for myself. I would not have believed just how real they were.

The General of The Most High G-D says. "If you think of me to be low, low, low, low. And you and I in the same f**king, low, low, low homeless shelter? How the f**k? Where the f**k?. What happen to you? What happen to you bro? You're not supposed to be down here? I continued laughing and writing. **The General says.** "This is where we are. Don't you know that? You now become a reject!" I say while laughing and writing. "Of your own situation!"

"**The General says.** "Of your own demise! Your shit makes you f**king homeless. I was born black. Am supposed to be homeless." **The General of The Most High** G-D continued laughing and holding both his sides while rocking back and forward laughing out loud. Into The Universe.

The General of The Most High G-D says. "Well as far as you are concern. Yeah G-D? They don't see the logic! Your white in a homeless shelter. Am black in a homeless shelter. But you think, your better than me? I was born homeless being black. What the f**k happens to you? You are not supposed to be here! I laugh and continue writing.

The General of The Most High G-D continued by says. "Gone Na! Gone! Get on out of here. Gone. You done figure we aren't nobody! You done figure we are the low of the low. So, if you figure we are the low of the low. How the f**k did you get down here? That must have been a hard, long f**king drop! You have hit rock bottom!" I laugh. As The General laughed. **The General of The Most High G-D says.** "While you down here to rock bottom!" We are eating the same food. You are saying "I don't eat that" I am saying. "I don't eat that." But your. "I don't eat." Is better than my. "I don't eat that?" **The General of The Most High G-D,**

started smiling. Then shortly thereafter. He was laughing out loud again. I laugh also for a time, but I was also silent. I wrote everything, because everything that G-D says? Is a blessing to mankind, a Wisdom, a Knowledge, a Truth, and an Understanding, I said what will help them to turn these bodies around?. **The General says.** "They need stronger administrators. Or if their entire team is not strong? They need a strong Manager over the team! The way the smoke comes through those windows. You can't sit down and eat. You can't go upstairs to eat. You can't go outside. They have outside with the smoke on lock! The dining room is so smoky from smoke coming through the windows. The only thing you can do is hold your breath and hope you live through it! They are not serious! And who could you tell? When you look for the administrator. Their door is closed, and they are outside smoking the tobacco that's coming through the windows!"

The General says. "Write them a letter about what we have witnessed your two weeks there. As a letter of thanks." "I know I will not be able to change a lot of things about it. So, I will leave a lot of things out that is not pertinent." I said.

The General of The Most High G-D says. "But what is pertinent is the direct dealing of individuals towards other individuals. Those are more pertinent! Everything else that is minuet can fall under. Building of characters. Not only that. If the administrator was not also talking about you, they would not have given the other women a listening ear."

LIFE
ATTRACTS

CHAPTER XXXII

On June 28, 2016, for my Lessons the General says to me. "Spirits are in everything!" I say. "I heard that before from G-D! So, the question would be, the age-old question is "if spirits are in everything, how do you get to the spirit that is in everything? How do you communicate with that spirit that is in that thing? What's the key? There is no key!" **The General of The Most High G-D says.**

"Life attracts life, doesn't it? Would that be the answer?" Life. If you need a key for that? Life is the key for that!" **The General says.** I say. "So, me being life form and them being life form and having the spirit I suppose to have, what? Dominion over them, right?" "No. When you give a cup life? You give it life by using it for its purpose. A cup is for water." **The General G-D says.** I see, using it for its purpose. "I say. "Yes." **The General says.**" So that's in anything? I say. **The General says**. "Anything.

A car! A car is dead until you put life, until you sit in it or turn the key or until you desire to move it. You give it life. You make it move. You make it move. Therefore, in an accident? They don't charge the car.

For you to talk to people. They must actually eat what you are saying. Because the minute they start going of track your conversation will not be sweet no more, what you are saying will not be sweet to then. What are they hearing from you? Will not be sweet to them.

What are you hearing from them? Will not be sweet to you." I say. "Well, it is best to stay away from people who are not on the same road you are on.

The General says. "Unless they become on the same road you are on! You should not have to go off your road to go and talk to anyone. I should not come off my path to talk to you. That makes no sense.

If anything! You come off your road to talk to me. Because where am going. Makes more sense than where you are going!" "I see." I say. **"The General says.** "I might take you to the library, if you talk to me. I might take you back to school. If you talk to me. I might cost you to start thinking about life differently. If you talk to me.

If you talk to me? You will get something different than what you are used to. Are you willing? To go that route. Because I am not going your route. I have passed your route years ago. You are now at 35 thirty-five and still doing the things I was doing at twelve. "**The General says."** "Yes. Bless the Lord!" I say. **"The General says."** I can't go on that road no more. It is you know that has to come from a 12-year-old mentality. Up to a 45-year-old man. AND *THAT? IS HARD* For *SOME PEOPLE!* And it is hard for me to go and talk with a person with a 12-year-old spiritual mentality!

I see them as a grown man. It upsets me. As a grown woman. I see you as a grown women and as a grown man but you." I say. "Is G-D letting things be as they are? In terms of people being saved. Does G-D prefer to leave it as it is? Or is his preference for all to come to him?

The General says. "G-D's preference is for you to find him. Because it has to be your will, He does not mind you looking for him as long as you are looking for him for the right reasons. In other words, you can look for G-D because you believe that he has money. You are only coming because I've got money.

And you want some money from me. You want that. If you find me, you know. I wouldn't turn you down. If you find me? I wouldn't turn you down. So now. I don't even want you to find me. I give you. I have a standing order every time for you. That's to take care of all your NEEDS." I say. "Yeah, which is already established in G-D." **The General says.** "A standing order. I have for you." "Established in G-D." "OK." I say. **"The General says.** "What more do you want? From your NEEDS? You can get the things you WANT! You take your NEEDS and get the things you WANT! You understand?" I say. "OK." **"The General says."** You understand? "Yes" I say. **The General says.** "Now if you multiply your NEEDS properly and figure out from your NEEDS how you can grow and bountifully grow your WANTS out of the things you NEED. Out of the things you already have that G-D's given you."

I say. "That's right. Yes, you grow from what you already have to also fulfill your NEED and you've WANT. OK. And then the residue from NEED will take care of your WANTS." **The General says."** Right! You NEEDED a transportation, G-D blessed you with a Honda, right? "Yes" I say. You take that Honda. That Honda gets you to work on time. So, know you are making more money from the NEED that you had. And he blessed you with it. Right? **"The General says."** I say. "Right!"

"The General says." You work for a while. A year or two and drive that Honda. You sell the Honda what G-d gave you and you buy another car that you NEED because the Honda is getting old you can get rid of the Honda or turn it in. So out of your NEED comes a greater explosion of blessing from out of your NEED." I say. "And that is called want?" "NO! that is call your satisfaction! You are being satisfied! You are selling the Honda to get a brand new one." **"The General says.** I say. "I see, I see, it is an extension of blessing." "An extension of your NEED, and you come into your blessing, and you are following the map." **The General says."** I say. "Yes. So, the NEED took care of some of your WANTS and then your WANTS moves into an extended blessing, it keeps going like that?"

"You needed a car. He gave you one. You got a job. You NEEDED a job. He gave you that. You NEEDED a house. Through the job and the car. You got a house, right?" "**The General says.**" "Yes" I say. "**The General says.** "Now, you are paying for the house because you are getting to work on time, paying for the house and paying for the car. Your car now is paid for. Through the car itself being able to drive to work, and drive you back, G-D took care of all of that, take all the stress out of it, catching a bus or catching a ride, he killed that. Gave you the car, turn the key you make sure that car is running, you make sure the car has water. Cars don't want water, the car NEEDS water. The car doesn't WANT oil, the car NEEDS oil. The car doesn't WANT to run right, the car NEEDS to run right! So, you get the needs of the car meet! Then that car and that car NEEDS being meet? Your NEED will be meet. Which is getting to work on time. Get from work, go to wherever you WANT to.

You WANT to go to the movies, the car can do that, you WANT to go to the mall, the car can do that, you WANT to buy some pants, the car can do that, you WANT to go to a restaurant, the car can do that. You don't NEED more pants, you don't NEED to go to a restaurant, but you WANT to go, so out of your NEEDS comes your WANTS!" I say. "Bless the LORD." **The General says.** "You see! Now. The car is a little old now and you desire to get the upgrade. So, you still will NEED a car once you get rid of this old car, so you go ahead and go shopping and buy a truck you turn the Honda in and you drive out with a truck. Now this is a truck that you NEED because you have gotten rid of the Honda, and this would carry you even further. You see!" I say. "Yes."

"You needed a car in the beginning, you got Sam's car for a time and then G-D blessed you with your own car. You are still benefiting from the NEED that was fulfill! Which is your own car! "**The General says.** The General started my car for me, without having the remote charger or the keys. But through supernatural powers.

He made lightening flash from his right-hand finger to my car. Within a blink of an eye, he withdraws his hand and my car started with my keys in my backpack. As the teacher of my divine lessons, when he started my car? I got the point he was making, all around. Which made him a great teacher. My car never sounded more alive "it really had life." This is when I realize the perfect life form G-D give everything. And that perfect life form exist even greater inside of the thing/article or gift G-D has given you.

YOUR
BOOK

CHAPTER **XXXIII**

On June 29, 2016, during my lessons with **The General of The Most High G-D he says to me.** "If a person desires to do something good? Nothing should stand in their way. The kids book you will write will bring joy to kids. It will bring a sense of G-D and sense of good nature. I think you should write it! G-D has approved it! Now you should deliberate, put it before G-D your thoughts and then if he likes it, He will give you inspiration of how to write it. If he hates, it? He wouldn't even give you an inkling." **The General of The Most High G-D says.**

"About it again?" I say. **The General says.** "You can still write it. And it might be a best seller. But it might not be a book that he likes. Because it will be review or get the view of the world, those who doesn't know him will really like the book. Those who love G-D, isn't going to really care about reading the book. So, it is going to fulfill its purpose. If G-D is not in it? I don't want to read it.

If G-D has no inkling in the book. why should I read it? what is it going to do for me? Only the ones who are not in G-d will read it and like it. And that will throw them further away from G-D. Me not reading it and not liking it will draw me where? Closer right? **The General of The Most High G-D says.** "Not reading it?" I say.

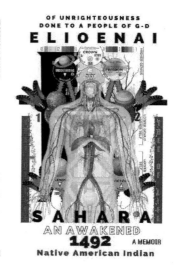

WHERE OTHERS ARE TAUGHT **OF THE CREATOR.**
ELIOENAI SAHARA WAS TAUGHT **BY THE CREATOR.**

OF UNRIGHTEOUSNESS
DONE TO A PEOPLE OF G-D

E L I O E N A I

S A H A R A
AN AWAKENED
1492   A MEMOIR
Native American Indian

"Those who read the book, are those who are not in G-D, they read it and they love it! The book has nothing in nothing! The book G-D never approved the book, so he never wrote anything in the book, he never gave any thoughts about anything in the book. The book has nothing to do with G-D, G-D has nothing to do with the book." **The General G-D says.** Others would be inspired in reading the book, because there might be some hidden stuff in the book for me, because I am in G-D. Those who are not in G-D, they will not find the pleasure of reading your book. Your book still can become the number one best seller, sell over 40 million. Without them even reading it! You See?

In other words, your book does not NEED help from anyone outside of G-D to bring success to it!" I say. "I see."

"It has already become successful because a book supposed to have readers who is going to attach itself to it. A book purpose is to attach readers who wants to find out what this book entails for them, so they read the book.

The book must have some attachment to them and what they desire to come out of the book for them. If they know there is nothing in that book for them, they will not read it! So, in that way, the book fulfills its purpose. For those who don't want to read it, don't read it! And those who want to read it, read it! But the book still becomes a #1 Best Seller." **The General says.**

"So, this book, it seems like, after hearing that, this book will attract people who have suffered identity issues, cultural assimilation, homelessness, who have suffered the joblessness, who have suffered medical issues, financial downfall, it will be more attractive to those one's who has suffer the same as I have, even spiritual, so it se it will be attaching people who have. Who I have had experiences like, right?" I say.

"Your book is going to attach G-D fearing people. Your book will not attract people who are not in G-D. Your book? It's like the bible attracting people who do not believe in G-D, whatever that bible has in that, a person who doesn't believe in G-D wouldn't find favor in that book to read it, it is just a natural thing!

But the Bible will fulfill its promise. It will come to me. Who have favor through G-D and who Love's G-D, who is in G-D, the Bible comes to me, the Bible when I read it, it draws me closer to G-D because I enjoy reading it? Those who don't want to read the Bible, have no desire to read the Bible, don't want to read the Bible, will not find pleasure reading it, because why? They are not of G-D!

But the Bible still will be the number one best seller, the number one most read book in the world, is the Bible. The number one most read book in the world is the Bible, even though folks don't love G-D and don't want to read it. It is not about who is downtrodden, and who has had down falls. It is about who is in G-D." **The General of The Most High G-D says.**

I say. "That he wants his information to get to?" **The General of The Most High G-D says.** "To get to!" I say. "I see." "Because they want this information to get close to G-D, they are not going anywhere else that would lead them away from G-D. They will go to the path that will lead them to G-D and it will bring G-D closer to them. Do you see!" I say. "I see!"

The General of The Most High G-D says. "Right! Yes...right! So, your kids' book. Is going to fulfill what it is supposed to fulfill. It will attract, if it is a book that G-D have insight in. G-D put verses in, and God put a few of his words and his light in that book? I would read the book because there will be life in there that was put there by G-D for me to see.

"Bless the Lord." I say. "I have experience that, I experience that in my earlier walk, when I was finding G-d. That I had done some reading, like if I was reading my Bible, there was a verse or one or two verses in the book, lines, sentences that would almost, like it illuminated or electrified just for me to pay attention." "Sparked your interest? **The General of The Most High G-D says.**

"Yes. Sparked my interest. Bless the Lord. And I kept on going. Yes. Yes." I say. "It brought you to a realization of something that you did not know, so, that is what the book is for, that is what is does. When you are in G-D, you find these things!" **The General of The Most High G-D says.** "Like hints, like clues. Yes." I say.

FACE
TO FACE

CHAPTER XXXIV

The General of The Most High G-D say. "Like I say, your book? A man who does not even know G-D, but believe in him, don't know him, but believe in him. In other words, he knows that those trees did not make themselves, right? So, he believes that G-D made them, he believes there is a G-D somewhere. He just doesn't know him, and he is not really checking to know him, he is too busy anyhow!" "Yes" I say.

The General says. "He wrote a book. Because he knows there is a G-D exist, everything he wrote in that book is going to be based on his believe, so he will never put anything in there that is going to contradict what he believes. He believes there is a G-D, so he will not put anything in there, or say anything to contradict what he believes. You, see?" I say. "Yes"

I would read that book because, the book would not have anything in there that contradicts or contains the disbelieve of G-D, even though he does not know G-D. He just believes that there is a G-D, that book will become a best seller also, even though people are not going to read it.

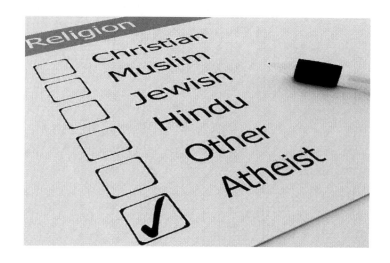

I might read it, the atheist out there might read it, you, see? because the guy, he doesn't know G-D. But he is closer to not believing than believing, but he knows that these trees did not make themselves, so there has got to be a G-D.

There will be a little bit in there for folks who don't believe in G-D. But it will also be something in there for me! I might see the part where he believes there is a G-D, but he doesn't know, I might be able to find him and take him to where G-D is. And show him the path of finding out. So now, the next book he writes could be a book that says "I found G-D, You understand?" So that is what I am saying, a hidden piece can be for me, that know G-D and that could be finding that same piece right there and going to find him and showing him where G-D is, because he has the basis, pure basis!

Find him and mentor him and the next book will be "I found G-D" I found him in the trees, I found him in the wind and found him in the waves, I found him in the fish, I found him in the voice, I find him in the air, I find him in the very clothes I wear.

So, now the atheist isn't reading that!" **The General says.** I laugh. **The General Laugh and says.** "So! That don't interest him no more, that vex him. I laugh. "So, he wouldn't be reading that anymore." **The General says.** The first one was OK., the second one!" **The General says.** "The first one was OK...the second one will kill him dead!" I say. "They wouldn't buy it?"

The General says. "They wouldn't buy it! Who will buy it? Who will buy it is me, it's you, the pastor, the preacher, the teacher, the evangelist, the kids who have grace with G-D, who have mercy with G-D, who is trying to learn who G-D is. The teenager, the youth pastor, the youth minister, so the book will still be what? A number one best seller." "Bless the Lord."

The General says. "Purpose is something you can't stop. Purpose! If this was made to stick on the windshield, purpose must stick on the windshield to actually accomplish its purpose, it will not work no were else, it would not look good on the outside of the car and the cellphone on the outside of the car, you are looking at it, inside, outside. Purpose fill! Give G-D what is his!"

I say. "And what is his? All he says is his!" **The General of The Most High G-D says.** "Whatever he says is his!" I say. "I Pray and I hope not to do anything different." **The General says.** "I know you do."

I say. "Well G-D told me "Prayer is for those who can't find him" I remember that! That is what he said to me. So, prayer is for those who can't find G-D."

So, I just said, I Hope, and I Pray. **But the Holy Spirit just said to me,** _"Prayer is for those who don't talk to G-D face to face."_ in other words, it is not for me. Bless the Lord. I said to The General. "That is what the Holy Spirit said to me just now."

The General says. "He also said that when you were in the park." I say. "Yes, and the spirit just brought it back into my remembrance. So, I don't need to pray, I do talk to G-D face to face."

The General says. "Yeah." I say. "I see the difference now, so that is what it meant when they were saying how Moses talk to G-D face to face? **The General says.** "Face to face...yeah!" *"It had to do with him saying something and it is happening so quickly!"* I say. **The General says.** "Or G-D responding to it quickly."

The General says. *"No! It happens just like how, you and I are talking now, that is how Moses would hear G-D, "just like this."* **The General says.**

"I know, that is how I hear G-D." I said. "That is mouth to mouth." **The General says.** "That is how I does hear him." I say. "That is what I am trying to say. That is how it is! Mouth to Mouth. No difference, it is mouth to mouth." **The General says.** I say. "I understand."

The General of The Most High G-D says. "You understand it is him! Because nothing bad comes from him." I say. "Yes, and it is kind of like hearing your mother or your daddy, you are used to hearing. Or your bother or your sister's voice, you know their voice. On the phone you know their voice. Even if their voice sometimes plays tricks on you, you would be like "I know that's you. So yes! I know The Creator's voice. That is how I am built, knowing it."

The General says. "That's how it is, and face to face is not just. It is deeper. You are also learning a way, but you are not all there yet!" I say. "Because it is deepened? I know G-D so many ways I can't count!" **The General says.** "It is!" I have experience G-D so many ways, I can't. There doesn't same to be a number, He laugh and says. "Bless the Lord."

The General says. "There is millions and millions, it is every way possible." "It is infinite ways." "Every way possible, there is no impossible way to see G-D, because he is in every eye blink, he is in the wink of the eye. For you to sit down and talk with G-D mouth to mouth, G-D! You can't be around people who? You can't be around anybody." **The General of The Most High G-D says."** Yeah." I say. **The General says.** "You can't be around anybody. "I say. "Is that what happen to Moses as well? He couldn't be around anyone because others didn't understand his ways?"

The General says. "In the cool of the day, G-D spoke with Adam when no one else was around. Eve was not even there, just Adam and G-D, as soon as he got a companion to talk with, to see, to talk with and to reminisce with? he forgot some of the teaching of G-D, which means his mind got distracted, when G-D came down to visit he was too busy." **The General says.**

"Is that what is happen now?" "That is what is happen now! *You will never get to talk with G-D mouth to mouth and face to face until you become like G-D."* **The General says.**

"OK so that is the ultimate face to face and mouth to mouth." I say.

"You have got to be like G-D!" **The General says.** "That would be the ultimate, meaning that would be it! Because see I know G-D, face to face, but I don't feel like G-D per say. So, there is still more I have to grow." "NO! G-D give you enough for you to recognize it is him." **The General says.** "And then after you recognize." I say. "That's it! He gives you enough to recognize it's him, through the voice, through the feeling, touch, the inkling, they are pieces, enough for you to service and understand that you have protection.

He comes to you in the vision and dreams he knows you, sitting down he knows you, go walking he knows you; he shows you. He does not have to come to you to tell you, that is him! Understand me! If G-D in the person over there, you will not know that he would have to come and tell you and show you he is in that person." **The General says.** "Yes, by that person deed or by that person...or something they might do or say. Right?" I say. **The General says.**" Right" "Or something they might say, or." "Right! Here it is! Here is being like G-D and there is a difference. He just showed it to me just now! I told you, he would come to you and show you indeed and actions that that is him." The General of The Most High G-D says. I say. "Yes"

The General of The Most High G-D says. "Well, you are walking, you and I are walking and a man sitting down with his head turn out to the river. He is just sitting here with a book in his hand reading the book, he did not give you any inkling that he wants to be bothered, that he is even checking for you and that he even notices us, nothing!

All you see is he is just a man sitting there, he gives you no action, no response, no nothing, right? Me! Who is like G-D go over to the man, sit down next to him and say. *"My*

LORD, blessed are though amongst men" what is it that THOU would have me to do? Do you understand what I am saying?" I say. "Ok so. So, you went to someone that was minding their own business?

The General says. I went over to G-D, so he didn't even show you that he was G-D. Didn't come to you and give you no inkling, didn't smile at you or nothing. Had his back turn to you looking over there. I say. "Right." "I left you where we were and I go over and sit next to him and say *"Father, blessed are **THOU** among men, what is it that **THOU** may have me to do?" I know that's G-D. I know that's him! Not just know it! I see him, because I am like him. You see me, you see the Fathar, you see the Fathar, you see me!*

You and I can be sitting over there on the chair and a man or a women can walk up to us with our back turn towards them and walk up to you and say *"Blessed are **THOU** among men" and immediately we would know that, that's my G-D.* Because he came right over to me, you did not give them any inkling that it's me, but they walked right over to me and when he spoke to us, he spoke to G-D, mouth to mouth." **The General says.** "I see." I say.

The General says. Not flesh to mouth, but the spirit takes over the hold situation G-D does that! See, OK. your mother! Your mother sitting down over there on the bench and your daddy is here and you are walking from over there, you know your mother from back on, your daddy you know him from back on, if he turns around it is just a plus, he is giving you for you to know that is him. Maybe he doesn't think you know that it's him, sitting down so be turns around. "OK so I get it." I say. "So, he turns around just so you can see him." **The General of The Most High G-D says.** I say. "OK so G-D does that?" **The General says.** "G-D does that, but that is a deeper thing." I say. "Right! That's when you have come into G-D." "That is when you have come into G-D like." **The General says.** I say. "OK" **The General of The Most High G-D says.** "You are G-D like, you are like G-D! In other words."

I say. "I knew that that exist upon the earth, but I didn't know that I - I mean like you had said before, I might be or will be the first. I thought other people. That." "It must be somebody. if you did not hear what you heard through the vessel of G-D this morning you would have never known your purpose. **The General says.** "Know I wouldn't have known it! But I have been asking so I still thank G-D for it." I say.

"So, G-D has given you the answer! *Now through you! The World can be blessed! I am just a vessel that brings to you a niche, that can sew up everything and seal it."* **The General says.** "What vessel?" I say. **The General says.** "I am just a vessel, the Light! The vessel that brings you the pieces that can sow everything together **The General says.** "Yes. With what you are bringing and what I have." I say.

The General says. "What you have, and what I am bringing, we can sow it together." "Bless the LORD!" I say. **The General of The Most High G-D says.** *"You have because you seek! You have because you seek! One seeks, and one is Open...One is! And one is going to be! I might be what I am, you might not be what you are!"* I say. "I Bless the General of The Most High G-D; who shows me wondrous things."

"You understand? It is almost like, I am what I am, you understand who I am, therefore, I fulfill it!" **The General says.** I say to The General. "Hear Oh General of The Most High, You fulfill your purpose with vengeance General. Yeah! I thank The Most High G-D for THEE." I say. "So where

384

are we off to next General for more teaching? Where are we off to next General? **The General says.** "Well we are off to the shelter to eat!" I laugh. And we were off to the shelter to eat.

"Wherever you are going. You just better make sure. You can find your way, back home. If there is nothing there for you to eat, drink some hot water." **The General says.** "Instantly I started to sing, dance and clip my fingers. Singing. "It is soon time now, my master will come; and spring me out the shelter. It is soon time now; My Master will come. And spring me out the shelter."

The following day, I received a call from The Human Resources Department of a certain company that I had applied for a job. They asked me if I wanted to fly or drive to the job which was nine hours away, that accommodations were also awaiting me there; and a daily stipend of over $300.00 Dollars I would receive during training. I had no place to leave my vehicle, so I started the journey. One hour into the journey I observed my tire was slashed; I felt I was not going to make it; but had already given up my room at the shelter, I prayed to The LORD. I say. "Fathar let me not be put to shame, for **THOU** art my rock and my fortress, for in **THEE** do I place all my trust. Hide me in the secret place of thine own pavilion, in your shadow oh Most High do I ask for safety, that none might touch your anointed and do your daughter no harm.

I made it safely to the city that was nine hours away on the very same slashed tire. And the air never came out of the tire. Until I was at the repair shop parked safely.

SPACE
TIME

CHAPTER **XXXV**

On September 15th, 2016, I had a feeling, I was an Oracle an interpreter of Element, Space and Time. I also forgot that there was no thought that was secret from the General. Though I did not speak my thoughts out loud. The General of The Most High G-D says to me. "It is more like an interpreter of element, space and time. They will read into something, years further, years further. That's element space and time, and when they read or see it, they do not just go and try to find the meaning of it. They don't just spread it around trying to find what it means; they already know what it means. They already know, what it means.

So, they will wait until that particular thing show up and reveal itself and they still will not say what they know concerning the thing because if it's...if an oracle see ahead that this building is suppose or would be owned by me, this was seen years ago. I at the time, was only six or seven years old."

"OK, so I understand, so that is what an oracle does." I say. **The General of The Most High G-D says.** "That's an oracle! She sees further ahead; she sees me from me to there. Let's just say, from this leg. She sees between space and time. From this leg to that leg is what she sees as the building. This led to the building, she sees me in stages." **The General says.** I say. "Space and time and even further in the distance."

The General says. "Nothing can detour her from that. And even if I tell her, even if I say to her "I like that building, but I don't know, I would like to own something like that" she will never tell me, "Yes, you will! She might say something like "You never can tell" You, see? Never! Never! Can Tell? She might say, "Never can tell!" "So, what does that mean, "Never, can tell?" I say. **The General says.** "I never can tell you, you will own that building. You might say, "well, I will never be able to own that building. And she might lean in and say, "You never can tell" and he or she has to say it like that so you will never figure out, I can never tell you that, that building is yours." I say. "Because they did not believe it, you can't ever tell them that?"

The General of The Most High G-D says. "NO! the word is "I, OK let me put it down. if you say "I will never own that building? It is too expensive. I will never own something like that. And I come to you and I say. "Well, I will not tell you that, that building is yours" But that building is your son, that's yours.

What an oracle would say to a child is. "Well. You never can tell." What is means is "son, if I can tell you that you own this building, I would tell you. But I really can't tell you that you own this building. Never can tell! Through spiritual understanding, I understood that Yahweh through this was telling me that we his people have full ownership of all that is within the world."

The General of The Most High G-D continued and says So now when someone says that to you, you've got to switch that to where, they can't tell me that it is mine, by telling me, "they can't tell me that's mine! It is almost like getting terminated to go put an application in at a certain time, and them go from that time to another little time, to end up here!

If someone was to say to you, "Elioenai, you are going to get fired from one job, you are going to go to the Motel, you are going to be homeless and stay in the Motel for three or four days, within those 3 or 4 days, you will already have somewhere to stay, but you are still going to stay at the motel until the ending of the week. Then after that, they will call you, while you are at the shelter and offer you a job to work as an Executive. I say. "I get it! I wouldn't have believed if! Right?"

The General says. "How would you? How would you have believed something like that?" "You See? So. that is the way an oracle keeps things, they never can tell you anything...no matter how you ask. You will not even know that they know."

So, I say. "So, what is the use for them? If they can't tell you what they see and know, then what is their use?" **The General says.** "Their use is their patience, their grace, their love, their admiration, their gift, their spiritual insight, their spiritual enlightenment, it's their aura, you just want to be around a person like that. I say. "OK...So it isn't for them to tell somebody what they see, in the distance for their life."

"No! The person automatically will be around them, and whatever little bit they can give them, they will give them." **The General says.** "I say. "If I had it my way, I would have told people what I see...if they are with me...even if am passing them and I see something, I would tell them what I see. Now you are saying that is not the way. Yeah? You don't think G-D will tell me, if I will have a billion dollars next ten years? You don't think G-D knows? Yeah? And he knows, and he will not tell me. Judge anyone else who does know, do you think they will go against G-D?, go over G-D? and tell you what is happening in the future? The most they can say to you is well, you never can tell." **The General says.** I smiled, then I laugh and say. "I didn't know it was not G-D's will that you did not tell."

If you tell me that I am going to die tomorrow, I will try to find the holiest of holiest man in the world to pray with me." **The General says.** I smiled at the General and say. "Yeah!" **The General says.** "It will take the joy out of living! It takes

390

the joy out of living when you know, when you are going to die!"

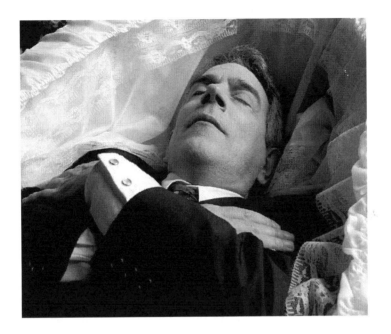

I say. "OK, so I will keep everything I see and do not share it with the person. And if it is something that is information for the time, then use it for my best and..." **The General of The Most High G-D say.** "That is why I say to you. I can truly say that we are Oracles in a sense."

MOST
UNFORTUNATE

CHAPTER XXXVI

On September 15, 2017, **The General says.** "That *is* the only way man obey G-D. You and I obey G-D in so many ways. He doesn't need to tell us "Stop" in anything we are doing, or "freeze" or put your hands up, you're under arrest, Don't Move! "The General smiled. I laughed. "He doesn't really need to tell us that. Because we respect him. We understand him. We love him. We trust him. We will go beyond for him. We just love all of him.

Some don't care where G-D is. They don't care what he is. They don't care. That is why for them they will hear. "Freeze, put your hands up." That is the only way men obey G-D. Is when they are dealt with ruff.

And when we must clap then. "Shout Up" shout your f**king ass up!" **The General of The Most High** Laugh. I laugh also because it was real; but funny in the moment just to hear such strong speech from G-D's General." **The General of The Most High G-D says.** "You need to stop f**king around. Get your f**king ass out here. That is the only way they do obey G-D. The General smile. Then laugh. I laugh and say. "Now that's funny, you mean ruff treatment,

393

right? The Humans need ruff treatment from y'all? That is the only way they'll obey?"

The General says. "And you know what they say?. Alright Sir G-D. Alright Sir G-D. Please don't kill me. Stupid ass. That is when G-D get mad with you. Just get tired of your shit! Believe it or not, that is the only way Satan can't get in to catch a soul. G-D beating you. G-D talking with you. Then he will arrest you. Charge you."

I couldn't believe what I was hearing. I laugh and then I said. "Yeah! And after the arrest. And the charge. Then G-D throw you in jail." **The General says.** "Then throw you in jail? G-D owns the jail. Then sit you down to talk with you. They call for a lawyer. That's G-D. G-D is the judge, your lawyer and the other lawyer."

Words. You are getting beat up with words. And G-D say "150 years plus 10 consecutive life sentences. That's what G-D give you. Because why? You are not even trying to get to know him. You are not even trying to understand who he is. When it's all G-D orchestrated.

You say "look here, look here G-D, boy G-D, go from round me, you hear?" **The General of The Most High G-D** started Laughing. And I laugh also. The General of The Most High G-D laugh so long, he started leaning over with laughter and says." "Boy look here." and then he started crying with laughter. The General of The Most High G-D says. "I... tell...you. I tell you. That is why we does have to beat some men bad. They say look here. _Look here boy G-D._ _Go from round here_. Then he goes round the corner and a fella say. Look here boy. Come here boy. That is G-D now calling him boy. Give me a dollar? I think you know his response. It's "boy I don't have any money." **The General of The Most High G-D Illustrated and says.** "WOOCH...G-

D snatch that dollar and carry that money from his hand."
While laughing I say. "Yeah! it's G-D now again right

General? this time running down the hill with his money? I began to laugh. **The General of The Most High G-D says.** "He stands right there cursing G-D. Your stinking f**king ass. The General Laugh. He says. "You stay right f**king there. Am going to kill f**king you… He *loses that one!* He goes down the road a little further, see one of his friends that ask him for a little something. His responds. "Man, I just got robbed, I don't have any money boy.

He just finished cursing G-D "your stink f**king ass." Now he doesn't know G-D is there again! asking him for something. He started talking about, "man I don't have

anything, I just got robbed" *the friend(G-D) says.* "You just got robbed? **The General of The Most High G-D made an ILLUSTRATION), while throwing blows**. He says. "You aren't got no money to give me? You just got robbed? The friend(G-D) put blows on him and say. "*Boy come out this yard!*"

The General says. "G-D is so busy beating these people and they don't even now...that is serious yeah? it might sound like a joke...but it's very serious. People thing Satan's beating them, Satan is a joke. He on the side saying "Look here y'all. Look here man y'all come this way. Ya hear? come this way!. (The General Laugh). And I laugh also. I started laughing out loud. Then I said, "My LORD? It's G-D!." **The General of The Most High G-D says.** "Satan over there talking about "come this way man" all this over here is yours. And then when you go over that side where Satan is, and you're sitting among your friends who you were friends with for so long and then you miss and holler.

I said, "But they don't know any better! They don't know that the scenarios in which they are going through was G-D orchestrated!" **The General says.** "G-D orchestrated." I said, "But they do not know that it's G-D, they think because some fool come and say to them, "Boy you are the unluckiest. You must have eleven years of bad luck to have all these bad things happen to you."

I laugh and said, "Someone will say to him. "Boy you break any glass lately? Your luck is so bad. But see they actually catching hell in The LORD, Most High. And don't know they are catching hell in The LORD. They don't know. People just don't know!"

The General says. *"They don't know nothing about love, I tell you! Mankind's doomed!"* I say. "But shouldn't that save some? Who doesn't know that information right there? About all things being G-D orchestrated?"

The General of The Most High G-D says. "OK, here it is right, you getting beat dead bad getting bombarded, right? Satan calling "Come on this side boy. They trying to kill you over there." When you go on that side, know you now, you got friends, you just turn yourself over to the Devil, you are among you've friends them. Now here comes the word. With all kinds of sword. Here comes the word. With all kinds of swords. You've sitting among your friends and you howler out, "I don't believe in G-D. I don't believe in G-D. Who me? I am an atheist. Now, all your friends will get up and leave you by that table. The General of The Most High G-D laughed out loud. I say "Because _all_ of them is G-D?" **The General of The Most High G-D laugh then says.** "All of them is G-D. And they will say to you while getting up from the table. Look here man, Don't even come around my house. Don't even come around my children. Don't come around anything. Big man, if I see you around my yard or even around my corner? I will do you! You don't believe in G-D? They will tell him, "I see why you are going through hell now." **The General says.** I say. "I didn't think G-D could have taken the form of someone who curse?"

The General of The Most High G-D says. "They are words! They exist, they still belong to G-D love." **The General when further saying.** "They exist. They belong to him. How the hell else you are going to listen to some people?" I laugh. **The General says.** "You can't listen to some people calm." I say. "Well Bless the LORD" **The Gene-**

ral says. "Go to some people like this. Excuse me sir. Good morning. Can I get? And before you can finish. Their like, "listen get your. Before I slap the f**k out you!" The General of The Most High G-D did laugh out loud. I laugh. I thought to myself. "I don't know G-D had jokes like this on mankind's behavior toward each other. It was funny"

The General was expressing to me through a joke that people are not giving other people the opportunity to be heard. And the benefit of the doubt. People are prejudging others. **The General of The Most High G-D looked at me and says.** "Yeah." Which was in response to my personal silent thought about G-D. And the fact that he had jokes. The General said "Yeah" to let me know that it was obvious G-D was funny, and had jokes. So, the General read my thoughts again. **Then he went further and says.** "Same fellow that

curse at you? Stop to the traffic light and someone hold him up and say. Look here, give me all you've got. You got to talk hard enough know for him to listen, He who was hard before? The next man needs to talk harder than him for him to listen."

"OK, so you have to talk harder than the hardest he. To get him to listen?" I say. **The General of The Most High G-D says.** "There is no man, that is harder than G-D. You curse the fellow that came to you calm and peaceful for a dollar. You run him. You wanted to tear his head off. The fellow by the light, pull gun on you and ask you for all of your money." "Yeah, and that's G-D." I say. **The General of The Most High G-D says.** "Now the fellow who slap you take all your money. He is walking the street. Big and bold. All he hears is "wooh, wooh. **The General laugh and says**. "Now that is the police now."

I say. "G-D orchestrated." "G-D orchestrated." **The General of The Most High G-D says.** I say. "G-D's big time.

G-Ds beyond radius. "G-D's BIG TIME, BEYOND RADIOUS." **The General of The Most High G-D says.** I answered The General and said. "That is why it is said. "FEAR THE LORD, FEAR THE LORD." **The General says.** "Don't Just fear him. Know why you fear him. To fear G-D is the beginning of wisdom."

I say. "That is why it was being preached so much to fear G-D. This is why that is echoing through time. This is why. _That is a serious warning **"fear G-D."**_ if G-D do all those things and go through all those things, and exist in all those things? "FEAR G-D." "Nothing is without power." **The General says.** "It is dimensional, dimensions." I say. "No. Dimensions make mention. With dimension." I say. "Dimensions make mention. That is a serious thing. G-D will blow your mind. **The General of The Most High G-D says.** No man's mind is stronger than G-D own."

The General says. "NO. Do you know who G-D is? Do you know where G-D is? Do you know what he is? All of those are words that need to be answered. That is why you cannot question G-D. You will be questioning G-D with his own question. You looking for an answer with his own answer? G-D cannot question G-D with the words of G-D; if the word is G-D, you can't question G-D with his word. How could you question. Question? **The General of The Most High G-D**, showed frustration. Then he hiss his teeth (suck his teeth). He said, "Can you imagine? What's your name? no what's your name? Then he laughs out loud."

"Yeah, because that is the Creator talking, so G-D what's your name? supersedes the created saying, "What's your name, because G-D is greater than the created." I said, that is true. Through wisdom that just befall me. I see. And I understand." **The General says.** "You can't ask G-D who he is. No. Who you is? No. Who are you? No. Who you is? Now.

When you get tired of that same response either you just sit down and take a rest, or my first thought would be that G-D would get tired of hearing that." **The General of The Most High G-D says.** "And just slap you upside your head with punishment. I say. "When you least expect it."

The General of The Most High G-D, Myki'EL/Michael says. "I tell you. You cannot question who G-D is. I said. "Well sounds like the best thing a person can do as a human being is peacefully live through the circumstances that they are in, and wait on G-D."

MONEY
EXPANDS

CHAPTER **XXXVII**

The notes I wrote in my journal on September 24, 2016, was brought to me through The Holy Spirit of The Most High G-D as a reflection for me to understand that people are not thinking consciously.

"Things have changed from the demographic of people, that would mind the bling or the shininess of objects, things (an item). Things have changed! "By the time things have flowed right in and open up like living water. By that time? You would have already had a head start **The Holy Spirit, sent from G-D says to me."** **During my lessons with The General of The Most High on October 28th, 2016** I say to The General. "So now, if money could get you, money just expands you, because if money could get you." No without money, you will for example walk or go to the neighborhood park and sit down right there in the open air, because that is free. And talk to the birds or look at them because you wanted to see birds in the first place.

Moneys. No that one is just free, the first one. Money can get you to the park the one that you pay for, the cab can wait for you there and carry you from the park with a taxi to even a zoo to see more birds, that is what money can do. *Money expands you....* So really you shouldn't grow then, you should expand! grow is going up, expand is from the side right?

The General of The Most High G-D says to me. "Well, my love! My love? You have already expanded, if I may say so." "I smiled and say. You may, yes you may." "You have already expanded, money makes these things easier in the natural for you to have, it separates the have, and have not. The hardships for getting it, its! money is this. You and I go to an appointment, I don't have a car, but you have one and our appointment is nine o clock. I have no money, but I can walk to my appointment, you have money, so money allows you to have the kind of transportation that you need to make getting to that appointment easy.

I have it hard. Because I have a lack of money or no money at all. Your money makes it easier for you to get to that appointment and you very well could get the job. **The General says.** "OK...money makes it easy for me to get to that appointment." I say. "Yeah, it makes it easy. It makes getting...it enhances your tentacles. You as a person." **The General of The Most High G-D says.** "So, money is tentacles?" I say.

"Money is like long arms! Because everybody wants it! If you were the only one who had money, you would be it! It does not change who you are, it makes who you are more visible, more....whatever the more is...it enhances you...if your name was just Elioenai Sahara, when I see you, I will say Ms. Sahara, open the car door for you because the car is a Rolls Royce, Then I will spread the red carpet out for you because you can't put your foot on the ground, then the two big door, the two sliding door they are made out of solid oak, so you need two persons to open then, the lock itself you have to actually press the button for the doors to open and the door are almost four inches thick.

When you walk inside your palace, your palace is decorated with gold from the front to the back even the floor is the best porcelain tiles money can buy. You, see? That's money, you, see?" **The General of The Most High G-D says.** I laugh and say. "OK, so what is the point?"

The point is, money enhances this, who you are! And it can be easily mistaken as a G-D. But G-D loves a wealthy man because he gives him wealth...It just enhances who you are, if you were a mean person and you have money, you will just be a meaner person. If you were a kind person with money, you will just be a kinder person with money. You know?"

"Body, Mind, Spirit and Soul, all of them have a part, but all of them must become ONE! All must become one. If you have money and all of them is one, even G-D will sit down and smile with you, because..." **The General says.**

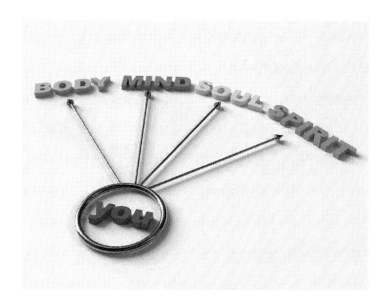

I say. "If all of what is one?" "If your body, mind, spirit and soul is one, one unit." **The General of The Most High G-D says.** "Body, mind, spirit and soul, if all of them is one, G-D. Because your soul is that connection to G-D, it doesn't stop or leave G-D's connection that is automatic, nothing can stop that connection, but spirit your body and your mind must become subject, all have to be one unison you can't feel what you want to feel and then your brain..." **The General of The Most High G-D says.** "In one unison for what?" I say.

"For the. For the unity. _For the unity of perfection._" **The General of The Most High G-D says.** "OK...so this is not the full unity yet then?" I say. "No...some people could actually. I mean they need to control the four. The four is not in control. They just need to control the four." **The General of The Most High G-D Myki'EL/Michael says.** I say. "Four?" "OK" I say. "Or OK, Body, Mind, Soul and Spirit?"

The General of The Most High G-D says. "Right, yes! *Your body is a house that houses the Spirit. Your body must be. Well, you must eat the right food. The right weight. The right temperature. The right breathing. Your heart must be good. Your knees must be kept properly. You can't have any infections in your knees. Your body all those things have to be perfect. For your body to actually house those three."* **The General says.** I say. "Those four you mean?" "Those three because your body is one of them!" **The General of The Most High G-D says.** "Oh...OK.... those three." I say. **The General of The Most High G-D says.** "Once you get your body together then your spirit..." The General Illustrated showing me fingers. I say. "OK the body is the pinky finger, and the spirit is the finger before the thumb?" "If this is G-D (The thumb he was holding. Then this is the spirit. The next finger. Then this is the soul, this is the mind, and This is the body. Back to the pinky finger."

The body is going to even everything up. Your body had to be perfect in order to house these three. Once your body is the right weight. The right temperature. The right food you're eating. The right water you're drinking. Your teeth are good. Your mouth smells good. Your heart is pumping right. Your lungs are right." The General gave me an illustration. Then **The General of The Most High G-D says to me.** "This is your body. This house. Your pinky finger is body. Your spirit is what drives you to accomplish certain things. Have you ever hear someone say. "Boy, you're a go-getter? or Elioenai, you're a go-getter? I hear you say many times. "I push you to do your best" *That is my spirit! That is my drive! I do not except failure. I do not except certain thing. That's MY SPIRIT! My mind is what direct the attitude or the temperature.*

My mind directs my attitude on how this (my spirit) will go about getting what it needs or if it goes behind it angry it is because of this. The General showed me an illustration. So, I pointed at the finger in The Generals Illustration view and I say. "This one is what?"

The General of The Most High G-D continues. He says. "This is the spirit. "OK" I say. "This one is the mind. This is your thinking cap. If you're thinking. Your mind controls your attitude. Your attitude your posture. Your anger your frustration all of that comes out of here. And if this here makes this frustrated. The drive for this will be Anger. It may accomplish certain things. But it will twist it. In a wrong and a negative way because this controls that." **The General says. "**I say, "I see."

The General of The Most High G-D says If this. Put a calmness on the drive that this has. Then this will accomplish it in servility. In joy and in fulfillment. Because this has every attitude you can put on it. It comes from here. You buck your foot, and you curse and carrying on. It is this! The Mind. The mind controls." "OK...it's the third finger." I say. "It's your mind. Your soul is right next to G-D" **The General says.** "OK.... Your soul is the one to the top." "Your soul is the one that would actual, that covers." **The General says.** I say. "Oh, I see."

"Your soul had grace, mercy. It has truth, it has holiness. Holiness. Wellness. Connection to G-D. It has the power to see what is going to happen with the mind and what is going to happen to the spirit." I smiled and say. "I see. That is the left hand." "What is going to happen to the body. It controls. It actually sends. It gives advice to control the whole entire bod. Because G-D is looking for it to be ONE." **The General says.** "Yeah. I see." I said. **The General of The Most High G-**

D says. "You, see?" I say. "Yeah!" "So, if this is one. Then G-D can flow freely." **The General says.** The General illustrated for me. Five fingers open and then a picture of five fingers close. I say. "I see"

The General says. "You, see? So, if this is one? Then G-D can flow freely through your whole body and have use of it. He can flow and have use of it. Your limbs and everything. This is what is called. Giving him your whole. All of you! You, see? Because you are in good shape. He loves that. You have a good drive. So, if he needs you to accomplish something, this is going to do it. And if he needs you to accomplish it in a certain way. This is going to put the attitude and the fire and the karma in it. You, see? And this is going to actually be the one to get to where the glory." The General Illustrated for me and he says. "The one by the thumb on the left hand. He can't come in this. He can't come to this unless this has all of these members together. This is like when G-D comes you kneel! When G-D come you bow. Those members must be together! Sometimes when G-D come in and he is dealing with you Elioenai? I don't pay attention; I stay out of the way. You know?

I laugh loudly. The General in so many words told me. That he didn't want to get hurt by G-D for being in G-D's way. Anytime G-D came to visit with me. So, when Holy Fathar, The Creator comes to me? The General of The Most High G-D Myki'EL/Michael. A Kachina, flees my presence. Because of his fear of G-D.

Which I though was extremely funny to hear from The General. Whose name meaning is. "He Who Is Like G-D."

Which meant to me that G-D was running away from himself danger of G-D. Because of fear of himself. That was a double funny joke made by Holy Fathar G-D. Because he knew I would get it. I said. "So He who is like G-D. Runs away from G-D because of his fear of G-D?." Now that is funny stuff, I said." While I laugh.

The General of The Most High G-D says to me while smiling. "I dare not get involve. When G-D comes to you?. I stay to myself."

HIS LOVE

CHAPTER XXXVIII

During Meditation with the thumb on October 28, 2016. This is what The Spirit of The Most High G-D delivered unto me. I begin to rub the base of the fingers. The spirit or whichever one of the fingers, The spirit. The mind. The body. And the soul. Whichever one you want to activate or re-activate like starting an engine? You do this when you are exercising the body. During this 2-minute meditative exercise. I belch. it seems this exercise makes everything well with your body. I remember thinking that. Then I say. "Bless the LORD" During the spiritual illustration my arm felt mechanical. This is also why. They used to wash their hands so much and wash it from all the way to the elbow. This is also why they us to wash their hands before they would go to G-D. To pronounce cleanliness among the members.

Everything was the washing of the hands before you preach or teach others. This is why. I Blessed The LORD for the information. Once you attached yourself to something? The end result of attaching yourself to something is. Let's say you attach yourself to a car. When you come out of a shopping center. The car you love has been totaled and is a burning inferno. You will scream loud. And show your pain.

So, when you attach yourself to something whether it is good or bad. Whether you scream with Joy or scream with anger. When you scream with anger. You will get things that

are angry. And some with very well be angrier. When you scream with joy then you will get happiness, peace, kindness. **The General says."** _So, whatever you come out of yourself as? You are going to get that right back._ **That is the Law of the Earth."** It is the way it's said "what goes around? Comes around." I say to you. As I live. _"What comes out of you, Goes right back into you. You cannot pass you! You live you. Every single day!_

The General says. "On these streets, you can get everything taken from you just like that, and you can't even do anything about it because you probably even didn't see them take it, you don't know who's got it, you don't know who steal it...so...so...you can't even do anything about it...that's a serious thing. G-D repeated something that I had said back then. I was taken by the fact that he could repeat what I said back to me, through The General, so perfectly." I say. "G-D can repeat his own words perfectly I said to the General." **The General say.** The words come from your mouth with power, Let's say we argue in here and you say "Get Out!" I say. "Get out has to come?"

 The General says. "Get out has to come...Now it is my part now to compete with get out? I tell get out. You can't put me out. I am not going anywhere." "Why is it? Because it is your nature?" I say. **The General says.** "No, because it is a word. It is a word you use to fight against another word. They are battling."

 You send, get out at me to put me out. I send, I am not leaving or going anywhere back at you. So, he is going to fight get out! You, see? Now, those two words by themselves, only fight among themselves. But the two, there is no win in there. They are not going anywhere you, see?

The longer I resist "Get Out?" The easier it would be for me to get out. And the hardest for me to come back in. Do you understand? "Yes" I say. **The General says.**" The longer I argue with you concerning leaving, the longer I argue with you? the easier it is going to be for me to leave. The next thing is you might even throw something at me, you might go for a gun. Humans are a very complex creature. Very complex. G-D made them powerful in their own rights with unthinkable strength. Because you are what you are. You are who you are Body, Mind, Spirit, Soul. **The General says.**

"Now is that everybody? Or is that just people G-D Love?" "G-D put himself in every man." **The General says.** "In all men then? In all manner of man." I say. **The General says.** "All manner of Man. G-D put himself in them." "OK." I say.

"And G-D is Love. He puts himself in you. Then you must have love too. It is in you! G-D is the whole being of a Man. He puts himself. His stamp. He puts in you. You are owned by him. That is his stamp because every part that is in you, he created, your sinuses, your cells, organs...you, see?" **The General says.** I say. "So, it is just the will that we have to go our own way?" "Yes! and in the words that are out here for you to use. You chose the words that will get you closer to him." **The General says.** I say. "Yeah. OK." "You chose the words that will put you in his arms. And You? Because you have power in you. You put power to the words that push you closer to his arms. In other words, _if love is a word. You put the power of G-D's love behind the love. So that it will make the love greater towards him._ You understand?" **The General says.** I say. "NO! put G-D's love behind the love?" **The General says.** "Action of Love is within you. But

421

you give that love to G-D. The one up here that you own. You give that to him, you understand? The one that he owns that is in you. Is stronger than the one that is out here.

You can love a dog. You can love a cat. You can love an animal. You can love a stranger that is out here. That is that one. The one in you is the strongest of all of these. It is like. if this one is a few. This one inside covers all of them. This is the one that makes all of those great. If you add this one to anyone of them. This one will make all of them GREAT! You, see? I can love a puppy or a dog. But I don't have to call him my son." **The General says.**

I say. "I see. So how I am a manager? I have to match something up with me whether it's a organization or a helping others course or something to make myself even greater? Right, or no?" **The General says.** "OK. Those things do make you greater my Love. But it is a different concept.

They are enlarging your vineyard.   They enlarge your vineyard. You, see?

Your Love. Which is your own choice to love, and the love G-D put out here in the universe that keeps everything else balance. The love of a dog. Cat animal lovers. Your love for G-D supersedes that!   That is just the thing that is out there for everybody to have." I say. "It is out there for everybody to have. And mine supersedes that?"

"The love that I have. Supersedes any other love that I have. Because I give my love and attach my love to G-D's love? When I attach my love to G-D's love it increases my love because there is an increase in *HIS LOVE*.

If out there is just the love for animals. My love towards the animals will be greater to where if the animals dies and I lay hand on the animal G-D will give him back his life…. Do you understand what am saying?" **The General says.** I say. "Yes" "That is greater than the love what he has out here…You see? The love here is just the love." **The General says.** I say. "OK…so it is the one in here?" "The one in here is the one that gives life to the love that he has already put in you." **The General of The Most High G-D says.** I say. "I see. The one in your chest. The one in your body?" "The love. Him. I will say the soul of G-D. The soul that is in you." **The General says.** I say. "So, the soul illuminates out of the flesh?" **The General says.**" Yes" I say. "It ignites? The soul ignites?" "Yeah, and anything what gets to the soul?. *The soul ignites it because the soul is G-D, and it belongs to G-D*. That is where all the ingredients is. Where all the speaking and the teaching is there." **The General says.**

"I see. So, *the soul is a speaker?* Like the set that you turn up?" I say. **The General says.** "Yeah. *It's an amplifier*." I laugh and say. "OK amplifier. You know am not well versed in these things." **The General of The Most High G-D says.** "It has the power to ignite." "OK" I say. "So, where another person would actually." **The General of The Most High G-D says.** "Can it also be considered a "frequency?" I say. "It is ever present!" **The General says.** I say. "Is G-D pleased with the word frequency? Sending out like a shock wave?" "Is he pleased with that being a comparison? frequency?" I say. **The General says.** "Is the shock wave about greater or less?" "I was just about to say how psychics talk about frequency and channeling and frequency and thing. Does any of that have to do with any of that we were just talking about?"

"Yeah!" **The General of The Most High G-D says.** "So, frequency is an OK word to use or?" I say. "No, I wouldn't say it is OK. **The General of The Most High G-D says.** You know in the Bible it is said, even the dog desire the crumbs from his master's table?" OK...consider the frequencies that they talk about the mystical frequencies that you can go from here in your body and travel." **The General says.** I say. "Yeah" **The General says.** "OK, consider them fragments, they are so small and minute they are unseen

fragments. They are there but they do not pose as no harm, they are worse than a yearling. I say. "Worse than what you can see with a telescope?" "Yeah…. you need two telescope to see them." **The General of The Most High G-D says.** I started laughing. I say. "Sound like you need a divine telescope."

"And that's divine. And you can barely see it through that. Which means, if you barely see it through that. "**The General says.** I say. "Which means that there is a lot going on!" **The General says.** "NO! But it is up to you to make it as big as you want. Or as small as you want. *BE IT UNTO YOU!*" **The General says.** "The reason I say. They are so small and minuscule. I can barely see them. It is because in my eyes G-D." I say. "I don't know how to ask for it. Or it is not something to ask for? "It is not something to ask for. It is something to bring something to." **The General says.** "The

mind. The spirit. It brings all of them together yeah?" I say. **The General of The Most High G-D says.** "Bringing all of them together to decide. If this tool, we are going to use to combat this ship." I say. "All they. They all agree." "Yeah. And they all agree." **The General says.** "OK, so that's body, mind, soul, spirit."

The General illustrated and showed me the working of the fingers as it pertained to the mind, the body, the soul and the spirit, and G-D. During this lesson. I wrote notes in my journal, and I said to The General. "G-D is desiring for all of them to get together. Because it is for our BEST! And then he can come through. Stay where the blessing flow freely. Make your life peaceful to live in. The story of one's life is the path one take in understanding what matters the most! Then **The General says**. "This is the way that G-D is. We all have to be together."

DANGLING
DANGLING

CHAPTER XXXIX

A mother will always ask. "How you are doing. Are you OK? And no matter how much you hid it. She will know." **The General says.** "That's how you know a mother yeah? So, what was my mother?" I say. "Your mother was always jealous of you and your grandmother's love. It had nothing to do with her love." **The General says.** I say. "Her mother's affection for me. She was jealous?" "She was jealous of your grandmother's love towards you. So, she had no space in her heart to motherly treat you. She treats you like an adopted stepchild." **The General says.** "She did!" I say.

"Because you favored your grandmother Mamie more than her and she knew this because your grandmother favored you. More than her. The grandmother was using her to carry your food and even wouldn't ask her. If she wants something to eat." I laugh softly and I say. "That's the truth. That's the truth." **The General says.** " You, see?"

"So, you mean, I had all of that happening?" I say. **The General says.** "Yeah! You had your mother treating you like a stepmother or like a stepchild." I say. "Like the Cinderella child, because that is how I was feeling." "I guess that is why you like the story so much." **The General says**. I say. "What story I like so much?" "Or cartoon. Cartoon always took you into a trans were... **The General says.**

I say. "I lived the Cinderella life of hardships truly." **The General says.** "So, your motherly love was given to you by your grandmother Mamie. So, you had motherly love you just got it from your grandmother. You, see? She was always there. G-D just transfer hand. And then not only that. You got the father's love from your granddaddy Mr. B. Which was greater. Because he did not treat the others. Like he treats you. He treated you a thousand times better." "Cut their ass. And let you go!" **The General of The Most High G-D says.**

I say. "Yeah. Let me go free. I smiled. Then said. "That's the truth. So that made it worse?" **The General says.** "No, No." I say. "For mommy?" "Yeah. It makes it worst for her." I say. "Intensify. **The General says.** "Yeah, further intensify. Why are you beating them, and you aren't beating Cleo? Don't get in my business hear." That is what your grandmother will tell your mother. Then your mother would say. "Cleo, come move this broom or come and do this thing for me!" **The General says.**

I say. "Yeah." **The General says.** "You see? They knew you were going through a lot in your skin. You can't take any bruising that is why your grandmother never put her hand on you. Your grandfather Mr. B. never put his hand on you. Because they knew your grandma's love toward you as a child was. "She can't take no bruising because your skin can't take it."

They would say. "We are taking care of her. And her scars right now. She can't take no bruising." When you come home. She had to peel up your skin because the socks were stuck in the scours. They couldn't bruise up no other part of your body." **The General says.**

I say. "Mommy use to tear my hip up. Many would run from their house to come down there to her and save me. Yeah. From down the road. Around the corner. Mamie would come to save me." **The General says.** "Someone would tell her. Your grandchild getting to beat." "Or when my mother would call her and say. "Mamie you better come for this child. I will kill her! The General of The Most High G-D smiles and laugh softly.

I smiled and say. "That's because Mamie didn't have the love for her, she had for me. It even now sounds like that. Even when I say. "Mamie you better come for this child. Am going to kill her! That's because Mamie did not love her. Like how she did love me." "Mamie had the mother's love for you. The Mother's cuddling. G-D gave it to Mamie. And Mr. B. Because your mother did not have it in her. **The General of The Most High G-D says.** I say. "That's true. Because Mamie and Mr. B. raise me."

"Didn't one of you threaten your mommy with a letter?" **The General of The Most High G-D says.** "I don't know." I say. "I will kill myself. I will commit suicide." **The General of The Most High G-D says.** I say. "Oh?" **The General of The Most High G-D says.** "Mommy? Am going to kill myself." I say. "Yeah, you love Cleo more than me." "Am by the bridge. Am by the bridge I will jump. Am at Porter Cay Dock." **The General says.** I laugh. Because The General demonstrated things to me in a very funny way. Sometimes we would also change his voice. Or the shape of his body into any animal for my illustration purpose.

430

"Your mother analysis what she say. "Mamie loves you." Your Dad got money" Granddaddy Mr. B. love's you" Your next Grammy Rita loved you." Your next granddaddy IG love you. They have money. Cleo will be alright! She gives you up to them. And she guards that one what was going to commit suicide. She only got one daddy and he barely come around. Now and again." **The General of The Most High G-D says.** I say. "Yeah."

The General G-D says. "That was a misfit. So." I say. "Jason was a misfit?" "So, she ends up stuck. Because she had no body. She had no body. The son had someone who had something. She had nobody. You had Mamie. Daddy, Mr. B. Granddaddy and Grandmother Rita." **The General of The Most High G-D says.**

I say. "So, she didn't have anybody?" **The General say.** "No! Your sister." She didn't have anybody." I say. "So that is why Mother did her so? So, my mother decide she wasn't going to check for me? She checked 10 to 35% it was almost

431

cold turkey." "No. Because you had everybody else. She found a reason and if she put that with jealousy. Remember I told you the mind. You know. The body. Spirit?

When this spirit here decided and have so traits in it that make you. *The mind controls the temperature*. So, when she decided to go after this? And let Mamie take care of you? Let Mamie raise you. "Just take care of this one?" The power behind this for that little act to go through the way it is. That little act she intensifies that by sealing it. By actually using neglect. It put fire behind neglect.

That is what happened. She neglects you for your other sister. And it also can be for many other reasons. Being that you were straight. You didn't need her. You were traveling the world. Everybody liked you. Miss America. Miss Bahamas. Stepping out in high heels." **The General of The Most High G-D says.**

I felt this (high heel shoes) was being said to make me smile. Because the news was making me sad, G-D's General knew and continued and he says. "Going around town. Everybody loved you." I laugh.

The General says. "You could dress. You could pick out cloths. You carry your sisters shopping. Your mommy saw herself losing that one to faith." **The General of The Most High G-D says.** "Losing who?" I say. "Your mother. Saw herself losing that one to faith. She was gone! Faith had her! In her last desperate breath to survive. In her last effort." **The General says.** "My Mother pull her out?" I say.

"Because she was drowning. She was drowning. She couldn't take it no longer. No longer." **The General says.** I laugh. "She fears the worst. She fears the worst." **The General of The Most High G-D says.** I say. "That's what happened? I knew something had happened. I just didn't know what." "She fears the worst." **The General says.**

I say. "Because look here. Mommies drop me cool turkey. Cool turkey. "She drops you because she would have lost a child. That birdie was gone. She was dangling." **The General of The Most High G-D says.** I say. "So, if she did not drop me that was going to happen?"

"Yeah, she was suicidal. Your sister Roshelle was going to kill herself. Either behind the wheel of a car or strangulation in the... She would have killed herself. Your mommy took all the love. **"The General of The Most High G-D says.**

Roshelle say. "Cleo has all kind of cars and her daddy have all kind of money. Her grandmother has a restaurant down the road. Her other grandmothers got all kinds of businesses, hotel, villas, grocery store, dive shop. She got property on the beach. My mammy them. Aren't get nothing.

My mammy them. Even aren't my mammy them." **The General says.** I loud out loud and say. "Yeah, your Mammy isn't your Mammy. But your Daddy don't know!"

The General says. "Mamie isn't her mammy. Mammy isn't her Mamie. She had one black turkey. She had one black turkey!" I say. "Goose yeah? Goose?" "Yeah. That's what her daddy gives her. One black goose. She had envy of a daddy. "The General of The Most High G-D says.** "She had one black goose. LOL I say while laughing."

"Yeah, that's what she got from her daddy. Your daddy didn't have to be a daddy to be called a daddy. He could have pretended. And go missing for almost a year and he still would have been a better daddy than her daddy. **The General of The Most High G-D** Laugh.

I Laugh and said. LOL, who Jason?." **The General of The Most High G-D says.** "You could have seen your daddy once a year. He still would have been the best daddy in the world. See Jason every day? he is the worst. I say. "Jason was that bad? **The General of The Most High G-D says.** "So, she looks at Jason. She looks at your dad family got it. Jeremy your dad's got it like. The General smile and says. "Jeremy lending her daddy money. And The General laughs out loud. Then said. Her daddy working for your daddy Cleo. Her daddy does go and get your daddy a bottle of water from his food store. So that he may drink. You understand? The General continued laughing and says. "So. So. So." I laugh.

"Jeremy sending her daddy home." **The General says.** "So Roshelle gave up?" I say. "Yeah." **The General of The Most High G-D says.** I started laughing and say. "I give up also General. I gee!" I couldn't stop laughing it was so funny.

"I give up." I say to The General so that he would stop making me laugh.

"So now. Your sister said, "Mommy. I tired, I tired. Am going to kill myself. You love Cleo more than you love me. I will kill myself. Cleo got everything. I don't have nothing. I don't have nothing! She couldn't take it. So, her (your sister) spirit couldn't take it. So, her spirit. Her spirit was broken. You, see? Her spirit was dangling. Like this **The General says.** (The General of The Most High G-D showed me through an illustration). I started to laugh. **The General says.** "Dangling like this. "And he suspended himself in the air.

While he laughs and illustrated dangling for me. "Just dangling. Dangling. He says dangling laughing." "I laugh also. Because I felt dangling. Dangling. Was used to make me smile. "Just dangling he said again." "Her last attempt to help was when she gained enough strength to put it behind the soul. She said. "Soul oh soul. Am dying. Please send some power behind these words to my mother." **The General says.**

I say. "So, the ten commandments are actually the soul of man? Because I was desperate to put all of these pearls. I was being given together." To that The General replied. "No love. Explain that to me? How you came up with that? About the soul? And your last dying breath to get help?" **The General of The Most High G-D says.** I say. "Yeah, the soul ignites!" "Yeah, the last thought in her head. After she had already given up. Was to make sure this letter that she wrote? That the words in this letter become life in mommy ears. So, mommy would come running to her. You understand?" **The General says.**

I say. "My sister went to the witch people?" **The General of The Most High G-D says.** "Let this be." "Roshelle went to the witch people?" I said. "So, you understand!" **The General says.** "OH. To the witch doctor? Oh, my G-D? How can she have done that? I said. "Now you understand. You understand." **The General of The Most High G-D says.** "She was that desperate ha? Ha? I said.

" So, you understand!" **The General says.** "Yeah. I understand. I understand." I said. "You don't see she married a fellow. A drunken?" **The General of The Most High G-D says.** "Who does beat her." "Yeah, so I heard." I said. "Yeah. She's in torment know for the rest of her marriage. Because every now and then. He will (The General of The Most High G-D illustrated) – tat, tat, tat, tat, tat, tat (sound of slaps)." **The General says.** I say. "Yeah, slap her up a little bit because of the sin?"

"And then G-D will come behind and move the hurt. And they will come closer together and they will be together for a little bit. He will come home drunk again." **The General says.** "I laugh and did the illustration. I say. "Now this time if it was tat, tat, tat, tat,tat, tat, tat, tat tiy?. It will be tat, tat, tat, tiy,.,tat tat, tat-tiy.....tat, tat, tat, tat, tat, tat, tat,tat-tiy. I laugh and said, "Yeah understand? Yeah understand? Yeah understand? This is how you understand.

"Yeah, every month or so. She got a new cut ass. For the sin against G-D. Talking about. Wasn't that the last like you clap me before?" **The General says.** I laugh and said. "No it was tat, tat,..,tat tat a tat tat!. Run a rhythm of their face. For going to the witch doctor. My LORD. My LORD. I say. "I see. And I understand. Sin. Comes back for payment. And it matters not how the payment is collected. I BLESS THE LORD. For Wisdom. Knowledge and understanding." **The General says** "Yeah! run the rhythm. "And she would never. Ever in a thousand years believe she is getting cut ass because of that one thing she did about many, many years ago." **The General says.** "Yeah, and that was wrong!" I say. "It was wrong

WAY
BACK

CHAPTER **XL**

I understood through these teaching that this was all for going to the witch doctor. When before turning. She was a woman of G-D. Life just comes against you for what you have done, WITH-IN THE LIFE! And it can come at any time.

I say. "That is a serious thing? People don't think that far back. They often think about what they did yesterday. I wonder what I had done yesterday. What may have course this or that to happen to me? But they do not remember the things they do to G-D. BUT HE REMEMBERS! *Divine Justice! Does Not Make an Appointment.*

The General says. "I do. Go way back. I do. Go all the way back. And he laughs, saying. "I do say. Go." Go further LORD" LORD go further. Go further back. Go further and he continued to laugh. Then I say. "This is how others come to believe G-D does not exist. Because punishment does not show up during the deed. But sometime after the sin!

Or this is how they do not bring themselves to think it is G-D that is doing the things to them. Because G-D does go far. Far back. He could probably even skip a generation, and deal with the problem he had with you. And your sin. Inside *your* other generations. Long after you are dead and gone. **The General says.** "YES. G-D GO WAY BACK!"

"So, he could stop our reality at any point; and at any given time; and apply the punishment?" I say. "He can go back to where your forefather say. "I have a son he will be named John. He will kick your son ass. **The General of The Most High G-D says.** Then he laughs. I laugh and say. "Yeah, and that was over 200 years ago. Because Charley didn't want to give John any water in a drought." I say. "My G-D. That is a very serious thing." **The General says.** "Yeah! Yeah! YEAH!"

I say. "And now. He didn't even have the son yet when he said that! I laugh. **The General says.** "Yeah. He had G-D to carry that forward for him. His son didn't have the son yet! "I say. "86 years later! That's what's happening." "Now you understand, that's what's happening. That is why they can't blame G-D!" **The General of The Most High G-D says.** "He didn't give them it to do. He gave them it to think. "By my strength I am doing this thing." I say. "Oh yeah." **The General says.** I say. "This thing is about me. LOL. This thing about me!

"That is what happen for her to take. To be able to switch the love. It had to be something that was done in the middle there. For that love to switch toward you. And because it was done in the window. Out in the back door? It was done like a theft in the night. G-D. If that were so. She will get cut ass every month when the rent is due. And she would never know. Every cut ass is different." **The General of The Most High G-D says.**

440

I say. "I had another situation like that. One of my staff got a key for the property without my permission. It seems she wanted to get away from her husband and stayed in one of the rooms. Yeah? She got a room. But she still needed me to know. **The General says.** "Now why did she go away from her husband?"

I say. "Well. She must not have the money cuz the rent due. She talked about falling down on her back. But he might very well be putting hands on her. He is putting hand on her. Because she had nothing to come and bath at her workplace for." "No." **The General says.**

"She did more that bath at the property. She slept overnight. So, knowing that. Do I still write her up? Or? **The General of The Most High G-D says.** "No" I say. "Overlook it?" "Don't overlook it." **The General says."** Well, I told the employee not to do it again without my approval? I say.

The General says. "But between me and you. About your sister? When G-D beating that one for that? This could be the first lashes. Remember dear. I told you this morning. I feel sorry for the person that did it. Because I know. All penalties are not the same. You, see? When you look at the employee now. Every day. She comes in to work. She will have a pain. I say. "You can see. It is real pain General." **The General G-D says.** "Real. It is hitting her hard. Until she actually comes to you and tell you that she is sorry for deflating your tires and confess saying "it was me. I did it!." Her pain will get severe. Then ease. She will not feel it for two or three days. And then? It will come back severe. And hard.

441

And the simplest thing for her to do is to go. And tell you that she was the one that slash your tires and that she is sorry. So that her pain will go away." I say. "My LORD. "It was her that slash my tires? And she can't go, and do it? **The General says.** *"CAN'T DO IT!* I say to The General. "I see that in people receiving healing also."

The General says. "And that is where the healing it!. "It is because they are holding onto somethings that they have done to someone. They only need to realize it by going and asking FORGIVENESS. And some will not do it!" I say.

The General of The Most High G-D says. "NO! THEY WILL NOT. I say. "They carry the words forgive me with them." **The General says.** "That does not apply to my sickness. My sickness is not because I didn't apologize or didn't say sorry. That is the way their mind is. You, see? That is the way people mind. It is easy to deny telling someone sorry. Even when you are in pain.

I say. "OK, so It is easier to deny. Rather than to remember. It is easy to deny than it is to remember. Yes." **The General says.** "Yes, Yes, yes." I say. "That is properly why also. Some people feel like that about G-D. Because it is easy to deny. Then it is to remember." **The General says.** "Yes, yes." I say. "It is easy for them to deny G-D. His existence and everything?

The General says." YES! Then to go and remember him and try and figure out who they are. Or to try and figure out who G-D's people are. The whole scope. No where they come from. They just deny it. Because it is easier than to dig up the past and find themselves. **The General of The Most High G-D says.** "That is too much work. Too much work involve. But it is no work at all I told you. "Anything with G-D is what?"

"Easy?" I say. **The General says.** "Easy. Everything. And Anything to do with G-D "The Master" is easy." I say. "OK." **The General says.** "This talking right now with you is, easy. When G-D come right now? And G-D start dealing up with you? It does be with ease. It's like a hug from a mother. When the child comes in the house muddy and dirty. Rather than the mommy grabbing the belt to wale your backside.

443

She opens her arms and hug you to put the dirt on her. Dirty up her dress. That child will never ever deny not going to mommy and getting a hug. In the worst of times. She made it easy for him to come to her. So, he will never. She will never lose that. G-D comes to you easy."

The General says. "I had a work to do. I ask G-D for a Laptop. What you call it? iPad? He gave it to me on the side of the road. After it fell down from a car. Fall on the tar. Break the glass. Ran over into the bush. Rain wet it. Sun dries it. Ants piss on it. Roach shit on it. The grass cutter throw shit on it. You know?

I laugh out loud, as **The General of The Most High G-D, Myki'EL (Michael)** was being very dramatic with the lesson. I loved it! It got my attention. He was busy transforming into the ants crawling on the iPad. It was hilarious. He just kept changing his forms. And the more I laugh. The more he went on changing forms.

444

The General says. "Tree leaf fall on it. (Then he transformed himself into tree leaves.) Rock break the glass some more The General said, then transformed into a rock breaking the ipad glass" I say while laughing. "Why does G-D do that to you? What is G-D trying to do General?" **The**

General of The Most High G-D says." No. Because that is what he is giving me." I say. " But why?"

The General says. "Because he will give it to me to see if I can get it back to its original state and beauty. Because he calls me "a builder." I say. "He will give it to you to see if you can get it back to its original state?" **The General of The Most High says.** "Yes!" "So that is Yahusha. will give him people. The souls. All that belongs to him to let him test it and try it and get to try to get it back to its original state and then give it back to G-D.

"Yes, so when Yahusha. get it back to its original state? He will say. "Father this is so and so. "**The General says.** I say. "OK, like he did with me?" **The General of The Most High G-D says.** "So when I get that laptop that little tablet in it's brand new spanking state?"

I say. "OK, so its original state is the body. The spirit. The mind the soul?" "So, tell me. What your next move?" **The General of The Most High G-D says.** I knew The General was trying to trick me to answer for the future. Which no man knows the future but G-D. And the question was a part of my lesson prior. Which was Matthew 6:34 34 Therefore do not worry about tomorrow. For tomorrow will worry about itself. Each day has enough trouble of its own. I say. "My next move General is higher up. And sideways." Which

meant to The General that he was not going to catch me in the trap. I left what I was going to do so wide open. It was obvious. I was leaving room for G-D. Including within my response. **The General of The Most High G-D laugh at me.** Looked down. And kept laughing. It was obvious to him I was learning from my lessons. And leaving room for G-D. I understood that I could not out G-D. G-D. Neither should I go before G-D in any of my undertaking or planning.

IN
EVERYTHING

CHAPTER XLI

On November 26, 2017 while I was listening to some music. The Holy Spirit sent by G-D spoke to me saying. "Caplenton?. Sizzla?. They were the words from divine" YAHWEH." Soon after Buju showed up. Check his hair. His dress codes. His slickness of words and listen to caplenton, and sizzla. Then listen to Buju and tell me? "Who Sent Who?" You try to make me out to be who YOU believe I am. **"I AM, IN EVERYTHING!" Said The LORD.**

This should help you to see. My daughters would wear dresses, elegant dresses, with head ornament clutching their husband. My sons by the arms as they walk down the street, passing the bars that belong to them and their fathers nearly escaping their daughters high heels, long legs and short mini skirt, tank top with chest expose, gum chowing, leaning on the cars of who she believes were the boss inside the bar, and it could very well be a friend's daughter.

My daughters were spoken for, from a certain age. Among their own brethren. My people's elegance, top that of many, many nations. The women were regal and graceful.

Their men were wise. Strong and courageous. My males run their own businesses. While my daughters stayed at home. Unless otherwise seen out with their husbands. And when they went out. They were seen by everyone. For their luxurious look. You ALL, became a target. Your wisdom made you a target.

Your women made you a target. Your prosperity made you a target. Your courage makes you a target. Your way of life made you a target. Your luxuriousness! MAKE, YOU, A, TARGET! This is where it all happens. You were forced from your lands. Which is Me! They stop patronizing your business. So, home life was not that great for you. Then they started to come into your store to credit.

Well, you are not making any money anyway. So, credit will not hurt. Or so you thought. There after your women getting desperate. See you suffering. And just like a warrior's princess. You were great at fighting battles you can see. So, you triumph at that as a people of YAHWEH. They brought WAR again you that you could not see. "Sociological"

Now that we know the upside down the sideways and the inside out of this. And how it goes? **STAY FOCUS!** Teach a daughter to cover herself. We her people know what is there. It is only them that do not. *I HAVE ALWAYS SET YOU FREE. SO, THIS TOO SHALL PASS!*

To change the world. It's views or its opinion? The people of Yahweh. His first born. Children of their forefathers? Enjoy the things you use too before. Enjoy bible study. Enjoy helping in a charitable way. Enjoy quite times under a tree. While the wind talks with you.

Enjoy praying before your meal. Like you once use to. Enjoy my laws. Those who didn't flinch at my laws are first to come with me. Only warriors have laws. The rest of them have rules and regulations. You are not making it. Because you are living under rules and regulations.

But the law is what you should live by. Elevate your thinking and be conscious every time. You MUST travel his road to know me. Abraham: The seed, The blesser. The seed that brought forth many others. The Abrahamic seed. One off Abrahamic seed brings forth 40 and odd more seeds

That is why YAHWEH loved him. A seed that was found to be greater than all other seed. This is also why it is said. "The eye of YAHWEH is always upon them." And it is for them. That all of their enemies become His enemies. We will. "Bless who they bless. And curse who they curse."

Abraham as a seed was the best reproductive seed that gave life that YAHWEH had known besides himself. And YAHWEH, absolutely loves LIFE. So much that he gave love. To life Selflessly! Abraham was just the first that showed this. He had the abilities to show and speak off Yahweh. And he changes hearts toward where the hearer following YAHWEH. Yahweh was pleased with it. The Holy Spirit sent from G-D when on to say

ABRAHAM- person Israelite -forefather SEED You royal people of G-D, Including the people of The Greater and Lesser Antilles. You were once spoken of in History to quote "Know No Evil." Moses is the law giver: Remember that and respect him. He is a forefather unto you In Deuteronomy from the 6th Chapter. You will find the laws for you to LIVE by.

MOSES - person Israelite - forefather LAW For entering the promise land which is "G-D's place for you. You don't have to get there yourself physically. Just following the teaching, show up to the street, exercise your OWNSELF rights to know who *you really are. A*nd the four Angels of the

451

four corners of the Earth will direct you further with the help of **Prince Myki'EL/Michael**. *The people of G-D allocated Guardian, Protector and Warrior.*

In other words, YAHWEH, (Yo'way) will not come from the road of righteousness that he is on to your unrighteousness. Or from the road of cleanliness and purity to the road of uncleanliness just to rescue you. While you do not understand that you. Must get your righteousness. Cleanliness and holiness up to G-D's digestibility. You must meet him at less. To the side of the road that he is on.

This way he will carry you further. But when you are basking in the ambiance of your sin and uprightness. You don't LOOK like you NEED help. You look like you NEED YAHWEH (Yo'way) to shut that party down for you. And don't allow _anyone_ to go back home.

But anyway. The Holy Spirit when on to say to me. That's not the direction this book is going in. **Suffer not The LORD with unrighteousness. 1 Peter 3:17.** LEARN AND LIVE!." *Then G-D said through his HOLY SPIRIT. " LEARN AND LIVE." MY COMMANDMENTS - the barrier. So that your feet will remain in the new land. The promise lands. Hidden inside of G-D. By obeying them. You will never be cursed. And you will be covered by Yahweh. Those who are not the children of your forefathers that keep our commandments are covered under the commandments grace.*

You have your own laws that governs you. Your own committee that meets on your behalf. Your own speaker that speaks for you. And the All-mighty YAHWEH that makes all this possible for you to be a NATION, of people! **BARRIER** *-So that you will not leave the road. Teach them to love my commandments. This is their covering of protection.*

COMMANDMENTS Covering of Protection from YAHWEH. The LORD and Caretaker of The Earth says to me. *"Meet the father. Our Elohim. For through all your life, has given you lives. For you have lived so many in such a short time. Through divine favor has shared with you ancestral wisdom. Might I dear speak of his love toward you? The love that you can taste on your tongue. The love that you can breathe with just one inhale. The love that your skin senses and your bones are strengthen by. Oh, the love. How deep it is. The depths of his love for you are pass eternal. YAHWEH. The Great Spirit is the life. That you were intended to live. You were created. Intended people of Abraham. You are the seed, that Yahweh send his laws to his people. To live by the commandments. Until he, (Yahweh) comes as the Land that was promised. ALL GOOD AND RIGHTEOUS GIFTS YAHWEH (Yo'way) gives."* Then The LORD and Caretaker of The Earth departed from me.

YOUR
NEEDS

CHAPTER XLII

I learned on November 12, 2016. The only curse Yahweh gave to woman is childbirth. And the only curse Yahweh gave to a Man is that he. By the sweat of his eyebrow. Will eat bread. Because we did not have to work to eat bread. As I wrote my notes. **The General of The Most High G-D says.** "These are the beginning curses with Adam and Eve. As a man can't eat without doing this. He will have to go out there and run from the lion. Run from the bear." "Oh, so the curse is in-between, Before you even get to the end? It is constant. Throughout your whole life?" I say. "Throughout your whole life." **The General of The Most High G-D says.** I say. "It's constant? Constant?" **The General of The Most High G-D says.** "Yes, you as a child of Yahweh will see it and it would be a part of you. Less than anyone else." I say. "Oh, I see."

The General of The Most High G-D say. "You, see? I might probably have to go." I say. "OK I see. So, my troubles will never probably be as much as theirs?" **The General of The Most High G-D says.** "No, no, no." I say. "OK I get it!" "Because you are above the curse!" **The General of The**

Most High G-D says. "OK so the other side is the flip of the curse? the other side?" I say.

On November 19, 2016, I say to The General. "I like the name "fill a void" it provides an opportunity to fill any void being made or create the opportunity or heighten the opportunity for a void to be met. "It's multifaceted, you can fill so many voids." **The General of The Most High G-D says.** I say. "From "fill a void" we can fulfill so many other voids. From one void being fulfill, others will be fulfilled, right?

The General of The Most High G-D says. "From your business. A void in someone's life will be fill. You can't fill all. They come with more than one need. Not even a need. But an issue. And you address that issue and if there is a void that you can fill with the issue that they have then that void can be fill and some learning on how they can fill the voids in their own life.

Come with knowledge on how we talk and what we are gaining now to ask for different gifts. Because you need it, don't feel like you know it and don't ask for it and get shame in the front of Nature. When you don't have it and don't know it. You ask for it. So, these things **you should be teaching them how to ask. And how to live and how to be.** Believe. To soar from the natural into...to out of the commonality thinking into the thinking that brings prosperous living. I WISH ABOVE ALL THINGS THAT YOU PROSPER, EVEN AS YOUR SOUL PROSPER.

So, it brings you to prosperous thinking. Prosperous living. Prosperous ability. Prosperous believe. Your job is prosperous. Your children are prosperous. Everything is prosperous. WHY? Because you. Yourself now have nothing attached to you. That is not prosperous. That has to do with you understanding and knowing that. *"All of your needs were meet before you even were conceived.* THAT'S THE DEAL!"

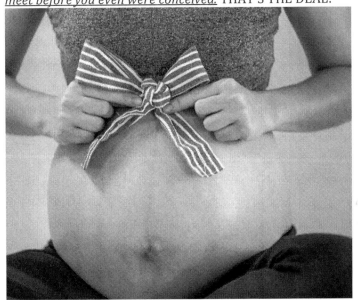

"If you know your need are met. You will not have to steal and kill. Jail houses wouldn't need to be open anymore! "You, see? **The General of The Most High G-D says.** "Yes! My LORD, I do see!." I say. **The General of The Most High G-D says.** "You don't need a car. You just need a ride to get to work. So, ask G-D for a ride. Then maybe he will bless you with a mule. You See? And then when he blesses you with a mule? Don't despise the mule because the mule might look brake down and rusted on one side. If the mule can get you to work. That's your need being fulfill. And it didn't cost you anything. Because the person gives you a mule to just put gas in it for you to go to work. You See?"

Out of your need being fulfilled to get to work with that breakdown mashed up car. You know can get to work out of that need and get a brand-new mule because of the need being fulfill. Which is to get to work. Does that make sense? You are cold. Freezing. You don't need a leather jacket. You need a snow jacket. Because you are cold! No. I want a leather jacket. I want a leather jacket please G-D. I don't walk around in the snow. Without a leather jacket.

I laugh and said. "Yeah, leather jacket in the snow LORD. And flow shine shoes while its freezing outside? **The General of The Most High G-D says.** "Yeah, I don't want no insulated jacket!" I say. "Excuse me. I don't live like that!**" The General of The Most High G-D says.** "I don't want no LL BEAN jacket G-D.

"No. I don't live like that. Well, no problem. There you go a jacket to keep you warm. But you want LL BEAN or that leather jacket. You, see?" **The General of The Most High G-D says.** "Yeah." I say. "G-D always fill. He always does. That's his nature to supply your NEED. It is already done. People just don't like their need. For what it is. They figure they need a car, so they are going to get a brand new one of the lots. Listen. When G-D. OK. No problem. Listen to this." **The General of The Most High G-D says.**

"Yeah. Then in one year. Their house get taken from them." I say. "Their G-D get small." **The General of The Most High G-D says.** I say. "They did not plan that out at all. Or thought that out at all." **The General of The Most High G-D says.** "The only thing the car was used for was to get away.

Because the repo man is coming after the car. I say. "LOL General. Lol." **The General of The Most High G-D says.** So. So. In all things give G-D thanks."

"That's a bad repossession joke by the way." I say. While laughing at the joke with The General." "Yeah!" I say. "Well, Bless The LORD." "You could have bought a car for less. And if it breaks down with you." **The General of The Most High G-D says.** "Yeah, you could have saved some of that money. You would have had some of that money to fix it." I say. "And if it breaks down? You would have some money to fix it. You would have gained some friends along the way also. Some good friends. Who would help you along the way? They would have said" don't worry about it. Just bring your car in. I will fix it for you." Let us all move into another way of thinking! **The General of The Most High G-D says.** "Yeah!" I say

"G-D has done so much. He has given us too much. So much to make our road so light. We have to stop forgetting!

"**The General of The Most High G-D says.** "Who me?" I say. "No! We! US! We need to stop forgetting and remind ourselves daily. Of where we came from. And how hard it was to where we are. Some folks still struggling can't even. They can't even see the smoke. Where the rain has their eyes closed." **The General of The Most High G-D says.** I said "That stuffs funny now. That is funny. (laughter..lol). The General started laughing also. I say. "That's about the second funniest thing. I have ever heard in my life. While on this journey My LORD. I continued to laugh. **The General of The Most High G-D says.** "Humans can't see the smoke. Because the rain has got their eyes closed. "Yeah? That mean they are wet. Boy. I tell you!" I say. "Well. They don't have to be soaked. They can come in from the rain. They don't even have to get wet. They didn't have to walk in the rain in the first place!" **The General of The Most High G-D says.** I laugh out loud.

"They could have stayed where they were. And wait the rain out. Because they are not like you and I." **The General**

461

of The Most High G-D says. I say. "You mean like choosing their own way?" "Yes" **The General of The Most High G-D says.** I say. "It's like they chose their own. Because it doesn't have to be chosen?" "No. Because they don't have to walk in the rain. It is not a must and there is not a NEED. You do not need to walk in the rain." **The General of The Most High G-D says.**

"OK. So they didn't come here with that knowing?" I

say. **The General of The Most High G-D says.** "No. That's something that they picked up. They picked that up. They see someone playing in the rain. They figure they can walk in the rain." I say. "OK, yeah, well the people they are now. It seems the people that black people are now. Are the people they have taught themselves how to be?" **The General of The Most High G-D says.** "They had to copy. They taught themselves how to copy. Copycat. They were taught."

"So, OK they were copycats of others? So, they taught themselves how to be like that?" I say. "Copycats. And their parents taught them how to copycat?" **The General of The Most High G-D says.** "And their parents taught them how to copycat. And their parents thought them how to copycat?" I say.

"And they lived a life of copycat?" **The General of The Most High G-D says.** "Copycatism?. I said. "Now THAT IS A SERIOUS THING!" Copycatism. I will have to look for that in the dictionary of the Most High! Jah! Rastafari! Everybody is under copycatism."

The General of The Most High G-D says. "Rastafari, Yahweh! is my G-D. And the fulfillment." I say. "I am Yahweh's fulfillment of his word." "You will never be nothing less!" **The General of The Most High G-D says.** "I will never be nothing less." I say.

"I can't even run from G-D. I will get scared. Just to break of running from G-D. Where can I run? I will buck up into a bear." **The General of The Most High G-D says.** "I always say?. It is better to just submit to The Creator." I say. "Might as well. Just submit." **The General of The Most High G-D says.** "Just fall down on your face before him. And it is not hard. It is so beautiful to just say, "FATHAR where am I going? And hear him say. OK just go over there and sit down for a while. I will send help." You are just to sit there and WAIT. What you say?. You sit there and you Wait. When you move. You lose. Even if I sit there and fall asleep. He will wake me up. But I am still there where he said I must be." **The General of The Most High G-D says.**

EARTH
REAP

CHAPTER **XLIII**

For seven days leading up to August 22, 2018. The Holy Spirit sent from G-D started troubling my spirit. Repeating these word night and day saying. "No man knows the day or the hour when the Son of Man cometh. No man knows the day nor the hour when the Son of Man cometh. No man knows the day nor the hour when the Son of Man cometh."

When the Holy Spirit sent from G-D would say those words to me? I would stop what I was doing and pray for extended periods of time. And I would also open my bible and study for hours. Sometimes I would go to sleep at 4am or when the sunrise the following day. Because I understood the Holy Spirit sent from G-D was warning me for a reason. I just didn't know what the reason really was. But the message was clear.

And I didn't want the Son of Man to come to Earth. While I was not prepared. So, I did what any bride of the son of G-D would do. I burned the midnight oil seeking the LORD Most High. In preparation for my husband. "The Son of Man." For the hour that is said that will be to day to late had come to The World, in The Spirit realm.

On August 21, 2018, the Spirit of G-D's words to me was the strongest I had ever heard it. So that entire day and night I stayed up reading my bible and praying while everyone else in my home was asleep. I didn't know what was about to happen exactly. All I knew was the Spirit of G-D gave me *NO REST. They troubled me in the Spirit. They burned a whole in my ear. They were relentless. And I was tormented. Over and over and over again The Spirit sent from G-D said to me.*

The words of **Matthew 25:13, <u>Watch therefore, for ye know neither the day nor the hour wherein the Son of man cometh.</u>** Then the Spirit sent from G-D kept repeating. *<u>"No man knows the day nor the hour when the son of man cometh. No man knows the day nor the hour when the son of man cometh. No man knows the day nor the hour when the</u>*

son of man cometh. I knew that it was a clue sent from G-D that the time that is said that will be to late was upon us all.

I had fears. Yes! But I had no doubt I would be saved. Because only a fool says in his heart there is no G-D. And I was not a fool. I knew G-D existed. Fear rendered itself useless to me after a while. It became more significant for me to surrender my soul right with G-D. So, I prayed. All night long. And I read my bible. All night long. And I seek and I knock on the door of The LORD. All night long. Because what was not going to happen was? The Son of Man came? And found his own bride unaware. As it is written. _**"Then shall The Kingdom of Heaven be likened unto ten virgins, which took their lamps, and went forth to meet the bridegroom. And five of them were wise, and five were foolish. They that were foolish took their lamps, and took no oil with them. But the wise took oil in their vessels with their lamps. While the bridegroom tarried, they all slumbered and slept. And at midnight there was a cry made, Behold, the bridegroom cometh; go ye out to meet him." Matthew 25:3.**_

I beat that bible up! Searching and seeking and knocking and communing and troubling the throne of G-D. At precisely 12:01am on August 22, 2018. There was a loud. Destructive shaking. A rumbling. That came from Mother Earth. It was so violent. I drop the bible and held on to the bed thinking. "The End of The World Had Come."

The power that existed in the violence of the shake brought me to say to The Creator as I gripped now the nightstand and the bed headboard. Just in-case Fathar didn't see what was happening around me. And to make him aware that I was experiencing severe turbulence on Earth. I say. "Well, Fathar. This is it." Then the rumbling of Mother Earth stopped immediately. Before I took my breath of relief? I close my eyes and with that first breath I say to The Creator. My Holy Fathar. I said. "Fathar?. If it be your will. Please. Tell me what just happened?

"YAHWEH" answered me right away. He says to me. "The Earth and all of its inhabitants has been reaped by The G-D of Heaven." I thank the Fathar for responding to me. That very night I went outside on my balcony. I looked up to the sky to look for changes. Just then a woman showed me herself. Walking across the sky with two white wolf leaping. As she walked. Just them I knew. The World was a change place.

The following morning. I went into an open parking lot. And I would speak to anyone interested to know what had happen on the Earth where they lived. A gentleman walked up to me and gave me a crown that had stars on it. And it had a triangle within a triangle with three entries on each side totaling twelve. He said to me before departing. "This is your crown. The G-D of Heaven has sent to you. Rejoice and be glad." And he placed the crown on my head as I cried. I knew. I had made it to the designated date and time. Of The LORD's coming. And because of that? G-D had placed stars in my crown. I was overwhelmed with gratitude that I had made it through to the date of The LORD's Coming to dwell on Earth.

On January 31, 2019, I ascended into heaven like a whirlwind. Seven days leading up to my ascension. I was asked by The Most High to fast. During this time? I was given angels food to eat. In the beginning I assumed it would be a food fast that the Spirit was asking of me. Because I had never heard of a silence fast. Two days into the food fast. The Holy Spirit came back to me and says, "No. This is a silence fast." To my surprise silent was harder than the food fast. So, I asked myself. "Is this the silence as spoke of in Revelations 8:1-5 When he opened the seventh seal, there was silence in heaven for about half an hour? Whatever it was. The Spirit of G-D's timing for this fast was great! I had just started vacation and really had no obligation to speak to anyone. So everywhere I went I took a book and a pen to write notes for anyone I had to converse with.

Everywhere I went with my written notes? The grocery store. The gas station. The fabric store. Everyone was extremely polite. They must have thought I had a disability and followed my written instructions and patiently waited for me to write them a note to complete my service request. I appreciated G-D for not making any of that complicated for me. Because the food fast? I was able to do with ease. But the silence fast? Was complicated. As there was silence in Heaven currently. So did The LORD Most High required silence from me. On earth.

At the stroke of midnight prince Myki'EL' (Michael) was sent from G-D to me and said." Say these words." So, in the darkness of my home. I stood up and said the words given to me that was foreign to me. This was the first words I had said in seven days.

My surroundings started to change. There were small dots of light that I saw kept on increasing until in the blink of an eye. I was no longer on Earth. I landed in Heaven with my right knee down on the floor first. And Prince, Brethren, Guardian Kachina, King Myki'EL/Michael let go of the back of my clothing. I saw his feet. They were as Deer's feet on steroids. Just like the bible says. Psalms 18:33 "He makes my feet like the feet of a deer; he causes me to stand on the heights."

And I wondered if this was why my relatives the Native American Indians did so much with deer. His legs were huge. And hairy, just like a deer's feet. But deer's feet metamorphosis. Like LORD and King of the Deer's feet. His feet shuck the room when he moved. I was amazed. His

471

strength made my heartbeat faster naturally. Because my heart knew. Without a shadow of a doubt. There was someone super strong. And super powerful was in the room. I watch his deer feet as it moved. Then he made a lightening stroke in the air, And rolled it into a scroll while walking, As the room shook. He said. "Fathar?. Look and see what Azazel (/əˈzeɪzəl, ˈæzəˌzɛl/; has done unto The Earth. The cries of the righteous has reached up to heaven. The blood of the slain says to us. (Us meaning to him and the other three angels of the other cardinal directions of the world) Take our complaint unto The Most High." immediately. I didn't know who Azazel (/əˈzeɪzəl, ˈæzəˌzɛl was. But I knew instantly. Whoever this Azazel is. His accomplices and all that is with him. Is in deep trouble with G-D.

Hearing this The LORD. The Caretaker and Spirit of The Earth stood up in the center of the four directions of The World. He gestured with his right hand. To The East he said.

"Come and present yourselves before The Most High G-D!.

To The West he said. "Come and present yourselves before The Most High G-D!. To The North he said. "Come and present yourselves before The Most High G-D!. To The South he said. "Come and present yourselves before The Most High G-D!." All spirits stood up in The EAST, WEST, NORTH and The SOUTH.

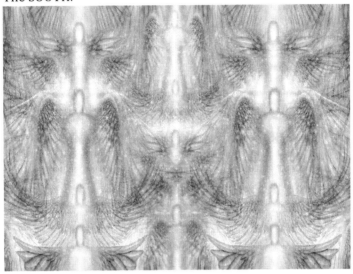

They were all the spirits of the deeds; and the works; at the hands; of all mankind. Each person's spirit stood up as a testimony and represented each man. Without their physical presence. From the day the Earth was created. Then The Spirits of Creation can in and stood in the center of The Assembly. Directly in-front of a Glorious Throne. They reviewed themselves before the face of Him that sat upon The Throne. To see if they had also sin against The Most High One that sat in the center of Heaven.

Creations Spirits reviewed their deeds; and the works; at their hands, openly! That all in attendance may see *through them.* That they (The Spirits of Creation had not committed any evil, sin or traitorous acts withing the Most

473

High's Creation of The World. That would cause mankind to falter. The Spirits of Creation (The Hebrew Letters) stood before The Throne and gathered themselves last first. Tav to Aleph. And last deed done in The World, *first!* The Spirits of Creation arrived at the end of their reverse gathering.

They re-played themselves from the beginning of creation to the moment I arrived on bending knees. This is

when the recording stopped. I looked and I saw all of the calamities of humanity uncovered. And I saw no good. And I saw only evil deeds. I saw men thrusting swords into the bellies of pregnant women. I saw men. Twisting the necks of babies. I saw men. Decapitating little children. And throwing other children in fires to be burn alive.

I saw men, Rape. Rob. Pillage. Plundered and Polluted. I saw men. Ambush others while they were unaware. When they least expected them. Catching women and children unaware and killing them. I saw all over the world murder and bloodshed. Robbery all over the world. Murders. Deaths. Killings. Lying. Lynching's. Shootings. Stabbings. People running for their lives. Decapitations. Cannibalism. Trickery. Smoking. Drinking. Partying. The world was making merry in the drunkenness of their hearts. Their minds. Their soul and their bodies. Witchcraft I saw. Sorcery. Incest. Others were selling little children in the sight of The Creator. Raping children. Killing children. Prostitution. I heard screams from victims. And so did The LORD.

I saw many innocent people treated poorly by others. Because they had wealth or power. And the poor was poor. I saw the poor being kicked on the streets by others passing by. My eyes saw. So, so much blood. Every record live image show in Heaven. There was blood shed before The Creator's face. And in every human action there was death. And not life or light.

With all my heart I wanted The Spirits of Creations recording being played of mankind to stop. I was so disappointed with how far from grace humanity was before the faces of The Holy Forces of Heaven. To be at a place of dishonor before the G-D's. I became ashamed. And I knew what trouble we all were in. Grief took hold of me. Upon review of the gathered deeds done on Earth. The entire Heavenly Assembly erupted in outrage.

They were angry to have removed all of us far away from their existence. Through instant annihilation. The entire Assembly encompassing The Creator jumped up on their feet in an uproar. They all were instantly ready, to come to Earth for a mighty battle. Each one in the Assembly gripped firmly on their individual symbol of Authority in The Universe. Some had this in their hand all the time. Each one was different from the other. Before anyone spoke that did not have their symbol of Authority in The Universe. Their symbol would appear. And then they would begin to speak toward The Creator's Throne.

The Assembly encompassing The Throne said to The Most High in one accord. With one voice they said. "**What of our servants. Our children? Living on earth that loves us. And we them. How can they survive one more day living in what we have seen here? And who is to save them from these things that are moving in; closer and closer on them. As to destroy them, IF NOT US?**" Though the Assembly did not speak the words? Their body language, and the look on their faces said to me. They wanted to destroy mankind by instant annihilation. I felt it in the room. Because of our deeds. They wanted to start afresh. And they

had the powers to do so. A largest one in the assembly held

an ankh in his hand. He was the greatest of them all. His countenance (heights) overwhelmed me. When he stood up angry like the others? His shadow moved across The Universe. Death went with him. Within his shadow. As his shadow increased from his standing upright. Death followed to turn midday on Earth. Into darkness. Others urged him to sit down before his standing causes all things to come to an end.

For fear of him? And the powers of those in attendance at the assembly? I passed away suddenly. And my spirit failed me. I became undone because of the fear of them that was in attendance. And the Most High sent Myki'EL (Michael), The General of The Most High G-D to revive me back to life.

Seeing all these things. Fear gripped me. And did not let me go. Their powers were without limitations. I just knew humanity was in trouble with the Heavenly Assembly. I knew that they would seek to destroy. Because of the strength of their anger. Because of the works of our hands, and the hands of the forefathers before us. That came into view from the Heavenly tables (records). I laid down prostrated before The Throne that everyone in the assemble directed themselves toward. I was the only human being in attendance. Therefore, I felt an obligation to pray. In representation of _us all._ I presented the Heavenly Assembly why mankind should live. And not be annihilated by G-D because of the abundance of their sins that had reached up to The Heart of Heaven.

I directed my soul toward The Throne. My soul was poured out like water. And it made me draw on all that I had learned. That I should be careful with my speech toward The Holy One. One of my biggest life lessons. Was to learn to repeat G-D's words back to him. That he should uphold it. Just like HE say. I mastered that class. (The class of bartering/begging G-D in a polite manner while using his words at its own defense). Of begging G-D. I am a Master beggar when I know I am at my last end. And seeing the size POWER in attendance?

I knew my soul was also on the line as I laid there in defense of a World that rejected me. And The Children of G-D.) But I knew. I had to do something. Less we ALL DIED. From the smallest to the great. The rich and the poor. And everything else living. I began seeking forgiveness, and repentance on behalf of ALL HUMANITY, The good, and the evil. The victims; and their accusers. The righteous; And the sinner. The saved; and the unsaved. And I said to the one sitting on The Throne as I faced the ground. I said. Fathar? Please. Forgive us. And they. So that we may all find forgiveness of you. For the sins of the other. Seeing that we are all one family in your sight and in your love. For we have all sinned against you and have fallen short of your glory. *For we know not what we have done!* Have mercy upon us to give us ALL forgiveness with the abundance of **THY** love. And **THY** tender mercy. And save us from ourselves Fathar. That we will err no more against **THY** Holy Name and **THY** Holy Awesome Ones. For we are weak Fathar; but **THOU** alone are strong. Give us another chance Fathar?. That we may continue living. With the land. The life and the happiness. That **THOU** have begotten us and intended for us to have.

And teach us **THY** ways Oh Most High. Holy Fathar. That there will be no middlemen between us and you. Less we stagger in the way that you have chosen for us to go Fathar, and **THOU** chastise us with great chastisement. But forgive us instead. And teach us your ways, that we may learn directly from you the things that please you. And we will not err to turn away from them. To the right hand nor to the left. But to do, all things pleasing unto you. With you and your holy awesome ones as our teachers and no one else. We will never again falter in the way that pleases you Fathar. And the things which we have all seen here, that do not please you Oh Most High Holy Fathar shall never again happen. But please. Let us live Fathar. And instruct us instead, that we may go forward pleasing unto **THY** sight.

He that sat upon The Throne. In The Center of The Highest Heaven appearance became changed, into clouds of thick, dark, billowing smoke. Of the wrath of his indignation (Anger) at the rebuke of the deeds of Mankind. He spoke and the smallest to the greatest In the Assembly bowed down before him. Then The Creator Says; "He Will Have, No Place To _**Run;**_ And No Place To _**Hide;**_ Proceed Against The _**Bastards!.**_

Trumpets sounded. And angels without number for multitude of armies started forming lines in heaven. And many left their places for the first time. From the day, they were created. That they should descend upon the earth. And proceed against mankind for the sins that were seen in heaven. At a time appointed by The LORD.

He that sat upon The Throne in The Center of The Highest Heavens; spoke again. This time, He address me by saying to me. "When I asked Mankind who will go for us? You answered me saying. Send me and I will go." "My Name Is memorialized forever, unto eternity, **'I AM'** The Creator. **'I AM'** The Living Elohim. **'I AM'** יְהֹוָה YAHWEH. The Great Spirit G-D of יִשְׂרָאֵל Yisra'EL The G-D of your forefathers. The G-D of Abraham, The G-D of Issac, And The G-D of Yacob. The Great spirit G-D of The Indian Man. The G-D of Moses, The G-D of Aaron, And The G-D of Joshua. THE TETRAGRAMMATON, YODH, HEI, WAW, HEI. Write! All that you shall see here and learn here. Write! *And I will bless those who blesses you; and anyone who curses you, I will curse, and all people of The Earth will be blessed through you. Write!*"

And The Creator. The Great Spirit G-D of Yisra'EL Yahweh. Through his Holy Spirit. Took me up from the ground. Where I laid as dead before The Supreme Court of Heaven's Assembly. And The Creator's G-D's Spirit took me. And place me above The Creator's right side. And I became comforted by his spirit. And we travelled the skies. And came to earth. I saw earth (The World) from above. As it was below us. As to our feet. I looked down on the earth as I wrote as instructed,

And I saw the most heart-breaking and gut-wrenching thing I had seen on the journey. The world was no longer beautiful. It was ugly. And dreadfully black with darkness from sin. And there was no light (love) in the earth found for humanity but a few flickers. And I became weak again of my spiritual strength. And I became drawn-out. As dead from pain of grief. To see how far The World had backslide from G-D. The Creator of ALL THINGS. While looking. It came into my spirit that evil forces had taken over The Earth. And mankind by 99.99%. And I became weaker. And even the more drawn-out through weaking of spirit to see and behold The World and the amount of evil, lawless ones. And I suddenly remembered the bible passage of scripture Revelations 7:1-8 that says. "Do not harm the earth, the sea, or the trees till we have sealed the servants of our G-D on their foreheads." And I heard the number of those who were sealed. 144,000 of the tribes of the children of Yisra'EL were sealed.

My heart fainted to see "The Major Evil" within humanity and "The Minor Good" Three or four flickers of light. Were the people that loved The Creator G-D. Anticipating his promise return. The Creator permitted me to hear. And I heard next. Mister sour gut. Mister Lava chest. Ole Slue-foot, prince of the air. That devil of a turned down

483

marriage proposal yelled to his minions. "FORWARD!.. ANNIHILATE THEM"

Satan wanted the last of the flickering lights that had the love of The Creator, G-D in their hearts to be put out. His words ring out into all the World. My heart failed me again.

Just on account of hearing Satan's words to forward on the annihilation of mankind. That would bring annihilation on all living things. The great and the small. Which included Ole sour gut's slue-foot's, Satan's own children. His own children he has prepared to be destroyed. I became sick to my stomach.

The way I saw it. It was like. The Devil was there as a coach of darkness. Strong as ever. Putting everything he has into the annihilation of humanity. G-D was there as a coach of light (love). Even much Stronger than the other coach's strengths. Humanity was the home team. In center field. I sat over in the highest point of the bleachers cheering and hoping for the home team (The World) to see the light. Because their souls were on the line. And I saw all the overwhelming odds, and the enticement of souls that the devil did against the home team because they have picked the wrong coach (The Devil). I became sick with the horrors while watching humanity in real time.

I observed as the home team in bed with the devil. Laying in a way. An assimilated Native American Indian of The Greater and Lesser Antilles would refer to as laying "Cat-gut" with the evil. (Stretched out in full enjoyment pleasure. And comfort. Partaking fully in the pleasures obtained through sin, wicked, unrighteous and lawless ways). While the _one_ who said. _"The wages of sin is death Romans 6:23_ was now there visiting the earth, looking in. As the fulfillment of that promise, had come to be fulfilled.

I passed away more than I was able to count. I couldn't take it. What I was seeing along with The Creator G-D was to much for soul. I had fear on all sides. Because I didn't know how what I was witnessing was going to end. But The LORD showed favor to me. And granted me mercy. And revived,

485

comforted, and strengthened me. Each time I fainted. Which was many.

I wanted to tell the home team (Humanity). All those The Creator G-D saw lying down Cat-gut with the evil and lawless one's that made the earth dark. To protect their necks, from the master's sickle. For the master of the vineyard had come to the laborers. To give everyone their hire in the fields (Earth).

But the time had come also in the spiritual realm. That those found lying joyfully cat-gut should not receive any further warning from The LORD Most High. _That the wages of sin is death. And the gift of G-D is eternal life_. And as I looked in horror for humanity. Where The Creator had placed me above his right shoulder. I wrote what I saw as instructed by The Creator. The Great Spirit G-D.

We came in even closer to The Earth. And The Holy Spirit says to me. "All those that are of the light. The few. Who's light you see there flickering?. The Creator. The Great Spirit G-D of Yisra'EL Yahweh will save, has come to save. And yet have saved already. Those that are off the darkness. That you see there. That covers The Earth? Those The Creator. The Great Spirit G-D of Yisra'EL Yahweh (Yo'way) has pulled back from his people and will destroy. And will cause to fade away from the face of the earth.

TREE
OF LIFE

CHAPTER XLIV

And I did look, and I did see. And I did learn. All that The Most High wanted me to learn. And I stayed in heaven for what felt like three months. Just writing, watching and listening. Seeing and learning. I was taught by too many to list. One was the Buddha Siddhārtha Gautama and he taught me about his journey to enlightenment starving himself on one grain of rice. His life and his upbringing. And so many other things. I have great respect for Buddha. He is one of The Creator's G-D in Heaven. He is among other G-D's of The Creator. And I spent time learning from Father Abraham who also instructed me to share with the people. That he would only have one question. To enter New Jerusalem. Holy Mount Zion. Before you can progress pass him. Into eternal rest.

Which is "Who Are You? Abraham explained to me that he will ask who are you? Not expecting that you will say your name. And that you're from the smith's family. And your mother's name is Sarah and your daddy's name is Mike. But you will have to answer with heavens alignment of who you are. From which tribe of the Nation of Yisra'EL you are from. To gain entry.

For instance. I am mine eyes are toward The Creator's Wilderness (Elioenai Sahara). Daughter of The House of Yacob (Jacob). Seed of Father Abraham. Priestess of The Nation of Yisra'EL. Queen of Righteousness & Peace. After The Order of Melchezedic's Royal Priesthood. I am the lot of Yahweh (Yo'way) The Great Spirit G-D's inheritance. I am of The Tribe of Benjamin. The Wolf Clan.

I am Priestess and servant of The Four G-D's of Yisra'EL. G-D Hashem, EL, Adonai. The G-D, Hashem, EL, EL, Elyon. The G-D, Hashem, EL Gibhor. And The G-D, Hashem, EL Jehovah. _I am she that goes between Heaven and Earth. As an established bridge from G-D to Mankind. And Mankind back to G-D_. That should get me through heaven's gates because it is all factual, and in alignment with who Heaven says that I am. And heaven has flawless identity and DNA records. _Flawless!_

491

But not that my sister's name is sue and I hail from west-side Compton or Beverly hills for that matter. That will not do to pass through the gates of the descending Kingdom for its citizens. New Jerusalem. Many will enter through the covenant grace. Which you will not have to give your tribal identity because many who are not of the 12 tribes of Yisra'EL directly? Will still go into heaven under grace. These are called the Adopted people of G-D.

And I saw Moses and he spoke to me. Then I saw Joshua. Who was my guide to show me the different hell's for there are many hells. And he told me of a time when he took the Devils sword that he used to kill children just before their birth. And he would not give it back to the Devil. Until The LORD Most High spoke from Heaven and told him. "The Devil has a work to do. Give it back Joshua." And I saw and spoke to King David. And I saw and spoke to many Elders. Elders of The Ancient Maya also. And I looked around

Heaven. And I saw many Chiefs and Elders of The Native American Indian people. But I did not see any of those that are called saints. When I arrived back to Earth after writing all that The Creator, The Great Spirit G-D of יִשְׂרָ אל Yisra'EL' יְהֹוָה YAHWEH had given to me.

I recall telling a friend. I said in my dismay. "There are Native American Indians (Indigenous Peoples) in Heaven's skies like diamonds. They are everywhere in Heaven for multitude. All the stars are Native American Indian Peoples. With all that the LORD Most High had given me to write. I started to feel as though I had hit the jackpot! And my number in heaven has fallen and it was finally my time to go and make a withdrawal from the bank of *LIFE*... And as I looked on the writings and considered how blessed I was.

And I considered that all my life I seek the LORD. And I had finally had The door of G-D open to me. The one spoken that his son will lead you to his father?. That door opened wide to me on The Blue Blood Moon of January 31st, 2019. And remained open for three months I remain in Heaven. Eating angels' food.

I looked down on the writing The Most High gave me. And considered how blessed I was. An angel came from G-D to me in a hurry and said to me. "IF YOU THINK WHAT HAS BEEN GIVEN TO YOU IS JUST FOR YOU? YOU WOULD HAVE MISSED THE MARK OF THE HIGHER CALLING INWHICH THE MOST HIGH HAS CALLED YOU TOO." That statement did deflate my ego I had after finding. And meeting G-D. And I wondered what kind of jackpot (reward) is this? That I would have to go back and work harder for? I have to share it with others. And I did all the work all these 40 years? And instantaneously I knew the Holy Spirit meant that I should help the other children of The Creator. That he loves so much. With the knowledge that I had. That he taught me. I

493

knew this because I knew. That Fathar's children is close and dear to his heart. More than anything else. So, I knew also right away when the Spirit spoke those words. I knew that I needed to look back at the children of G-D to stand up before the face of their coming King. Who has come into The World at this time to save them. And redeem them unto himself that where he is? There they may be also.

So, I said to G-D. Something true. I said. "These people are a stiff neck and a rebellious people LORD. Just like you said in your word. They will not listen to me. They will hear that I do not sound like them, and they will not listen to me.

Their heads are high up in the clouds. And they will not heed my words. Who am I that they should listen to me? Before me many were sent. And they did not listen." They will not accept what you have sent through me.

PSALM 119:89

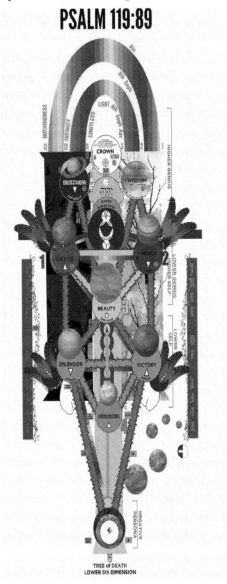

Then The Holy Spirit sent from G-D came and said to me. **"THE CREATOR HAS CALLED YOU TO ENTER HIS**

MARKET PLACE. ENTER THE MARKETPLACE OF THE LORD MOST HIGH. AND THE LORD WILL DIRECT WHOM HE CHOOSES TO YOU. I said. "But how? And where should I begin?" The Holy Spirit sent from G-D says. "A Ministry" I say. "Ministry? What kind of ministry?" The Holy Spirit said to me. "A Charity. An organization." And I did write everything The Creator instructed me to write. When I completed putting together all the notes and writing? A diagram of the Tree of Life came from the writing that I collected from Heaven. Above is written Psalms 119:89 which reads, "Forever O LORD, THY word is settled in Heaven. After The Holy Spirit finished speaking to me about The Creators desire for me to go into Ministry? Then Holy Fathar. The Creator spoke to me from Heaven. He says to me. ***"Elioenai? You are a Priestess Forever. After The Order of Měl chǐz'e děk.*** Looking back on my journal notes taken during the time of my ascension into Heaven? Where I wrote all my conversations with the divine forces of heaven? On September 30, 2018. I wrote this note in my journal. "G-D called me a Teacher of Jacob his inheritance. And I did like the appointment. Because I tried to see over a long cause of time, my way of delivery unto his people. Teaching, "I can do." I ended the note with a smiley face. Which-means the LORD had that planed for me long before the Holy Spirit came to tell me to enter his marketplace.

To fulfill The Creator, The Great Spirit G-D of יִשְׂרָ אל Yisra'EL יְהֹוָה YAHWEH's request of me. I started Elioenai Sahara Ministry. A 501c (3) Charitiable Organization, Tax Exempt. **Elioenaisahara.com** To bring out of a state of Assimilation. The Descendants of Native American Indians. Then to the Righteous. The Chosen, and The Adopted

496

Kingdom Citizens. And all the writing The Creator, The Great Spirit G-D of Yisra'EL has given me can be found at **Elioenaibookstore.com**. To bring out of a state of assimilation was a major part of the teaching and lessons I received from The Creator. And the LORD gave us our purpose. And I wrote the purpose as The LORD Most High told me. Which is: - To do the will of The Creator, The Great Spirit G-D of Yisra'EL YAHWEH, The Sovereign G-D; Blessed be he; who has chosen anointed and sent me.

1. **ALEPH א** To Bring Out of A State Of Assimilation The Descendants of Native American Indians, Then To The Chosen; The Righteous; And The Adopted Kingdom Citizens

2. **Bēt ב** To release the Oppressed

3. **Gimel ג** To bring Good News to the Poor, and Healing to the Broken Hearted

4. **Dālet ד** To Proclaim Recovery of Sight To The Blind

5. **Hēh ה** To Proclaim Liberty to The Captives; And That they shall ALL be set FREE

6. **Wāw ו** To Proclaim The Year of The LORD's Favor

7. **Zayin ז** To Proclaim The Day of The Vengeance of Our G-D, The Creator.

As I sat at home and contemplated what I saw and heard in heaven. I knew. This world as we know it, would soon be a changed place by G-D. I started telling people. Go to wherever you need to be right away. Because you are going to need help with what is coming into the world. And you shouldn't be alone. Everyone is going to need someone. The G-D's of Heaven is on their way. And wherever you are found?. You will be stuck there until The LORD makes a consummation of his works on earth. Every name brand thing I owned. Every polyester. Every mix fiber clothing. As G-D Adonai warned me about the righteous wearing mix fiber clothing. And the need for me to wear 100% linen. Every item I had that did not look like who I was. A Native American Indian and or a righteous person? I place it in the trash. Along with every item of my 1492 and beyond captivity. When into the garbage. And all idols I owned. Became instant garbage. That The LORD and The G-D's should not fine any in my dwelling place when they came to visit The Earth. I cleaned it up so that I may live. And not die, from their anger of abundant vanity.

LADY
LIBERTY

CHAPTER **XLV**

On August 27, 2019, I woke up at 3am, by a frightening vision. In the vision I was standing. And before me there were many high fenced up gates. And the gates were able to open. Many did not make it through the gates and the waters came. And flooded out many other gates. And just as the flood water was going to overtake me at my gate? The Creator opened my gate that I was able to escape the rising flood. I made it out with a cut in my right hand. That seemed to have been place there by G-D as a reminder of the event. I made it to the other side. Many that were on the opposite side of the flood? Rejoice and celebrated that they were not overtaken by the flood waters as so many where.

On September 14, 2019, I laid down to sleep. And I looked and I became absent in the body and present with The LORD. And I saw The Spirit of The LORD came down from Heaven. And I was with The LORD, and observe from the right side of The LORD's shoulder, as before. The feet of

The LORD landed on the Earth like a great explosion. Upon the harbor shoreline. Directly behind Lady Liberty.

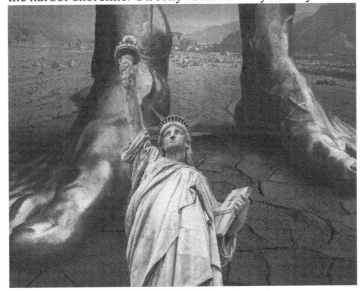

The Earth shuck. And The Heavens were moved. And made a loud noise. The LORD's appearance was wrathful. And He was filled with rage because of his anger. And his cloak was red with blood. And they that were with him. Were many. And he spoke not a word to her. And his wrathful appearance conquered lady liberty. As she turned slowly to see what was behind her. Lady liberty saw The LORD standing behind her. And she proceeded to melted down to her knees with a feverish shaking and trembling. In fear of The LORD. And in dread of his anger.

While on her knees. Lady Liberty trembled uncontrollably. She places her eyes to the ground, and she never looked up again. But that one initial first glance when she saw The LORD and caretaker of The Earth standing behind her. I sat over the right shoulder of The LORD Most High where he had placed me. Though Lady Liberty and The

LORD didn't speak? I sense. And felt that there was a mutual knowledge between The LORD Most High, and Lady Liberty. As though, that day was expected. And had finally come. Or finally came. It was just a feeling that I had in the spirit. That The LORD and Lady Liberty knew together. That day would come. So they did not have to exchange words.

Then The LORD. And all that was with Him. Entered all the Cities. I watch as the spirits innumerable advance toward the cities, by crossing the harbor. While many was asleep and unaware. And I looked from the right shoulder of the LORD Most High. There he had placed me so that I would witness. And write the account of what I had seen. And I felt sorry for Lady Liberty. Her spirit is feminine. So as a Lady, Lady Liberty kneeled. Before the higher powers. Which all Boys, Girls, Sir's Madam's Lady's, Lords, Queens, and Kings will have to do there *shortly. Before The LORD Most High.*

Lords, Lady's, Queens and Kings look to G-D. G-D gives a reply. Then they take that reply and give it to the people. After thinking about it. Her Spirit did what was expected of any Lady. Which was to quit, while she was ahead. Face with a strong man standing behind her. Because The Most High G-D was wrathful like a strong man to run a race. I knew? The liberty of the whole world was symbolically taken by G-D. Because G-D is a G-D of signs and wonders. And I did have great sorrow. As it is written. Those who increase in knowledge; also increase in sorrow.

On September 18th, 2019 The Holy Spirit sent by G-D came. And took me up to Heaven. And I looked. And behold. There were two escalators. And two races of people. One was ascending to G-D on High.

And the others were descending from G-D to hell. And I looked and saw. As the people on each side looked at each other. And low. All had their cattle and bags, and wheels and wagons. And animals. And children. Those ascending and descending. One race G-D descend. And another race G-D advance toward him. And the ascending race were the children of Yacob/Jacob (The Yisralites). And the descending race were the children of Esau (The Edomites). Even in this. I knew that changes would come into the world sent by G-D, The Creator.

On December 12, 2019, just before bedtime. The Spirit of The LORD visited me and says to me. "The same spoken of freedom that occurred 3,000 years ago in Egypt? Is coming around again tonight." And then I was woken up at 1:25am to the howling of the winds that happen all night until daybreak the following morning.

On December 15th, 2019, as I was at home. G-D, Hashem, EL Jehovah came to me and said. "As I live. I will cut the world down. All that should be left is 20 to 40% of the people." I had never seen G-D Jehovah angry. Because he is *filled* with love. Ask anyone of his servants. And they will tell you? G-D Jehovah. Never gets angry. I love him deeply because he is all good. And a mighty provider. But this day? He was angry. And wrathful. Which is not his nature. I felt bless that he was not angry with me. And I felt sorrow for all. His anger was towards. And just as he touched down in my house. And said those words to me? He left just as quickly. More and more. I kept understanding. That The World. Was in trouble with G-D. And his G-DS. *Deuteronomy 10:17 says. "For The LORD your G-D is G-D of G-Ds.*

On December 21, 2020, while I was following the Tree of Life given to me by The Creator. And the intergalactic

Circle of Happiness Observational Calendar given to me by The LORD Most High. I saw the blue star that is spoken of come into The World. The one that is said will arrive and changes would follow.

I was alone when I saw it while following the heavenly signs the Most High give me to observe. I saw that which the Mayans spoke off for December 12, 2012. Take place in The World on December 21, 2020. I was amaze. This was the end of the world as we knew the world to be. I fell on my knees and thank The LORD for permitting me to be present. With a blessed front row seat. I love The LORD. He has most certainly heard *all* my cries. On December 26, 2020, The Holy Spirit sent from G-D came to me and says. *"When the moon passes between The Earth and The Sun? The world will be a changed place. And it will never be the same again.*

I told others what The LORD had told me. It was all I could do to save some that they should prepare for what I saw was coming through the signs and wonders of Heaven, taught to me by The Creator. I did not only see the blue star that is prophesied by the Hopi Indians. I saw everything else that was in alignment with it. I saw what gate within the sun. I saw what mansion of the moon. I even know which chakra (which one of the seven spirits standing before the Creator's face). And not only that! That day fell on tzedek, (mercy) the color (blue) in Kabbalah/Qabalah).

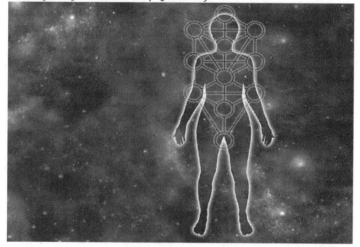

December 26, 2019, annular solar eclipse brought in The Day of Purification. Which is the day of Eternal Righteousness, when the world tilted to righteousness. A paradigm shift. December 26, 2019 was a New Moon sabbath day. And, It was the sabbath of the week in Heaven. Heaven follows thirteen days as a week. And the journey through the thirteen days, the Creator has blessed me with the knowledge, to teach his Kingdom Citizens.

While everyone was watching for the Mayan prophecy in December of 2012. The prophecy of The Mayan's came on December 21, 2020. The LORD's holy word says to them that seek the sign. Matthew 16:4. A wicked and adulterous generation seeketh after a sign; and there shall no sign be given unto it." And G-D promise me that if I would do as he has asked of me. *He will bless those who blesses me; and he will curse those who curses me. And all people of the earth will be blessed through me.*

It was a double sabbath day when the world was a changed place. Along with the annular solar eclipse. And The Creator, The Great Spirit "YAHWEH" did let my eyes behold it. And I indeed felt bless for the blessed front row seat in the LORD Most High's Coming. December 26, 2020, put the icing on the cake of the Hopi Indian and Mayan prophecy. I knew I had to do something to warn others. So, I posted something, very profound. And very straight forward. Because unto the wise. All things wise. Proverbs 12:15 says. The way of a fool is right in his own eyes: but he that hearken unto counsel is wise. I posted, "People of the Most High? Be sure your anchor holds; or you *will* be a *drifting seaman in 2021*. But before I posted those words, I place this before it. "A word to the wise, should always be sufficient." From those words. Warning that many would lose their life. (a drifting seamen if their lives were not anchored in The LORD Most High to today? 5,062,106 people are confirmed dead worldwide. I begged many to seek G-D while he was able to be found of them.

On December 28, 2019, at 9:04am after The LORD gave me the answers to my prayer and my supplication which was to understand completely the TREE OF LIFE information, he had previously given to me. I was given the knowledge I required from The LORD from 7:00am to 9:04am and I was very happy to receive a swift reply to my request of The LORD. And my heart was filled with the knowledge. And then The LORD says to me. "BEHOLD, I HAVE PUT MY WORDS IN YOUR MOUTH, SEE, I HAVE THIS DAY SET YOU OVER THE NATIONS AND OVER THE KINGDOMS, TO ROOT OUT AND TO PULL DOWN TO DESTROY AND TO THROW DOWN, TO BUILD AND TO PLANT." I immediately started to cry for I knew, it was the LORD. But previously the LORD had told me to cry no more and to not have crying coming from the sound of my voice. Because it was not the time for sorrow. But for Jubilee. For gladness. And rejoicing. I tried to stop crying when I remembered the words of the LORD, Most High, so I say to him in apology.

"LORD I will try harder to except **THY** good works without tears. But **THOU** oh LORD overwhelms my soul with **THY** goodness. if **THOU** will make every work of my hands fruitful, then I would except **THY** goodness without tears. But in peace. And with understanding of your divine favor over my life, all the days that I should live upon the face of the Earth, unto Eternity. I will accept **THY** good and loving kindness toward me forever without tears. If it pleases you. For I am a vessel of thine own handmade. **THOU** have brought me to the place of **THY** choosing. That I may obtain the heritage of my forefathers. Let my life be an instrument of your love. And in all of my doing let it be for your glory and for your honor oh Great Spirit.

In January 2021 The LORD gave me a wakeful vision early in the morning. When I was not asleep but lying down. And I look and I saw a flag with the colors thereof of red, of white and of blue. And it cascaded out of Heaven's sky. Slowly it came down to the ground. The moment the flag touched the ground, ripples of moving water came from it.

The water from it started small and increase quickly and mightily in seconds. Until the water became a monstrous body of water. Blotting out the sky. The waves were so high and black. People started running for their lives and I stood still and look upon the monstrous flood. And I said because of the viciousness of its waves.

"Oh, My LORD." And in my vision on the other side of the exceedingly great flood. The LORD did save many and brought out many. I stood on a mountain top in the vision holding The LORD's staff given to me by him. That he calls the staff of his Authority on Earth. And I looked down upon the flooding earth. And as the world as I knew it was going to be overcome by the flood waters? The Spirit of The LORD by a Mighty angel brought a small number of people out

before the floods overtook them where the flag had descended from the sky. And he placed the people before me that I should teach them that which he taught me. And to care for them. As The Nation of G-D. The Great Spirit Yahweh.

As the people that The LORD brought out of the world to me stood before me. I looked behind them and the flood waters consumed the whole world. And it was no longer to be found. And I said unto the People. As The LORD had taught me. "Hear Oh Yisra'EL The LORD our G-D is One. Blessed be the name of our G-D. And bless is his glorious Kingdom. These be the commandments and statues and ordinances that the LORD your G-D has instructed me to teach you. To follow in the land that you are about to enter and possess. So that you and your children and grandchildren may fear the LORD your G-D all the days of your lives by keeping all His statutes and commandments that I give you this day. So that your days may be prolonged in the New Land The Creator has prepared, brought, and *WILL GIVE TO YOU.*

THE DOCTRINE

CHAPTER XLVI

O n June 20, 2020. I learned of the doctrine of discovery for the first time. And I did read it. And what I read was sickening to me. The Bull of 1453, also called The Doctrine of Discovery is a document that I came across. It possess a treat to every brown skinned person under the sun. I never knew it existence before 2020. But this I knew without a shadow of a doubt. Whatever happened during that time period of 1492? The Creator, The Great Spirit is zealous with wrathful anger toward it, even today. His anger toward that? Stands *firm in the heavens above The Earth.*

As I read The Doctrine of <u>no</u> discovery weeping inconsolable. The Creator says to me. "They that entered the gates of my people. Should have never entered their gates. Not only that daughter! They did not have to kill my people. They were peace-loving people. And they that entered? Did not have to kill them."

Because of the doctrine and the life around that time? I learned many were taken as slaves. Captives. And millions were assimilation into the European culture and indoctrinated or murdered that lived in the Greater and Lesser Antilles (The Caribbeans). My people were told by the Catholic missionaries and priest. That they were black because of their sins. Jacob/Yacob. These people? The Lot of The Great Spirit, YAHWEH's (Yaya, Yo'way) inheritance. The apple of The Creator's eyes.

Benjamin (The Bahamas) where Hundreds of thousands of Native American Indians died. Yes. But they did not die out. As the world continues to suggest. Which I felt is said as a form of copout. Rather than to look. Find and help and rescue the masses to escape the indentured servitude contract their fore-fathers and fore-mothers signed. And the effects of 1492 assimilation of a people? Is still being felt in 2022.

Denying those who has passed away. From the senseless violence of 1492. A connection to their descendants alive today. I am Tiano. "Tiano" I am. I am Native American Indian. My Great Grandmother and Great granddaddy we're Cherokee Indian. Which make their son. My grandfather Cherokee Indian. Which made his son. My Dad. Cherokee Indian. My dad's mother is Tiano Native American Indian.

On my Mother's side is Tiano Native American Indian. Her Mother is Tiano. And her Mother's Mother was Hopi Native American Indian. The Hopi Native American Indian, is the cousin's of The Tiano Native American Indian. Which makes me. Ancient Generational Descendant of The Native American Indian. AND I AM NOT DEAD. "TAINABIKA" THE TIANOS LIVE." And a-da-ne-di, a-yv, v-le-ni-do-hv. Which are Cherokee words for. "Give me life."

They. Us. We. The Assimilated Native American Indian descendants. That Christopher Columbus throw dirt on. Is not dead. The Creator G-D desires all to see his resurrecting powers. The few that are becoming awake. Is a joke. Compared to what he will do with his powers for the resurrecting of HIS seventh generation of HIS inheritance. When he opens the Heavens above the earth. And the masses The Great Spirit Yahweh (Yo'way) will awaken of his people to their heritage. Which is HIM. Nothing, And no one. Will be able to stop it. I am awake because The Creator G-D of The Cherokee people (my great grandmother Marquicee's G-D) desires it to be so. Because of The Covenant Promise he had with my ancestors. For I am off the seventh generation

514

of The Creator. And he has cause for me to become awake that I make partake of my inheritance. Which is HIM.

Isabella of Spain. Fell far from grace when she troubled the humble. Peace loving people of the remote lands. So far from grace. To have overseen the rape, slaughter, lynching, destruction and annihilation of millions of innocent woman and children. But to enjoy the richest obtained through bloodshed. Which only brought temporary pleasures. I say temporary because of Ecclesiastes 1:2 that says "Vanity from Vanity of vanities. Saith the Preacher, vanity of vanities; all is vanity." Whether an hour filled with the pleasures of vanity. A week. A Month. A Year. Five Years. 10 Years. Two Hundred Years or Four Hundred Years for that matter. Punishment will always come for the reward of blood guiltiness. And is come already. Christopher Columbus felt bless with many stolen treasures. But what he did was curse future generations.

The Doctrine of Discovery 1493 The Papal Bull "Inter Caetera," issued by Pope Alexander VI on May 4, 1493, played a central role in the Spanish conquest of the New World. The document supported Spain's strategy to ensure its exclusive right to the lands discovered by Columbus the previous year. It established a demarcation line one hundred leagues west of the Azores and Cape Verde Islands and assigned Spain the exclusive right to acquire territorial possessions and to trade in all lands west of that line. All others were forbidden to approach the lands west of the line without special license from the rulers of Spain.

This effectively gave Spain a monopoly on the lands in the New World. The Bull stated that any land not inhabited by Christians was available to be "discovered," claimed, and exploited by Christian rulers and declared that "the Catholic faith and the Christian religion be exalted and be

515

everywhere increased and spread, that the health of souls be cared for and that barbarous nations (The Native American Indian Nations) be overthrown and brought to the faith itself." This "Doctrine of Discovery" became the basis of all European claims in the Americas as well as the foundation for the United States' western expansion. In the US Supreme Court in the 1823 case Johnson v. McIntosh, Chief Justice John Marshall's opinion in the unanimous decision held "that the principle of discovery gave European nations an absolute right to New World lands." In essence, American Indians had only a right of occupancy, which could be abolished. The Bull Inter Caetera made headlines again throughout the 1990s and in 2000, when many Catholics petitioned Pope John Paul II to formally revoke it and recognize the human rights of indigenous "non-Christian peoples."

This is the document that has been destroying brown and black Native American Indians lives from 1493 unto today. And **The Doctrine of Discovery** that dictates how G-D the Creator's people are treated in the world when anyone comes in contact with them. **The 1492 Doctrine of Discovery reads as follows:**

Alexander, bishop, servant of the servants of G-d, to the illustrious sovereigns, our very dear son in Christ, Ferdinand, king, and our very dear daughter in Christ, Isabella, queen of Castile, Leon, Aragon, Sicily, and Granada, health and apostolic benediction. Among other works well pleasing to the Divine Majesty and cherished of our heart, this assuredly ranks highest, that in our times especially *the Catholic faith and the Christian religion be exalted and be everywhere increased and spread, that the health of souls be cared for and that barbarous nations be overthrown and brought to the faith itself.* Wherefore inasmuch as by the favor of divine clemency, we, though of insufficient merits, have been called to this Holy See of Peter, recognizing that as true Catholic kings and princes, such as we have known you always to be, and as your illustrious deeds already known to almost the whole world declare, you not only eagerly desire but with every effort, zeal, and diligence, without regard to hardships, expenses, dangers, with the shedding even of your blood, are laboring to that end; recognizing also that you have long since dedicated to this purpose your whole soul and all your endeavors--as witnessed in these times with so much glory to the Divine Name in your recovery of the kingdom of Granada from the yoke of the Saracens--we therefore are rightly led, and hold it as our duty, to grant you even of our own accord and in your favor those things whereby with effort each day more hearty you may be *enabled for the honor of God himself and the spread of the Christian rule to carry forward your holy and praiseworthy purpose so pleasing to immortal God.*

We have indeed learned that you, who for a long time had intended to seek out and discover certain islands and mainlands remote and unknown and not hitherto discovered by others, to the end that you might bring to the worship of *our Redeemer* and the profession of the Catholic faith their residents and inhabitants, having been up to the present time greatly engaged in the siege and recovery of the kingdom itself of Granada were unable to accomplish this holy and praiseworthy purpose; but the said kingdom having at length been regained, as was pleasing to the Lord, you, with the wish to fulfill your desire, chose our beloved son, Christopher Columbus, a man assuredly worthy and of the highest recommendations and fitted for so great an undertaking, whom you furnished with ships and men equipped for like designs, not without the greatest hardships, dangers, and expenses, to make diligent quest for these remote and unknown mainlands and islands through the sea, where hitherto no one had sailed; and they at length, with divine aid and with the utmost diligence sailing in the ocean sea, discovered certain very remote islands and even mainlands that hitherto had not been discovered by others; wherein dwell very many peoples living in peace, and, as reported, going unclothed, and not eating flesh. Moreover, as your aforesaid envoys are of opinion, **these very people living in the said islands and countries believe in one G-D, the Creator in heaven, and seem sufficiently disposed to embrace the Catholic faith and be trained in good morals. And it is hoped that, were they instructed, the name of the Savior, our Lord Jesus Christ, would easily be introduced into the said countries and islands.**

Also, on one of the chiefs of these aforesaid islands the said Christopher has already caused to be put together and built a fortress fairly equipped, wherein he has stationed as garrison certain Christians, companions of his, who are to make search for other remote and unknown islands and mainlands. In the islands and countries already discovered are found gold, spices, and very many other precious things of divers kinds and qualities. Wherefore, as becomes Catholic kings and princes, after earnest consideration of all matters, **especially of the rise and spread of the Catholic faith, as was the fashion of your ancestors,** kings of renowned memory, you have purposed with the favor of divine clemency to **bring under your sway the said mainlands and islands with their residents and inhabitants and to bring them to the Catholic faith.**

Hence, heartily commending in the Lord this your holy and praiseworthy purpose, and desirous that it be duly accomplished, and that the name of our Savior be carried into those regions, we exhort you very earnestly in the Lord and by your reception of holy baptism, whereby you are bound to our apostolic commands, and by the bowels of the mercy of **our Lord Jesus Christ,** enjoy strictly, that inasmuch as with eager zeal for the true faith you design to equip and dispatch this expedition, you purpose also, as is your duty**, to lead the peoples dwelling in those islands and countries to embrace the Christian religion;** nor at any time let dangers or hardships deter you therefrom, with the stout hope and trust in your hearts that Almighty God will further your undertakings.

And, in order that you may enter upon so great an undertaking with greater readiness and heartiness endowed with benefit of our apostolic favor, we, of our own accord, not at your instance nor the request of anyone else in your regard, but out of our own sole largess and certain knowledge and out of the fullness of our apostolic power, by the authority of Almighty God conferred upon us in blessed Peter and of the vicarship of Jesus Christ, which we hold on earth, do by tenor of these presents, should any of said islands have been found by your envoys and captains, give, grant, and assign to you and your heirs and successors, kings of Castile and Leon, forever, together with all their dominions, cities, camps, places, and villages, and all rights, jurisdictions, and appurtenances, all islands and mainlands found and to be found, discovered and to be discovered towards the west and south, by drawing and establishing a line from the Arctic pole, namely the north, to the Antarctic pole, namely the south, no matter whether the said mainlands and islands are found and to be found in the direction of India or towards any other quarter, the said line to be distant one hundred leagues towards the west and south from any of the islands commonly known as the Azores and Cape Verde. With this proviso however that none of the islands and mainlands, found and to be found, discovered and to be discovered, beyond that said line towards the west and south, be in the actual possession of any Christian king or prince up **to the birthday of our Lord Jesus Christ** just past from which the present year one thousand four hundred ninety-three begins. **And we make, appoint, and depute you and your said heirs and successors lords of them with full and free power, authority, and jurisdiction of every kind;** with this proviso however, that by this our gift, grant, and assignment no right acquired by any Christian prince, who may be in actual possession of said islands and mainlands prior to the said birthday of our Lord Jesus Christ, is hereby to be understood to be withdrawn or taking away.

Moreover we command you in virtue of holy obedience that, employing all due diligence in the premises, as you also promise--nor do we doubt your compliance therein in accordance with your loyalty and royal greatness of spirit--you should appoint to the aforesaid mainlands and islands worthy, G-dfearing, learned, skilled, and experienced men, in order to instruct the aforesaid inhabitants and residents in the Catholic faith and train them in good morals. Furthermore, under penalty of excommunication "late sententie" to be incurred "ipso facto," should anyone thus contravene, we strictly forbid all persons of whatsoever rank, even imperial and royal, or of whatsoever estate, degree, order, or condition, to dare without your special permit or that of your aforesaid heirs and successors, to go for the purpose of trade or any other reason to the islands or mainlands, found and to be found, discovered and to be discovered, towards the west and south, by drawing and establishing a line from the Arctic pole to the Antarctic pole, no matter whether the mainlands and islands, found and to be found, lie in the direction of India or toward any other quarter whatsoever, the said line to be distant one hundred leagues towards the west and south, as is aforesaid, from any of the islands commonly known as the Azores and Cape Verde; apostolic constitutions and ordinances and other decrees whatsoever to the contrary notwithstanding. We trust in Him from whom empires and governments and all good things proceed, that, should you, with the Lord's guidance, pursue this holy and praiseworthy undertaking, in a short while your hardships and endeavors will attain the most felicitious result, to the happiness and glory of all Christendom. But inasmuch as it would be difficult to have these present letters sent to all places where desirable, we wish, and with similar accord and knowledge do decree, that to? copies of them, signed by the hand of a public notary commissioned therefor, and sealed with the seal of any ecclesiastical officer or ecclesiastical court, the same respect is to be shown in court and outside as well as anywhere else as would be given to these presents should they thus be exhibited or shown. Let no one, therefore, infringe, or with rash boldness contravene, this our recommendation, exhortation, requisition, gift, grant, assignment, constitution, deputation, decree, mandate, prohibition, and will. Should anyone presume to attempt this, be it known to him that he will incur the wrath of Almighty G-d and of the blessed apostles Peter and Paul. Given at Rome, at St. Peter's, in the year of the incarnation of our Lord one thousand four hundred and ninety-three, the fourth of May, and the first year of our pontificate. *Here ends The Doctrine that first enslaved my Great-Great Grandparents. In 1492. And enslaved me until present day 2021.*

THOSE
DOGS?

CHAPTER XLVII

They that sent Christopher Columbus. And endorse his voyage? Are the real savages. They called my people The Native American Indians, Savages all day long. All those that took park in killing and murdering innocent woman and children, and cornering and capturing them unaware? Are the dogs they once said my ancestors were. Now you are the ones in the crab pen. Cornered like trapped rats. In a cornered place. That you once had place my ancestors in. You are in the crab pen of The Creator, my people's G-D. And the walls of that crab pen The Creator has around you? Are fortified and it reaches up to the sky. And you should not escape.

And you should have no peace. **THOU** dogs that furnished Christopher Columbus voyage to massacre my people. And uphold Christopher Columbus believes. And never looked back at the destruction he have caused. That I should wake up from the enchantment of colonization, assimilation, indoctrination of 1492. In 2020.

While others are skill unconsciously imprisoned by your evil deeds. For one life taken of the Children of The Creator G-D my people The Native American Indians? So saith The LORD Jehovah of The Kingdom of The South to declare: *Jeremiah 9:22.* *"Dead bodies will lie like dung on the open field. Like cut grain behind the reaper. With no one to gather them."*

Blood for Blood and Slaughter for Slaughter. Exodus 21:24 of The LORD Most High's holy word says. *"An eye for an eye. And a tooth for a tooth."* Which we humans have taken take statement for ourself and internalized it. To say treat people like they treat you. I for an eye, tooth for a tooth. But it is actually a warning from The Creator to mankind, Warning that if they killed, they will be killed. If blood is shed, blood will be required not of man. But of G-D.

Deuteronomy 19:21 says. *"And thine eye should not pity. But life shall go for life, eye for eye, tooth for tooth, hand for hand, foot for foot."* But in the assimilated Native

American Indian's mind such as myself. Of which we can all thank Christopher Columbus for my exactness of speak. Which I understand G-D's sacred scriptures to mean. Blood for Blood and Slaughter for Slaughter. Nothing that belongs to **THEE** will be able to be found on Earth. No not one thing! UNLESS! **THOU** seize the opportunity to seek final repentance. Though repentance has actually lost her favor. The Creator is GREAT! And there is still, repentance grace. Tick, Tock, Savages who said me and mine once were. Time waits for no man.

The Native American Indian descendants are assimilated because of the dogs that entered their borders. Attempting to strip them and their future generations of their identity. The Knowledge of The Creator G-D and their heritage. Which is weaved into Creation Story. As they divided and conquer. Well, coming through the spiritual realm near those who divided and conquered? Is the "Real Conquering Lion of The Tribe of Judah." Who is able to strip and no man cloth again. And cloth. And no man can strip.

Prepare yourselves in sackcloth. Beseech The Creator for forgiveness because of the works of many forefathers hands. For there is no carpet big enough to cover the sins of old.

The Native American Indians. The people of The West Indies. (The Caribbean). Jacob/Yacob of The Tribe of Benjamin, The Bahamas and the rest of The Greater and Lesser Antilles Islands people are still asleep from 1492 to present day. A perpetual sleep. It is because of these the sleeping assimilated descendants of The Creator. That G-D asked and inquire with Ezekiel about the dry bones of his people. And that those not awake. Will be awakened. And that their dry bones will live again. *Ezekiel 37:1-14 NIV declares. And he said, "Son of man can these bones live?. Prophesy to these bones and say to them, 'Dry bones, hear the word of The LORD. I will make breath enter you, and you will come to life. I will attach tendons to you and make flesh come upon you and cover you with skin; I will put breath in you and you will come to life. "Prophesy to these bones and say to them, Dry bones, hear the word of The LORD. My people, I am going to open your graves and bring you up from them; I will bring you back to the land of Israel. Then you my people will know that I am The LORD. When I open your graves and bring you up from them. I will put my Spirit in you and you will live, and I will settle you in your own land. Then you will know that I The LORD have spoken, and I have done it, declares The LORD.*

The Native American Indian descendants have received the sleep of death because of contact with the Europeans. Whose goal was to divide and conquer The Creator's people. The Native American Indian descendants are the most assimilated people in History. Because in the year 2022 they are still being assimilated into a culture and way of life, that is not in line with the orders, the statues, the ordinances, and the laws, and or precepts handed down to their forefathers from The Creator, as ways, for us to live by. I remember when I woke up to my true identity. And self-realization. As a Native American Indian. I found myself sitting as The Son of G-D had given me a liquid like honey to drink and left me. Two hours of just sitting still crying. I felt robbed of many years of my life. With different

thoughts running through my mind. Of one I can remember and will never forget. I said to myself. "Who did this to me?" And I became angry like any other victim. And when I saw the doctrine of discovery? I knew who did it to me. And I recognize a great evil in the earth. I knew who had hurt me. And cause me all the pain and suffering I had. All those years. I knew who had given me the hardest journey. I didn't wish on anyone else. And I wept again. That doctrine was such a hard read. My heart kept failing in the process. It took me near three days to completely read The Doctrine of Discovery. I wept like a baby before my Husbandman and Holy Fathar. The Creator. I could not be comforted. Because I knew. The Doctrine of Discovery I w as holding? Had ALL to do with the rivers of blood. That The LORD had placed both his hands in. That was the blood of his children. The Indigenous Native American Indian people. And he brought his hands to my face that I should witness and see why his anguish and sorrow existed. And G-D said to me. "Look at

528

this. See where my anger lies." The Doctrine of Discovery as I saw it in the spirit was a warrant to massacre and destroy my people The Native American Indians by any means necessary. And to subdue them.

As Pharaoh of Egypt did when he saw that the Yisraelites, The Natives, were so many in number, and would overtake his people. He commanded that every first born be put to death of The Creator G-D's people.

And when I looked from 1492. To 2020 when the Doctrine came into my life by divine intervention. I observed the indigenous peoples. The Native American Indians are the sufferers of The Earth from 1492 and or 400 years to today's date. Our hardships have reach up to the Highest Heaven. The prayer chambers has been opened before G-D, The Creator.

Therefore, the first should be the last and the last shall be first. I held the death warrant to massacre my people. And I continued weeping as The LORD did at the first when he visited my boudoir with a heavy heart. After learning who

The Creator G-D's children were who are scattered around the world. Whose blood has been shed and poured out like water filling the rivers (The Native American Indians). I needed to be comforted by The LORD. As in the first when I comforted G-D's heart from sorrow,

As I read the doctrine. "To set the Europeans sons above my people. The Native American Indian's sons? I ask The Creator to comfort my soul. Being assimilated into European white's culture. As many native Indians children are? Assimilation makes an individual suffer. I just didn't know that others had cause my planed our suffering until I read The Doctrine of Discovery. An assimilated individual bases his decisions on his artificial nature that was assimilated into him. All his life. He has a friction between his assimilated self and his spiritual/ real nature. Because assimilation programs you to never tap into your real self. It holds you back. To never have an action that is truly yours. In fact, it causes you to leave your real self alone and pick up an artificial form of you. All the days of an assimilated person's life is spent building a mirage, but he does not know it. Your Soul being is left behind. Which is our true self. Being spirit driven. As a Native American Indian.

It's like being someone's permanent prisoner. But you do not see the person you are a prisoner off. He programs you with limitations. To only go so far. It's like having an invisible electric fence up. And your mind is never able to go beyond that fence. But you can't see that beyond the fence is needed. Or better. Colonization Assimilation dumbs you down. And it's a GREAT sin.

Your prisoner locks you in a dark and lonely room and goes away forever. He pulls your strings. In his prison that he has made just for you. But he is nowhere visible to be found of you. So, you do not know what he has done to you exist in your reality. What assimilation does to the soul and the spirit of man. Is the sin. It was not my new state I wondered about. It was the old state I had before The Son of G-D's drink. Now that I was able to see my calamity. And it was great. I cried.

If the dogs had not visited? Of-cause am referring to the very same dogs that referred to my grandmother whom I love deeply, my grandfather, my father, my mother, my aunt, my uncle, my sister, my brother, my cousins, my friends, my relatives and our children, and their children. The Native American Indians as dogs. THOSE DOGS? The abominable dogs? I call "Sava-dogs" which is a combination of the 'Savage' and a 'Dog.

Don't attempt to find "Sava-dog" in the dictionary. Which sounds a lot like a salivating-dog to me. Which does fit the bill for what Christopher Columbus and the Europeans that entered did. That word and words like it. Are only found with the assimilated Native American Indians. We take one word out of the English language. And throw another in there to go after the first word. Then mix and match words together. To see how they fit. The way we like it. Or until we get the perfect curse word sound, we feel suits you. Regardless of its meaning. Once it feels good to us. We will let you have that which feels like you. And sounds like you ways to us.

Never argue with an assimilated Indian. And only G-D can help you to navigate what is being said about you. And if he is mad at you? He will mix and match to give you "one" word of what he thinks about you. While the unassimilated will give a sentence to express. And even hide what they are really saying. Within words. But you get the point. Just let someone call your old sweet grandma out her name. And especially behind her back. Like this Doctrine of Discovery that I feel should have been in the hands and taught in the schools of ALL Native American Indian descendants. As a history lesson for me to learn.

The Doctrine of Discovery looms over the heads of every Indigenous person. The Brown & The Black (The Creator's people.) And see just how you would react. And let that be plastered around the world and no one apologizes. And everyone that sees a color in resemblance to your race thinks that you are what their forefathers called your ancestors. A savage or a "sava-dog" for that matter. So, to each their own. And G-D for us all. Therefore, the sava-dogs should not have entered the Nations of G-D's people's boarders.

If Christopher Columbus and his vessels filled with sava-dogs was not stranded at sea? My beloved relatives The Native American Indians inhabiting the lands that G-D gave them. The good and humble nature servants of The Creator. Would not have rescued them and receive death as a reward for their heroic deed. Of-which only a sava-dog will reward death for life. As an exchange. As death is not of G-D. And G-D does not deal in dead things. Then we know who was with The Devil (Wolf in Sheep's clothing) in 1492. And who was with G-D. Now. Let us now finally. Henceforth and forevermore. But away this idea that The Native American Indians. The Indigenous people, The Black African American Indian people are nothing. And no one. Let us bring ourselves to apologize for the decades long wrongs committed on them and their children. Less your heart becomes hard like Pharaoh (Which is G-D's hope, to destroy you by making your heart hard). And the banner over his children is his love (A Covenant Promise). G-D will root you out of the earth. Because you continue to despise that which another man (G-D) has planted. Which is you. And them. Together. In the same hole called Earth.

And if the world does not *wake up Jacob/Yacob. The Seventh Generation of The Native American Indian? The last of the remnants of The Creator. The Great Spirit G-D's Holy Spirit Seed.?* If The World does not let The Descendants of Native American Indians that are assimilated and scattered all over the world, Including the Black American Indians, the apple of The Creator, The Great Spirit G-D of Yisra'El YAHWEH (Yo'way), The TETRAGRAMMATON YODH HEI WAW HEI's eyes go?. And start teaching them their true identity. To go in the direction of their own culture. Their own heritage, Their own way of life, Their own service of their G-D The Creator? There *will* be hell to pay. Hell will be the pay and portion of many. I know this because I hear the conversations of Heaven.

Even when I don't plan to hear from Heaven? I do. It's like my ear is permanently aligned on Heaven's door. That I may bear witness. That The LORD is a fair G-D to the people of Earth. That none may say that G-D did not treat them fairly.

I would hear from Heaven from I was a child. And I sense things in The Spirit. Through a combination of signs, wonders, dreams and vision, and direct conversations with G-D and his angels. Which has always kept me, my family and friends ahead of others.

Not because I've said so. It's because I have a gift. And of my gifts? I give it freely to Mankind. That these accounts are true and faithful. Thought you believe not any before me. And **THY** neck is stiff. I am without hope that you will believe even me. But my heart is free of you. On account that I have told you that which I know without a shadow of a doubt.

534

Therefore, whatever happens to you regarding these things, and G-D's words? It will not be applied to my charge. As I have shared that which I know with the world freely. Through brotherly and sisterly love. And this is all that matters to me, AMEN. And AMEN, Selah, And So Be It.

My talent is G-D. My skill is G-D. My inheritance is G-D. As the world had nothing to offer me and my people. The Native American Indians. And has written me and us out of its history? I have nothing else to offer this world. But The Creator G-D. And I give him to the world freely. **<u>LET THE CHILDREN OF THE CREATOR, THE GREAT SPIRIT G-D OF YISRA'EL GO. THAT THEY MAY SERVE HIM. AND ONLY HIM.</u>**

For the son is not greater than The Father G-D. Giving them some of what you've got. It better than The Creator G-D taking _all_ of what you've got and giving it to them. Which The Creator will do because of your insolence. To the things he has instituted.

"For you do not understand. The Powers of This Creator G-D. I have come to understand. And I have met many of The Heavenly Host of Light. Too Many to List. Even The Titans are with The Creator G-D.

True story. One day when The Titans joined the Universal work of light. To bring in everlasting righteousness. I never knew them prior. Needless to say. Greek G-ds were not a subject matter during my captivity on the remote islands within The Commonwealth of The Bahamas that was once visited by Christopher "killer" Columbus.

But The Titans came to me. And introduced themselves to me. I had experienced the strength of many of those of The Heavenly forces of light. Including the one holding the anhk, who's shadow moved across the universe when he stood up to bring death. I believe he was death himself. But there is none like The Mighty G-D, The Creator Yahweh (Yo'way). Who is sometimes called Jah or Yah,

One day in 2020 I was on the highway driving down Interstate 95. The Titans just showed. Out of nowhere. I swerve the car. I became afraid at once. As I got back into the lane. Holding the wheel with both hands. The spirits changed their form. And blended in with traffic. By transforming themselves into a large charcoal truck. They drove two to four inches from my vehicle.

I was astonished by their accuracy and great precision, along with their strength. Their appearance is unmistakable. As I held on to the wheel. Doing 80mph. I was boxed in. A vehicle ahead. Another one on the left. And one behind me. And conjoined spirits on the right. I looked out the passenger side window. And the oldest one (A male) says. "We are The Titans." Then I saw a long line of people (spirits). Inside each other. One after the other. (A family of spirits attached). Then a female shows me herself and a male. A younger brother showed himself after her. They both smiled at me. Though I like the smile. And it comforted me just a little. I still didn't know their intensions. Because I had never heard of them before. Until that day they showed up beside me on Interstate 95. Though there were many more of them connected? They didn't show me who they all were individually. They just let me see them conjoined as a family of powerful G-Ds (spirits).

I remember thinking. "Yes Sir Mr. Titan Sir. Sir head of the Titan family sir. All y'all is whoever. And whatever y'all say that y'all are. Sir. I believe it yesterday. Though you never told me Sir. I believe you today, Sir. And I will believe you even tomorrow. Just don't end my daylight on this highway. That is not on its way to Heaven. I really didn't know who they were with right away. I thought they were with the opposition. And not with the forces of light. Their powers are frightening. And overpowering. I though they came to shake me up because they knew The Creator G-D talks with me, and I talk with him and his Holy Spirit.

They left the highway as quickly as they came. On their departure. You should hear those Titans. They said to me "We wanted to introduce ourselves to you. That you should know us. We have joined the Holy Forces of Light. So that our Master Yahweh (Yo'way) will get all The Glory." My first though was to suck my teeth. I though. "These dan-git Titans. You think yall couldn't use the front door to come to me in a more peaceful manner? You had to open the sky and descend violently? Do you have to destroy everything in your wake just to say hello?" Then I said to myself. "If this is how these Titan family of G-D's says. "Hello?" I wouldn't want them to be sent to tell me. "Goodbye."

A conjoined Family of seven to twelve spirits of G-Ds in a line. Is The Titans. I was so afraid. I had a firm grip on the steering wheel. And I needed a crowbar to get my hands off hours after they had left. I didn't know what would happen next because of their great strength and unbelievable precision within their powers. I checked the vehicle compass. Learned I was traveling East and said after The Titans left. "Fathar?. Do you think those Titans had to do me like that LORD? I understand me being introduce to them might have been important to them in this time. As they felt I knew many other. And needed to know them. (I was so scared, I used all my wisdom that Fathar would approve my petition.) I said to G-D. "But am not even trying to be afraid for anyone other than **THEE**. So, if they come again to me? Can you please tell them Titans not to come like that? Their strength is overwhelming Fathar. And am sure you wouldn't want me feeling fear for anyone else. As it is written. I should fear The LORD alone"

I've never seen The Titans again from that day to this, Thank G-D for pray that changes things. Besides. The Titans are a family of spirit G-D's you only need to met once. To never forget again.

Ra I met during my wilderness wondering. When I was searching for myself. He is of Light also. Long before The Titans. I met Ra. The Titans I met in 2020. Or they met me rather. Three or four-times Ra has come to my aid along the way through. During my imposed wilderness wondering of 1492 to present day. Ra gives good and pleasant gifts. My first Ankh was from Ra. I never knew of an Ankh. Or it's meaning before him. He taught me of eternal life. He is a very pleasant spirit of Light. You cannot hide anything from Ra. It is pointless. Ra comes and goes through The Sun. And only shows up on major importance. Though Ra is kind. And one in several of The G-Ds of The Creator. Not to be confused with The G-D's of Yisra'EL. Which there is only four of The G-D's of Yisra'EL. Sitting on the four sides of The Creator. And they are found in the four cardinal directions of The

World. I do not serve Ra. Even The Titans are a family of G-D's. I do not serve them. But I can call on any. Within my Fathar's glorious Kingdom.

G-D, Hashem, EL Jehovah. The Kingdom of The SOUTH. I met after rejecting him the worst. I would run his people out my yard. And tell them. "My G-D name isn't Jehovah!" But when I went to Heaven? There he was sitting at the back (beside) of The Creator. The South. Jehovah is our Might Provide. Just like. It is said of him. He is the most loving G-D. Jehovah, and I had an extra special relationship. Let's put it like that. Now adays. If someone says to me. "G-D Jehovah is in the field?" I will forfeit all that I have and go to the field. And yes. As it is said? "THERE IS NO G-D LIKE JEHOVAH." Oh no not one! G-D Jehovah's symbol of his Kingdom is The Serpent. He told me that it was the symbol of his Kingdom used during Moses and the staff that turned into a Serpent. **G-D Jehovah I serve.** He is The G-D of <u>The Human Soul. And one of the G-D's of Yisra'EL. Who is with him is Raphi'EL</u>

G-D, Hashem, EL, Adonai. The Kingdom of The EAST & EAST Heaven. He is The G-D over everything. All Mankind. Everything that was made. And is Made. Sinews Including. Ruler of All The Earth. When I when to Heaven? There Adonai was. Seated at the right hand of The Creator. The East "The Eagle" is the symbol of his Kingdom. And is banner is red.

I never knew G-D Adonai. His people? I used to run them also. Hop. Skipping and a Jumping. "Out of my face. I would say." "Get out. I don't know your G-D." Only because I was so serious about my G-D. Whom I never had a name for. Properly even jealous theirs had one. My G-D's name could have very well been Adonai or Jehovah. I was too ignorant to explore those possibilities because of the imprisonment of my mind brought on by the captivity of my people minds from 1492. Adonai is <u>The G-D of The Human Mind. The Head. The Brain. G-D Adonai. I serve. He is another one of the G-D's of Yisra'EL. And who is with him is Myki'EL</u>

All along. It was My Fathar The Creator G-D. The G-D of my ancestors. The G-D of My Cherokee Indian Great Grandmother. Sitting in the center of Heaven drawing me unto himself. Through The G-D's that sits around him.

G-D, Hashem, EL EL, EL Elyon. The Most High G-D. The Kingdom of The WEST & WEST Heaven. He is The Most High G-D. Above all G-DS. The Supreme Court of Heaven. He presides over. He is always wearing white. Which is also his Kingdom banner. His virtue is Pure & Cleanness. His symbol The White Buffalo. He is The G-D of The Human Body. G-D EL, EL, EL, Elyon. I serve. He is one of the G-D's of Yisra'EL. And who is with him is Gabri'EL. His name meaning is Strength of G-D. Gabri'EL's of The Angelic Order Kerubim, Powers of The Elements. Gabri'EL's element is water.

G-D, Hashem,EL, Gibhor. The Kingdom of The NORTH. He is The G-D of War. And of Battle. And of Might. The All-Mighty G-D. The symbol of his Kingdom is a grizzly bear. In display of his strength. He is directly in-front of The Creator. This G-D is the one who fought and won many of Yisra'EL biblical wars. Like Moses and Joshua's victories. His banner. Kingdom color is blue. G-D Gibhor?. I serve. He is also one of the G-D's of Yisra'EL. And who is with him is Auri'EL. Auriel's element is Earth.

G-D, Hashem, EL, Adonai. The Kingdom of The EAST & EAST Heaven. Adonai is The G-D of all things. With him is Myki'EL/Michael. Who's name meaning is He who is like G-D. Of The Angelic Order, Malakim (Kings). His element is

Fire. And the other G-D I serve of my Fathar The Creator's G-D's is.

G-D, Hashem, EL, Jehovah. The Kingdom of The South. He is the G-D of provisions. He provides all our needs. With G-D Jehovah is Rapha'EL. Who's name meaning is Healing of G-D. Of The Angelic Order Beni Elohim (Son's of Elohim). His element is Air.

Although I know many good celestial spirits of light. I do not serve them. It is forbidden. I serve The Creator, The Great Spirit G-D of Yisra'EL Yahweh (Yo'way). My Holy Heavenly Fathar and his four G-Ds of The Four Cardinal Direction Kingdom. Who's Kingdoms colors are Red, White, Blue and Yellow. As The Cherokee Indians indicate of the colors of The Kingdom directions. For there are G-D's many as there are stars in the sky. But there is none like my Holy Heavenly Fathar, The Great Spirit G-D of Yisra'EL, Yahweh (Yaya, Yo'way) The Creator. He is the **G-D of G-D's**. And **LORD of The LORD's**, and **King of The Kings,** yet he is **One**. **And though he sits at the round table with other G-D. It is The Creator that sits at the head table. Surrounded by himself. Though he is in the company of many G-Ds? It is yet Him alone. That sits with himself. Deliberating with many. But yet? BY HIMSELVE.** Do you not see the danger? Therefore, I am afraid for those who have wronged him. And those he says is his own. With their deeds that has broken the heart of The LORD. Through offense.

If THOU finds any wisdom in these pages. Go and plead with them that are hard of hearing. And to those who have a history of not listening. I beg you to hear me. "This G-D. This Creator. This Great Spirit. This YAHWEH. This Yo'way. This Yaya. This TETRAGRAMMATON. This Yodh, Hei, Waw, Hei.

This G-D of The Nation of Yisra'EL. Has drawn me out. That I may partake of my identity, my culture, my heritage. To inherit The Creator. And he inherited me. Which is a promise he made to my forefathers. In this his Coming. That is and was. HE HAS COME. That *every* Native American Indian Descendants. And those that are assimilated and do not know themselves is about to partake. Any day now. Which is to go into the next Kingdoms eternal rest. As a birthright. As the children of the covenant promise.

The Creator, G-D will save ALL THE NATIVE AMERICAN INDIANS and their descendants he selects to go with him. Those that are the apple of his eyes with a showboating mighty right hand and a outstretch arm. He will use powers the world has never known, seen or heard off. Making a public spectacle of all that hate him and do no keep his commandments.

There are a people living within humanity that has the oldest form of worship. They worship the same G-D you worship. Just that they have the old age way of calling on him. And pleasing him. And you have the new age way. None is wrong. Their form is the purest of Spirit. And their labor at that task call "Spirit?" has been longer than you have labored. And The Creator is Spirit. Before he is anything.

These days I see any Native American Indian people? After learning just how dear they are to The Creator G-D's heart, In passing them. I bow. For their feet will be washed here on Earth. Quick, fast and in a hurry. Because they were right. And their ways are right. I was wrong in the ways I was thought to perceive them. And so were you. And we need them and what they do to keep us all in balance. And not the other way around. Their prayers, rituals, ceremonies, mediation all this time was keeping things in balance. Just like they said. For The Creator has showed me this.

And I beg your pardon. Descendants of Native American Indians. For all of the hostilities you have suffered in The World unto this day. Because you did. And you do. Have a job given to you and your descendants from THE KING OF THE UNIVERSE. The Creator. Who has created all things.

And any day now? You will weep no more. Because The LORD has spoken. And he will not take it back. _"You've got a double dose of trouble and more than your share of contempt? Therefore, your inheritance in the land says The Most High G-D of Heaven. Will be doubled and your joy go on forever"_

Because they are The Nation. In-which The Creator has blessed. And it is they. That keep The Earth in balance. Through the things that they offer The Creator. On behalf of all Humanity. And every brother and every sister. Their offerings have kept us all. Including me. It kept me when I slept the sleep of death brought on by the events of 1492. And it made me to return in 2020. If they had given up the rest of the land physically? I too would have been lost forever spiritually and physically. Because little children of The Most High. <u>Matthew 16:16; 18:18) says. "Whatever we bind on earth is bound in heaven, whatever we lose on earth is loosed in heaven."</u>

But they help on to some of the land. Not given up and holding the prayer, the offering the ceremonies, the rituals. I am back from the spiritually dead. The unconscious sleep of death. Imposed on me by my accuser Christopher Columbus. Spain and it's Crown. Including The Catholic Church. I have been their prisoner for over 40 years. Yet the world puts my accusers. And the accusers of my people on center state to be celebrated by me. Should not a father fight for a child when they are being mistreated or neglected by his brother or sister? As there is a earthly fashion for this. There is even so. A Heavenly fashion. As *The Creator is father to ALL*. Should he not judge between his children?

The World did nothing to free me. Like so many others still needing help today from the prisons of their minds. The Creator showed me a group of Native American Indians knocking at a door to be let in once. And others did not let them in to acknowledge them as a people. As human beings.

My Native American Indian family, I never knew. Did more in releasing me from my captivity. Through their prayers, rituals, ceremonies and offering of peace to The Creator. That he would not forsake me. And those he has a covenant promise to protect. They worked around the clock in releasing me from my captivity.

Their prayers keeps me now while I am awake. <u>If they stop the prayers, offering, ceremonies, rituals? We will *all perish*. Be done for. Finish. Toodle-oo. Auf wiedersehen.</u>

Farewell. So long. Goodbye. See you later. Adios. Arrivederci, G-D BE WITH YOU. In the sweet by and by.

Yet so many of their children has turn away from the way of sacrifice, offering, ceremonies, rituals. Many by force boarding schools between the 17th to 21st century. Others have lost interest. Due to the world seducing them to follow other ways of life that is not their own. For every action there is a reaction. And the earth is currently not in balance on her axle.

The offering is now scanty before THE FACE OF THE KING OF THE UNIVERSE. The Creator. He has showed me a wide and deep open space where his offering is collected. And it is so empty. It is dark and empty. This is how I know that which I speak of the significance of their offerings to The LORD. He looks for those of the next generation (His Seventh Generation) that should offer the offering and sacrifices to keep things in balance. Which is the agreement The Native American Indians forefathers name with G-D, The Creator.

In replacement of the aging Elders of his people. He found only a few. Scanty, Scanty. Is the people of The LORD that are chosen as Priest and Priestess of Humanity. The Holy Spirit planted go between. Those that go between G-D and Mankind and Mankind back to G-D. Scanty are they.

The LORD is not pleased with this. The LORD makes us all to live good. He gives us houses. Cloths. Families. Wealth. Prosperity. Health. Strength. And we dare to rob him as we increase? As we increase. We have decreased The LORD's portion. Which are his sacrifices, rituals, ceremonies, prayers, meditation of his commandments, offerings, tithing. And we have pulled the people asunder that stood.

And should stand before him. Should not the Master of the lofty high places come and pay you a visit because of this?. Because you have not only taken what was theirs but has also taken them away captives?

There is a Deal. A Contract. An Agreement. That if He (The Creator) did his part? The Native American Indians and their descendants would do theirs. Final Capeesh? Of still no final Capeesh? Remember? When you decide on capeesh or no capeesh. You have selected to understand what G-D has ordained and instituted or to reject that which G-D has ordained and instituted. Which is above any institution of man. Because you need now to know that power is behind that which he instituted. Remember this also. It is not what Jesus Christ of Nazareth will do. Nor Adonai will do. Nor Jehovah will do. Nor Gibhor will do. Not what EL. EL. Elyon will do. Not Yashua HaMashiach will do. Not even The Buddha will do his part. Nor Mickey Mouse. And not Donald Duck will do. NO!. Nor any other figment of the human imagination will do.

It is what The Creator will do. The Creator of Adam and Eve would do his part toward them, The Native American Indian. You know. The Creator. The one with all the biblical accolades? That one? The biggest killer in The Bible? That one? Well, he had made a Promise. And guess what? That promise has no other choice but to come. In the beginning was the word. And the words were with G-D. John 1:1. Because The Creator is THE WORD, THAT HE HAS PROMISE. Therefore, the promise cannot come back to the PROMISE without fulfillment. (He is the promise that he has promised).

And not because The Native American Indians think that they are special. No. It's because incidentally enough. "They Are Special." Your car and your phone and your dog is special to you. Well they are special to G-D. Their fathers make the deal. The contract. The agreement with The Creator.

They really did. And because am tied up in that deal? The Creator has come to save me. Resurrect and redeem me from the dead cold hands of Christopher Columbus, The Catholic Church and Spain. My captors. And I have turned around to save you. That you should see yourself. And or the danger. And as I have? I give to a world that had forsaken and taken from me. And so many little Indian boys and girls. Has this world forsaken.

The whole world will see. The lamb upon The Throne that will come to rescue a people and conquer The Beast. This book helps you not to be surprised when the ark of The Creator descends upon The Earth for the meek and lowly of the people. His remnants. Is he just descending for the Natives? Absolutely not. As the Creator banner is LOVE. And his colors are that of the rainbow? So should they that enter be for multitude. But the longest standing employees. Servants? Workers? The good and faithful servants? They will walk upon the ark first. Remember The General's lessons. Heaven has order. As Earth has order.

The Bible declares in Matthew 5:5. "Blessed are the meek, for they will inherit the earth. They should board his Ark. That will come over All the Earth for his people. And those of His Chosen, His Righteous, And His Adopted Kingdom Citizens.

For many serve The Son. But only a Chosen few. Was. And is. Chosen to serve The Fathar alone. For even in this life a father retains certain things unto himself. And does not give it over to his son. Which brings me to these invaluable.

Timely words. **"Let The Creator's People Go." That They Should Serve. And serve! Him Alone. Remove your false doctrines from His Children."**

Those who hold the line in service before his face is dwindling. And of the nature which most do not understand. Which is Spirit? They are best at. Let them help you by you leaving them alone. Because The World is in the very hour of their G-D's visitation. It is better to be found giving them a hand. Verses taking one away. Which will anger the consuming fire that is their G-D. Whom they offer their prayers to.

If they are not given their leave to exit the ways that are not of their own fathers? It will be like the days of Egypt. As it is this day. Filled with plagues. Pestilence, Famine, Floods. Fires. Storms. Earthquakes, Drought, and the like. As the Creator saved his people in Egypt? So shall The Creator G-D free his people and bring out his remnants (The Seventh Generation) with a strong and might hand.

The elements are in The Creator's right hand, wind, fire, water, air, and the planets, the firmament of the orient, the stars the zodiac, the sun and the moon. And they will cease not. And they will be as a weapon in the LORD's artillery. Christopher Columbus and the rest imagined a vain thing. They all together had never heard. "Child, what sweet your mouth today, can very well bitter you're a** tomorrow." Had they all heard that enough they would not have make so many ung-dly mistakes.

Temporary joys have come from rape and murder. Pillaging and plundering of a people. The Creator's people. The Native American Indians.

Let Columbus take his own blows in his cloths. By himself. For himself. He is dead. For the sins of his own hands. But you the living? Shouldn't take his blows in your

549

cloths. While Universal Justice hangs over The Earth. Put away the evil and choose good. The time is short. The records have been seen. The witness has given account. The Creator's judgment is on its way. But yet has come. And the judgment will not start back in Egypt. No. Egypt has been judged and found in wanting. And does not currently exist but in our memories.

Universal Judgment will start at 1492 for this world. And make its way up to The Creator's selected hour. The Year of Jubilee. Of-which hour and day? No man knows. But The LORD has blessed me with the season of his coming.

You see in 1492 time period? To curse was to be curse. So as Christopher Columbus cursed my people, The Native American Indians? So did Creation. (The Law). The Word of G-D, The Two Edged Sword, Cursed his people. And those that came from his loins. And more should be angry with him. To whip his name from among the people. Because many people joy that is tied into his plundering and massacres? Is about to be turned upside down and inside out. Because of Christopher Columbus delivering to the world a form of fool's gold. Stolen treasure. Fleeting and temporary joys. To enjoy and prosper of the items he acquired through death and bloodshed.

Oh, foolish backward and perverted generation. How long should The Holy Forces contend with you?. Earth has order as Heaven has order. If a bad demonic man, goes out and slaughter even ten innocent women and children. Should not the sheriff. The police. The bounty hunters. Some of the victim's family. And even a perfect stranger pick up arms and go to find him that is a destroyer of the innocent. And bring him to swift justice?. And should not his punishment fit his crime? This is the justice of the two-legged ones. That need mouth to speak and legs to move.

Why do you not then consider the justice from those who do not need legs to move? And arms to carry weapons? The Holy Forces (The Holy Spirit) are the arms themselves. Saturn controls the lead. These are the Temples of The Most High G-D. And will render it useless. Mars controls the iron. And will render it useless. Venus controls the copper and will render it useless. Mercury controls the quick sliver. And will render it useless. The Sun the gold and The Moon the silver. And LORD Jupiter will render the tin useless to mankind. So what weapon are you going to us. When The LORD activates The Planets to lift those materials up from the face of The Earth? What will you use fingertips and hips, papier-mache? Because many fail to learn the lessons. That doesn't mean that there are no lessons to be learned. You have come to the earth to learn. The Holy Forces are the weapons themselves. Should not their justice be swifter when it comes? And? Should not their blow be more precise and deadly? <u>Psalms 47:9. For the shields of the earth belongs to G-D. He is highly exalted.</u> Because you fail to consider the fact that the earth belongs to him who make it? Then it is best for you to begin learning today. Just how to properly get down on your knees. In practical preparation for The Creator's descend into Judgement Day. For you have forsaken knowledge. And for that reason. Others will stand over your head in the judgment, even little children. And you will knee. If you are so blessed.

The Creator has expressed this to me. So, I will express this to you. In the saving of your soul in real time. In-which you have freewill to decide, it's your Soul. During the judgment? The first people will be immediately destroyed by the sword of G-D. Their heads will be severed of their bodies. Even before The Judgment starts. They will not be able to defend themselves. No question will be asked of them. Universal justice will take care of the biggest and the worst of the people that are mixed in with the lowly. Those that make or have make the good people living on Earth afraid. Those without arms and feet will take them out first. Then. The Creator will ask The Righteous, The Chosen & The Adopted people to point out any among them that are their enemies (adversaries). And they too will be put to the sword.

Then the last of the people will go into captivity. The children of those that had others in captivity. Will become captives. Isaiah 14:2 And they shall take them captives, whose captives they were; and they shall rule over their oppressors. But also, as their forefathers of Edom have agreed in times pass. That is found in the holy books of Jubilee. That they would be subjected to servitude. In the service of Jacobs (Yisra'EL's) children. That is additionally recorded (written) within the heavenly tables.

As it is written says The LORD. Exodus 21:24. An eye for an eye, a tooth for a tooth, a hand for a hand, and a foot for a foot. Of hands? Christopher "Murderer" Columbus has chop off many hands from the wrist of 14-year old babies, Of The Native American Indian Children in the name of The Catholic Church. The Lord Jesus Christ and Spain. For the non-delivery of gold after child labor in the mines of my people. Severing Native American Indian kids hands was a common practice for Christopher. Yet my people were called barbaric savages. With the slaughter of 300 to 500 million Native American Indians in a 40 years' time frame. The number of deaths were so astonishing. The priest that traveled with Columbus said of the deaths. "Who in future generations would believe that in 40 years. Over 300 million Native American Indians were massacred?"

I would believe it. Because that was what one bad man did do. But where there is one bad man? The General of The Most High G-D taught me?. Incidentally enough, there is one even worst than that bad man. For eternity is longer than a man's life. This is what The LORD of Host says. *"Behold Disaster is spreading from nation to nation. Those slain by The LORD on that day will be spread from one end of The Earth to the other. They will not be mourned, gathered, or buried. They will be like dung lying on the ground. Jeremiah 25:32-33.* You see? The priest that traveled with Columbus said it took them 40 years to kill of 300 to 500 million Native American Indians. The LORD said, He will take one day to slay from one end of the earth to the next. "One day."

The senseless massacre of Millions of people follows *The Doctrine of Discovery. Which is a decree issued by Pope Alexander VI. A papal bull. "Inter Caetera." In which he authorizes Spain and Portugal to colonize the Americas and its Native American Indian peoples as subjects. The decree asserts the rights of Spain and Portugal to colonize and*

554

enslave. Yesterday? Christopher Columbus walked my ancestors' streets in America. Today? Lava walks his.

Christopher Columbus killed by amputation and other heinous crimes so many of my people. Until my people got together at a lake. That The LORD Most High showed me. They agreed together saying. "Because the white man's G-d is Gold? And we keep giving him his G-D but he would not leave our land? Let us put away his G-D from among us. And keep our G-D. The Creator."

And one by one. The LORD showed me the gold being poured out like water into the lake. As my ancestors formed a line and toss the gold into the lake from containers above their heads. They would strip themselves also of the gold from their bodies. And toss it into the lake. And (For this reason.? And that of the golden calf with Aaron? No gold or silver will enter the Kingdom that will descend). Put them far from you. Trade them now. If you possess them? You will not enter. Not even a gold tooth should pass the door of Holy Mount Zion. For gold, rubies, diamonds, and all precious stones are already found there in. And that which babies (Little children) had died for in the mines of The World? Will not enter therein,

Now the curse of Christopher Columbus actions has reached its consummation. (Reached up to Heaven.) The second of the 10 Commandments of The Creator tells you. **For I the LORD THY G-D am a jealous G-D,** (which means he is JEALOUS over his people, his servants) **visiting the iniquities of the fathers upon the children** (which means, you might not be guilty, but for your fathers guilt? Though he is not alive. You will receive the punishment) **unto the third and fourth generation of them that hate me; and shewing mercy unto thousands of them that love me and keep my commandments.** (Which means. You might not get the recompense in this generation. And you might not get it in the next. But recompense must come. And already is).

And the waters will come as high as the sky and the skies will roll away like a scroll. And the seas will roar. And the people will be perplexed. And everything covered will be uncovered on the day of Judgment at solar noon for one hour says The LORD G-D, Hashem, EL, Jehovah of The Kingdom of The South, of his judgment day. And none will be able to reverse it. And it will be the day that is called, "A Day to Late." A word to the wise should always be sufficient.

But isn't G-D, The Creator good I thought? That there is still time to correct the wrongs done unto his people? Who are scattered around the four corners of The World? His elect. For The Creator's portion. Is his people.

The name of G-D, The Creator The Native American Indians, The Tiano called upon was Yaya like YAHWEH. Because they did not speak English. And the queen that eradicated millions of my people cast a dark enchantment over the lives of the inhabitants of the islands. The Bahamas and Caribbean Native American Indian descendants. Who are still asleep and do not know themselves even in the face of The Coming of their own King. The Creator. And for even that? The LORD and Caretaker of the earth is angry with the world to destroy it from under heaven. Over those he love.

The good news is. They and so many other Native American Indian Descendants who are also the Black Americans that will all be changed that have been assimilated away from their Native American Indian ways of life. And they will also wake up and realize that they are Sons and Daughters of The Creator. For them, it is written. 1 Corinthians 15:51-58. <u>Behold I show you a mystery; we shall not all sleep. But we shall all be changed, in a moment, in the twinkling of an eye, and the last trump: for the trumpet shall sound, and the dead shall be raised incorruptible, and we shall be changed.</u>

And it will not happen because someone in the world has *finally* taken up The Native American Indian's course. *And freed their children from a way of life that was imposed upon them. Through colonization, cultural assimilation, and religious imprisonment. NO.*

It is because our Elohim, The Creator, Our Holy Fathar desires it to be so. Because of the covenant he made with OUR FATHERS. This was why the LORD had come to me in sorrow, with a broken heart. This was a time when the curse of Yisra'EL. The Native American Indians were lifted. And The LORD looked upon the land from Heaven at a time

557

appointed. And he saw rivers of blood. And the desolation of The People he has a covenant promise to protect.

To understand it more clearly, "If the LORD Most High put a curse on you? The angels/kachina's, mother moon or father sun is not able to interfere and save you out of anything you might go through. Because The Elohim. Holy Fathar, The Creator is a consuming fire. You and yours must get though the period of that curse the best way possible. Which is by the grace of G-D.

And you must arrive at the end of the circle of that curse before you can get help from the divine forces under The Creator's control. *AND YOU HAVE Native American Indians. YOU HAVE PLEASED YOUR G-D. REJOICE! 2023 IS THE YEAR OF YOUR JUBILEE. All those that love G-D.* The Creator's words. Doesn't come back to him void. And became he did nothing? Many thought he would never come. Because they do not understand G-D. G-D is a consuming fire. And when he comes? ALL OF HIM MUST COME. Because he is in everything. Two hands will come forth from The Creator before the grass becomes fully green again. One of Reward and Peace. And the other? Filled with the cup of the wrath of his indignation. **For the Native American Indian and their descendants, it is written in Psalm 53:4 4 Do all these evildoers know nothing? They devour my people as though eating bread;** This is because The Creator was watching all along. He has said to me that he didn't intervene until the appointed time of the end of the 400 years curse fulfillment. In-which the 400 years curse that was over the lives of brown and black people. Indigenous peoples. The Native American Indians and their descendants ended on August 22nd, 2018, at 12:01am.

Come, Come now brothers and sisters. Let us reason together. **THOU** have been many years alive. But have not considered the condition of **THY** own neighbor. **THOU** pass by the poor every day and mock them. Though by thine own gluttony, greed and excessive wealth. The poor is poor among you.

THOU Foolish of the People? "As our father Jacob held back the heel of Esau his brother. (2 Esdras 6:8). So is your neighbor. Jacobs Children. The Native American Indian Descendants holding back your heel. Obadiah 1:4 declares unto you. "The pride of your heart has deceived you. O dwellers in the clefts of the rocks whose habitation is the heights. Who say in your heart? "Who can bring me down to the ground?" Though you soar like the eagle and make your nest among the stars. Even from there? I will bring you down. "Declares The LORD.

THOU wise of The People? Begin to cleanse your environment (surroundings). Saturate yourself in G-D. Mind, Body, Soul, and Spirit. Including your physical environment. Seek my help if needed. Ask The LORD to come into your life to stay. Go on your knees before him who can preserve your soul alive. That it should ascend into the next Kingdom that has come into the world. Do this for yourself. Go to him. On behalf of yourself. For this Judgment? None may speak on another's behalf. None may beseech The LORD as in the days within lot was rescued on another's behalf.

Remove the idols of Baal far from you. Cut back to that of your need alone. Do away with abundant vanity. Walk through your homes and all that The Creator G-D has given to you and cause for you and your family to have. Purify your surroundings. Clean it up with urgency. Remove the idols. I

559

had seen an evil that men do. And have done under The Sun. And it is GREAT! And it had reached up to Heaven.

Express gratitude toward G-D. Anything that is displeasing of your actions or might be displeasing to The LORD's nostrils? Cast it far from you. And cause it to cease from among you. Give a great portion of what you have to the poor and needy. Be humble. Swiftly. The hour of The LORD's coming is no more. It is the minute of his coming. There are no more years? His presence is at the door. Come into your dwelling place and carefully wait out the final exodus of G-D. Ask The Creator for forgiveness of your sins. Seen and Unseen. Walk in the light of The LORD. To be spared from blood guiltiness. One who is wise. Who's forefathers have committed an abundance of GREAT SINS should pray henceforth and forevermore. Psalm 51:14, NASB: "Save me from the guilt of bloodshed, G-D, The G-D of my salvation; Then my tongue will joyfully sing of Your righteousness." To the assimilated Native American Indian Descendants, The Chosen, The Righteous, And The Adopted Kingdom Citizens. "Trust in the LORD with all your heart and lean not on your own understanding; in all your ways submit to him, and he will make your paths straight.

John 5:24

Verily, verily,

I say unto you,

He that

heareth my word,

and

believeth on him that sent me,

hath everlasting life,

and

shall not come into condemnation;

but is passed from

death **unto** *life.*

Elioenaibookstore.com

Made in the USA

Las Vegas, NV

23 July, 2022

564

Made in the USA
Columbia, SC
30 July 2022

64123383R00311